FUNDAMENTALS OF PERFORMANCE TECHNOLOGY: A GUIDE TO IMPROVING PEOPLE, PROCESS, AND PERFORMANCE

Second Edition

Darlene M. Van Tiem
University of Michigan - Dearborn

James L. Moseley
Wayne State University

Joan Conway Dessinger
The Lake Group

International Society for Performance Improvement
Silver Spring, MD

D1288555

Fundamentals of Performance Technology

A Guide to Improving People, Process, and Performance, Second Edition

Copyright © 2004, by the International Society for Performance Improvement.

ISBN: 1-890289-17-5

Published by
International Society for Performance Improvement
1400 Spring Street
Suite 260
Silver Spring, MD 20910
301.587.8570
Fax: 301.587.8573

Visit our website at www.ispi.org. To order books, log on to www.ispi.org/bookstore.

He who does not improve today
will grow worse tomorrow.

—German Proverb

Dedicated to

Phillip M. Van Tiem

Dariusz Strzalkowski

Gary J. Dessinger

Special Appreciation to

Joseph (Jerry) Lapides, University of Michigan - Dearborn

Rita Richey, Wayne State University

About ISPI

The International Society for Performance Improvement (ISPI) *is dedicated to improving individual, organizational, and societal performance.* Founded in 1962, ISPI is the leading international association dedicated to improving productivity and performance in the workplace. ISPI represents more than 10,000 international and chapter members throughout the United States, Canada, and 40 other countries.

ISPI's mission is to develop and recognize the proficiency of our members and advocate the use of Human Performance Technology. This systematic approach to improving productivity and competence uses a set of methods and procedures and a strategy for solving problems for realizing opportunities related to the performance of people. It is a systematic combination of performance analysis, cause analysis, intervention design and development, implementation, and evaluation that can be applied to individuals, small groups, and large organizations.

Website:	**www.ispi.org**
Mail:	International Society for Performance Improvement
	1400 Spring Street, Suite 260
	Silver Spring, Maryland 20910 USA
Call:	1.301.587.8570
Fax:	1.301.587.8573
E-mail:	info@ispi.org

Certified Performance Technologist Designation

The Certified Performance Technologist (CPT) designation is awarded by ISPI in affiliation with the American Society for Training & Development (ASTD) to experienced performance improvement professionals whose work demonstrates adherence to the 10 Standards of Performance Technology and the Code of Ethics. For more information and to download application forms, visit www.certifiedpt.org.

PerformanceXpress

Published 12 times a year, *PerformanceXpress* is an electronic forum for timely communication to professionals in the field of performance improvement. The newsletter includes articles addressing current issues; monthly columns focusing on trends, measurement, and job aids; and a marketplace for promoting products and services. For the latest issue, visit www.PerformanceXpress.org.

TABLE OF CONTENTS

List of Tables vii

List of Figures viii

List of Job Aids ix

Foreword x

Acknowledgments xii

Chapter One	**Fundamentals of Performance Technology—A Guide to Improving People, Process, and Performance**	
	Performance Technology–Defined 2	

Chapter Two	**The Human Performance Technology Model**	
	What Is the HPT Model? 6	
	Is PT Just a Passing Bandwagon? 13	

Chapter Three	**Performance Analysis**	
	Introduction to Performance Analysis 22	
	Organizational Analysis 26	
	Environmental Analysis 33	
	Gap Analysis 38	

Chapter Four	**Cause Analysis**	
	Introduction to Cause Analysis 46	
	Lack of Environmental Support 51	
	Lack of Repertory of Behavior 56	

Chapter Five	**Intervention Selection and Design**	
	Introduction to Intervention Selection and Design 62	
	Classification of Interventions 66	
	Performance Support Interventions: Instructional 67	
	Performance Support Interventions: Noninstructional 71	
	Job Analysis/Work Design Interventions 79	
	Personal Development Interventions 87	
	Human Resource Development Interventions 92	
	Organizational Design and Development Interventions 99	
	Organizational Communication Interventions 107	
	Financial Systems Interventions 113	

TABLE OF CONTENTS

Chapter Six **Intervention Implementation and Change**

Introduction to Intervention Implementation and Change 124

Change Management 125

Process Consulting 133

Employee Development 138

Communication, Networking, and Alliance Building 145

Chapter Seven **Evaluation**

Introduction to Evaluation 156

Evaluation Models Show the Way 161

Formative Evaluation 164

Summative Evaluation 171

Confirmative Evaluation 176

Meta Evaluation 181

Chapter Eight **Performance Technology in the Workplace — A Word to the Wise**

Introduction 190

Reflagging and Managing a New Hotel: Marriott International – Detroit 191

Conclusion — Skills and Knowledge Needed by PT Practitioners 201

Citations 203

Glossary of Terms 207

References 211

Index 219

Appendix One **Standards of Performance Technology and CPT Designation Program** 227

Appendix Two **Moving from Theory to Practice: Standards of Performance Technology** 235

Authors' Biographies 245

TABLES

Table A-1   Case Studies by Section iii
Table 2-1   PT Scientific Foundation and Evolution 8
Table 2-2   Gilbert's Behavior Engineering Model: Overview 8
Table 2-3   Job Applicant Weaknesses 14
Table 2-4   Sample Performance Outcome Indicators 16
Table 3-1   Anatomy of Performance 23
Table 3-2   Linking Analysis Techniques to Purpose 25
Table 3-3   Analysis Techniques, Purposes, and Tools 25
Table 3-4   Organizational Analysis Component of the HPT Model 26
Table 3-5   Various Strategic Planning Definitions 26
Table 3-6   Environmental Analysis Component of the HPT Model 33
Table 3-7   Gap Analysis Component of the HPT Model 38
Table 4-1   Gilbert's Behavior Engineering Model 47
Table 4-2   Behavior Engineering Model Adaptation 48
Table 4-3   Cause Analysis Tools 50
Table 4-4   Gilbert's Behavior Engineering Model: Environmental Support 51
Table 4-5   Gilbert's Behavior Engineering Model: Repertory of Behavior 56
Table 5-1   List of Interventions 63
Table 5-2   Performance Support Interventions Component of the HPT Model 68
Table 5-3   Learning Levels and Characteristics 68
Table 5-4   Action Learning Guidelines 69
Table 5-5   Self-directed Learning Guidelines 69
Table 5-6   Job Aid Viewpoints 71
Table 5-7   Job Analysis/Work Design Interventions Component of the HPT Model 79
Table 5-8   Japanese Safety Approaches 83
Table 5-9   Personal Development Interventions Component of the HPT Model 87
Table 5-10   Typical Career Assessment Instruments 88
Table 5-11   Human Resource Development Interventions Component of the HPT Model ... 92
Table 5-12   Organizational Design and Development Interventions Component of the HPT Model 99
Table 5-13   Organizational Communication Interventions Component of the HPT Model 107
Table 5-14   Advantages of Information Systems 108
Table 5-15   Conflict Resolution Do's and Don'ts 109
Table 5-16   Financial Systems Interventions Component of the HPT Model 113
Table 6-1   Gregorc's Learning Styles 145
Table 6-2   Populations in Automotive Job Categories 148
Table 6-3   Number of Students by Technology Format 149
Table 6-4   Number of MVAC Students Over Time 150
Table 7-1   Full Scope of Evaluation 157
Table 7-2   Overview of Evaluation—Type, Purpose, Timing 157
Table 7-3   Comparison of the HPT Model and the Dessinger-Moseley 360° Evaluation Model ... 163
Table 7-4   Traditional and Alternative Formative Evaluation Methods 165
Table 7-5   Advantages and Disadvantages of Alternative Methods of Formative Evaluation 167
Table 7-6   Six Options for Managing the Performer and the Performance Improvement Package 177
Table 7-7   Tasks to Perform During Confirmative Evaluation Phases 179
Table 7-8   Timing and Purpose for Type One and Type Two Meta Evaluation 181
Table 8-1   Evaluation Systems at Marriott International—Detroit 200

FIGURES

Figure 1-1   Human Performance Technology (HPT) Model 3
Figure 2-1   HPT Model 7
Figure 3-1   HPT Model: Performance Analysis Phase 22
Figure 3-2   Grant and Moseley Customer-Focused Performance Analysis Model 27
Figure 3-3   Rothwell's Environments of Human Performance 33
Figure 3-4   Kaufman's Definition of Need 39
Figure 3-5   Rothwell's Six Cell Gap Analysis 39
Figure 4-1   HPT Model: Cause Analysis Phase 46
Figure 5-1   HPT Model: Intervention Selection and Design Phase 62
Figure 5-2   Components of Job Design 82
Figure 5-3   Interventions for Organizational Design and Development 100
Figure 6-1   HPT Model: Intervention Implementation and Change Phase 124
Figure 6-2   Example of Project Management Gantt Chart 128
Figure 6-3   Career Guidance Model 150
Figure 7-1   HPT Model: Evaluation Phase 156
Figure 7-2   Matrix of Evaluation Decisions 158
Figure 7-3   Geis and Smith Evaluation Model 161
Figure 7-4   Dessinger-Moseley 360° Evaluation Model 162
Figure 7-5   Kirkpatrick's Evaluation Model 163
Figure 7-6   Adaptation of the Kaufman-Keller-Watkins Model 163
Figure 7-7   Equation for Confirming the Value of a Performance Intervention 176
Figure 7-8   Moseley and Solomon Confirmative Evaluation Model 178
Figure 7-9   Preliminary Checklist for Confirmative Evaluation 178

Job Aids

Job Aid 2-1   Situational Analysis 12

Job Aid 2-2   Organizational PT Effectiveness Measurement 19

Job Aid 3-1   Organizational Analysis Survey 30

Job Aid 3-2   What Is Happening?* 37

Job Aid 3-3   Sample Priority Matrix 43

Job Aid 4-1   Probing for Environmental Support Drivers (or Causes) 54

Job Aid 4-2   Probing for People's Repertory of Behavior Drivers (or Causes)* 59

Job Aid 5-1   Intervention Selector* 65

Job Aid 5-2   Performance Support Template 73

Job Aid 5-3   Evaluating Training 75

Job Aid 5-4   Performance Support—Intervention Planner 76

Job Aid 5-5   Task Analysis Checklist 81

Job Aid 5-6   Studying a Workstation 85

Job Aid 5-7   Hand and Wrist Protection from Cumulative Trauma Disorders 86

Job Aid 5-8   Feedback Checklist 90

Job Aid 5-9   Planner for Selecting a Mentor 91

Job Aid 5-10   Human Resource Development—Skills Set 96

Job Aid 5-11   Retirement Planning—Determining Net Worth 97

Job Aid 5-12   Retirement Planning—Monthly Income/Expenses 98

Job Aid 5-13   Evaluating Team Attitudes 104

Job Aid 5-14   Communication Networks Planner 112

Job Aid 5-15   Multiorganizational Arrangements Analysis 117

Job Aid 5-16   Basic Financial Statements 118

Job Aid 5-17   Templates of Basic Financial Statements 119

Job Aid 6-1   Change Management Planner 131

Job Aid 6-2   Change Management Evaluator* 132

Job Aid 6-3   Process Consulting Planner 137

Job Aid 6-4   Employee Development Standards 143

Job Aid 6-5   Networking Is Necessary 152

Job Aid 6-6   Skills Development Worksheet 153

Job Aid 7-1   Types of Evaluation: Addressing the Issues* 160

Job Aid 7-2   Planning a Formative Evaluation of a Performance Improvement Package ... 170

Job Aid 7-3   Guidelines for Planning a Summative Evaluation 174

Job Aid 7-4   Determining When to Conduct a Confirmative Evaluation 180

Job Aid 7-5   Why Do We Need to Conduct a Meta Evaluation? 187

Job aids also found in comprehensive case study of Marriott International in Chapter 8.

FOREWORD

What are the fundamentals? The concepts and tools necessary for understanding how to improve workplace performance. Why do some people perform well and others poorly in the workplace? This book provides an answer: People do what they do because that is what they have learned in the workplace!

- If people loaf on the job, they have been taught to do so. How? Perhaps by supervisors or managers making confusing or contradictory demands, discouraging people who are diligently trying to do a good job. Perhaps by learning that doing a good job is ignored whereas loafing is fun until the boss comes by and screams (and then goes away again). Or perhaps by learning that it is more fun to loaf with peers than to be punished by peers for working hard.

- If people "don't think" on the job, they have been taught not to. How? Perhaps by having their ideas and suggestions ignored. Perhaps by being punished for showing initiative, or asking tough but important questions, or for doing things better (but differently) than the boss wanted.

- If people engage in highly productive teamwork, they have been taught to do so. How? Perhaps by learning how to do work that has been designed for a team. Perhaps by taking part in on-the-job problem-solving teams. Perhaps by being trained in teamwork behaviors that are then supported on the job.

What is performance technology (PT)? This book provides an answer: It is "the systematic process of linking business goals and strategies with the workforce responsible for achieving the goals." (The workforce includes everyone: a salesperson, a third-shift setup mechanic, the CEO, the CFO, the receptionist in the human resources department, and everyone else.) PT is a technology for linking people to organizations in mutually beneficial ways. PT is about supporting people's efforts to:

- Learn how to perform competently.
- Perform competently.
- Learn how to perform even more competently in the future.

PT is about making sure that the people side of the business works. What makes the financial side of the business work? People. What makes the technical side of the business work? People. PT is about making organizations work by helping people work. PT is about helping people work by creating organizations that support high levels of performance. PT is about installing instructional systems and performance support systems. PT is about establishing win-win relationships between organizations and people.

That's a lot. What is performance technology not about? It is not about a specific type of intervention (such as training, incentive systems, quality improvement, reengineering, cost reduction, or right sizing, etc.…). PT is about improving human performance in the workplace; it is not about specific techniques for improving performance. PT is about making systems work; it is not about making parts of systems work better (whether or not doing so actually helps the organization work better). PT is about wholes, not parts.

The mission of the International Society for Performance Improvement (ISPI) states it clearly— "Improving human performance in systematic and reproducible ways." PT is not about changing light bulbs and hoping performance improves; it is about improving performance in systematic and reproducible ways. It is not luck. It is not charisma. It is not the fad of the month. It is a systematic and reproducible approach.

What is the PT approach? This book provides an answer: PT practitioners select the right tools for the job and evaluate progress to assure that the tools are doing the job. This book is organized around the flow of PT in action. The PT flow chart, as shown in many ISPI publications, was generated a few years ago by Bill Deterline and Marc Rosenberg. It shows that one begins with a performance analysis to find gaps between what is happening now and what should be happening now or in the future. Cause analysis identifies the causes of deficient performance and, at the same time, identifies what is necessary to achieve high levels of performance. After specifying desired performance and identifying the variables that support performance, the next step is to select and design an intervention that will enable people (and organizations) to perform at the levels specified. The next step is the one that takes the most time, resources, and ingenuity: implementing the intervention. The final step, evaluation, is a final step only in a flow chart—it is integrated throughout the entire PT process. PT is a data-driven process: Unless evaluation (data-based decisionmaking) is integrated throughout the process, it is not performance technology.

This book describes each part of the process and provides case studies and job aids to help people perform each part of PT competently. In other words, it shows people how to do performance improvement projects in systematic and reproducible ways! I wish a book like this had been written years ago.

Does the book enable readers to learn everything they must learn to be highly competent PT professionals? No. Readers who use this book well will be the ones who already know a lot about human behavior in the workplace. Perhaps they are managers who have heard about and want to understand and use PT. Perhaps they are total quality management (TQM) professionals looking for ways to make TQM initiatives succeed a little more often. Perhaps they are human resources development (HRD) professionals who want to get out of the training box. Perhaps they are graduate students in instructional design who want to make sure their designs add value. The book will be most valuable to people who know a lot about related matters, e.g., some of the many interventions used in PT.

Does the book provide something that those new to PT would benefit by knowing? Yes. It is a handbook for doing PT. Stolovitch and Keeps' *Handbook of Human Performance Technology*, 2nd Edition (1999), is a handbook about PT that is rich in material for doing PT. Darlene Van Tiem, James Moseley, and Joan Conway Dessinger have produced a handbook for doing PT. I think of them as companion volumes, each valuable but in different ways.

Does this book provide anything for experienced PT professionals? Yes. It is the only book available that takes the reader through the whole PT process. It is a journey that experienced professionals take often and, with the help of this book, one they might travel more competently the next time out. It, like Langdon, Whiteside, and McKenna's *Intervention Resource Guide: 50 Performance Improvement Tools* (1999), shows many different interventions PT professionals can use. Even experienced professionals tend to be competent in using only a few of the interventions and would benefit from learning more about the interventions that can be used.

Is the book flawed in any way? Of course. It is flawed in the same way that Deterline and Rosenberg's marvelously useful flow chart is flawed. It shows a systematic process, but it doesn't show the PT practitioner how to think systematically. Does that flaw diminish the book's value? Not really. If a PT practitioner has learned to think systematically, the flow chart is an added tool. If a PT practitioner hasn't learned to think systematically, the flow chart, used often, will enable her or him to add value while learning why systemic thinking is so very important.

Dale Brethower

ACKNOWLEDGMENTS

Second Edition

This second edition of *Fundamentals of Performance Technology* includes new information about the Standards for Performance Technology and the Certified Performance Technologist (CPT) designation developed and instituted by the International Society for Performance Improvement (ISPI). To make this certification available to more performance improvement professionals, ISPI and the American Society for Training & Development (ASTD) affiliated to bring this opportunity to ASTD members.

The CPT designation represents an important phase in the history of performance improvement. By instituting the certification of individuals as CPTs, the profession demonstrates a commitment to common expectations regarding the way performance technology practitioners work in collaboration with clients or organizations.

We are privileged to revise our book to include the Standards of Performance Technology and the Code of Ethics. *Fundamentals of Performance Technology: A Guide to Improving People, Process, and Performance, Second Edition*, discusses each of the 10 Standards and provides steps and guidance for accomplishing each Standard, abiding by the Code of Ethics.

This second edition will be useful to many potential audiences, including performance improvement specialists, trainers, instructional designers, consultants, analysts, intervention specialists, evaluators, change managers, human resource developers, and those in academic environments. From novice to expert, readers at every level of experience can benefit from this book.

After reading this book, the HPT practitioner will be able to:

- Gain significant insight into the landscape, structure, and dynamics of human performance improvement.
- Describe the essential components of the Human Performance Technology (HPT) Model.
- State the linkages among performance analysis; cause analysis; intervention selection, design and development; intervention implementation and change; evaluation; HPT Certification Standards; and Code of Ethics.
- Articulate why HPT adds value to the nature of work, the worker, and the workplace environment.
- Use the HPT Model as a roadmap and reference guide to embrace the business of HPT.
- Assess readiness to apply for the CPT designation.

The CPT designation represents the best of current thinking and professional practice. Experience, reflection, and changing times will lead to more improvements. But we now have structure and Standards that encourage innovation and creativity, plus a Code of Ethics that challenges us to be the best we can be.

We personally thank Dr. Judith Hale and her "Kitchen Cabinet" of more than 30 performance improvement professionals who developed and implemented the Standards of Performance Technology, Code of Ethics, and the initial application forms and procedures. During the 2002-2003 grandparenting period, more than 800 experienced performance improvement professionals became CPTs, demonstrating the wide acceptance and respect for the credential.

Sincerely,
Darlene Van Tiem, PhD, CPT
James L. Moseley, EdD, CPT
Joan Conway Dessinger, EdD, CPT

Acknowledgments

First Edition

There are no problems we cannot solve together, and very few we can solve by ourselves.
—Lyndon B. Johnson, news conference, Johnson City, Texas, November 28, 1964.

Our colleagues and students have influenced this book immensely. Students questioned and challenged us to account for human interaction and its consequences as we worked with them on projects and helped them solve real workplace problems. University colleagues provided insights and contrasting opinions. Practitioners and professional association members provided situations to ponder and assess. In addition, this book meshes three minds and three sets of lifetime experiences.

Ann West, of The Leadership Group, provided an invaluable perspective and critique. Ann's areas of expertise are psychology, leadership, and career development. She has worked in the field of organizational design and human performance for more than 30 years. She understands the projects and challenges of performance technology. However, Ann's background is sufficiently different so that she could take a reader's point of view and avoid making assumptions common among professionals in the same field.

Matt Davis, director of International Society for Performance Improvement (ISPI) publications, provided feedback during the process of revising the Deterline and Rosenberg model of human performance technology (PT). As editor, Andria Brummitt, director, Leapfrog Communications, saw the manuscript through the eyes of someone outside of the PT profession. She challenged our assumptions and encouraged us to think again, using unbelievable diligence and patience.

As teachers, we are especially indebted to our students and our classroom experience. Many of the job aids and case studies were based on instructional activities, which have been improved over the years. It was Karen Miller's master's degree research project (University of Michigan - Dearborn) that helped me realize an entry-level, application-oriented performance technology book was necessary. Students wanted to better understand how to apply the HPT Model in their internships and work environments.

The insightful cartoons, contributed by University of Michigan–Dearborn student Jed Veir and his partner Buck Jones, were originally published as a daily feature on the American Greetings website (www.americangreetings.com).

In addition, graduate students helped with the initial writing of some chapters. Their scholarship is noteworthy. The following people contributed to sections of the book:

Douglas Swiatkowski ....Cause Analysis
Kristin Olin-Sullivan ....Organizational Design and Development Interventions
G. Kevin Sullivan ....Organizational Design and Development Interventions
David Grant.................................Job Analysis
Leonard Constantine, Jr. ....Financial Systems Interventions
Nancy Copeland ....Performance Gap Analysis
Deborah Armstrong ....Performance Gap Analysis
Cathy Tishhouse ....Human Performance Technology in the Workplace
David Maier.................................Organizational Communication

Others who made significant contributions are Priscilla Davis, Diane Moorman, Elizabeth McQuiston, and Johnnie Boone. A special thanks is extended to Annetta Ellis for her proficiency in word processing and for producing chapters with expediency.

Case studies provide vivid real-world examples for applying concepts. Each chapter illustrates the challenges addressed by and the successes made possible through the HPT Model. We are indebted to our personal colleague-friends.

Nancy Lemkie helped us track our progress while writing the book. Nancy monitored the Gantt charts, ensuring that everyone was making progress. Finally, Kathy Laing and Nancie Long, of Triad Performance Technologies, helped us put the icing on the cake by designing the book's cover.

Thanks again!

Darlene Van Tiem
April 2000

TABLE A-1: CASE STUDIES BY SECTION

Section	Source	Workplace	Type of Industry
What Is the HPT Model?	Don Blum, Michelle Goad, Jonathan Campbell	Visteon Automotive Systems	Manufacturing
Is HPT Just a Passing Bandwagon?	Don Davis	Health Alliance Plan (HAP)	Health Maintenance Organization
Performance Analysis: Organizational Analysis	Joan Dessinger	Unidentified	Professional Association
Performance Analysis: Environmental Analysis	Joan Dessinger	HPT Legend	Glass Manufacturing
Gap Analysis	Deborah Armstrong	University Development Center	Higher Education
Cause Analysis: Lack of Environmental Support	Douglas Swiatkowski	Injection Molding Firm	Automotive Supplier
Cause Analysis: Lack of Repertory of Behavior	Douglas Swiatkowski	Plastic Exterior Trim Manufacturing	Automotive Supplier
Performance Support Interventions	ISPI	J.C. Penney Company	Retail
Job Analysis Interventions	David Grant	Aerospace and Defense Corporations	Aerospace and Defense
Work Design Interventions	James Moseley	Michael James Clinic	Medical Group Practice
Personal Development Interventions	Elizabeth McQuiston	Simioni Company	Sales
Human Resource Development Interventions	ISPI	Aetna Life and Casualty Company	Insurance and Financial Services
Organizational Design and Development Interventions	ISPI	Morrison-Knudsen Corporation	Construction and Engineering
Organizational Communication Interventions	James Moseley	Bugaj, Incorporated	Retail Conglomerate
Financial Systems Interventions	Leonard Constantine, Jr.	Muller-Roberts	Clothing Industry
Change Management	Arlene Gorelick	Epilepsy Foundation of Michigan	Nonprofit Human Services
Process Consulting	Joyce Beasley	Roegan Enterprises, Inc.	K-12 School Improvement Planning
Employee Development	Debra Demeester, John Wisniewski	Henry Ford Health System	Managed Health Care
Communication, Networking, and Alliance Building	Rodolpho Morales, Jr.	Michigan Virtual Automotive College	Public/Private Education Cooperation
Formative Evaluation	James Naughton	Detroit Medical Center	Health Care – Hospital
Summative Evaluation	Joan Dessinger	Specialty Vehicle	Retail – Automotive
Confirmative Evaluation	Joan Dessinger	SWRL/Ginn Beginning Reading Program	K–12 Education
Meta Evaluation	Mary Jane Heaney	Detroit Medical Center Specialty Vehicle SWRL/Ginn Beginning Reading Program	Health Care – Hospital Retail – Automotive K–12 Education
Performance Technology in the Workplace	Cathy Tishhouse	Marriott International – Detroit	Hospitality

FUNDAMENTALS OF PERFORMANCE TECHNOLOGY— A GUIDE TO IMPROVING PEOPLE, PROCESS, AND PERFORMANCE

"MAYBE I DON'T WANT TO FETCH A PAIL OF WATER."

PERFORMANCE TECHNOLOGY–DEFINED

Too many phones are ringing to be answered promptly. Parts are being produced with flaws. Customers just won't buy the latest product improvement. Advertisements aren't catching shoppers' attention. Every workplace has challenges that seem unsolvable. Workers and managers have held meetings, written plans, and pledged new energy and resolve. Sometimes the new ideas work, sometimes nothing changes or matters get worse. It often seems difficult to control the workplace situation systematically. Why do the problems persist? Why do workers seem resistant to new ideas? Why do managers seem so "bossy" and insensitive?

Humans have tried to understand why people do what they do since the beginning of recorded history. Performance technology (PT) attempts to explain the observable aspects of workplace behavior, individually and collectively (such as through culture). However, PT does not pretend to be able to explain human behavior in its entirety; heredity, prior experiences, and other factors probably have an unbelievably great impact on any workplace situation.

Performance Technology—Defined

Performance technology (PT) is the systematic process of linking business goals and strategies with the workforce responsible for achieving the goals. PT practitioners use a common methodology to understand, inspire, and improve people; they study and redesign processes leading to increased performance in the workplace. PT systematically analyzes performance problems and their underlying causes and describes exemplary performance and success indicators.

PT attempts to:
- Analyze observable workplace behavior.
- Associate the behaviors with related environmental factors, such as organizational culture and mission.
- Determine the causes of exemplary and problem behaviors.
- Design possible solutions, called *interventions*.
- Put the interventions into action.
- Monitor and measure the results to document the effectiveness of the intervention toward designed change.

The Human Performance Technology (HPT) Model

The previous list may seem like the established standard used to understand human situations and make changes. In fact, the traditional approach to problem solving usually deals with groups or departments and focuses on a single defined concern. For example, reengineering usually focuses on a particular process or job design as an approach to improve productivity. In this situation, little attention is given to how performances are recognized and rewarded. The traditional approach fails to link employee behavior with organizational culture and to deal with the full complexity of work behavior.

In contrast, the HPT Model (Figure 1-1) acknowledges the complexity of the workplace and the interrelationships among all organizational factors. Careful analysis of multiple factors helps the PT practitioner to more accurately diagnose human behavior and its impact on the organization and vice versa. Finally, measuring the results of PT activities allows the PT practitioner to modify interventions and to verify success. In other words, each stage of the HPT Model helps practitioners understand why people do what they do.

Because human behavior is influenced by the reciprocal patterns of the workplace culture and individual factors, PT practitioners consider all of these factors simultaneously. Subsequently, an array of interventions are identified as potential solutions. The HPT Model also challenges upper management to create an environment that fosters success.

Book Structure

Fundamentals of Performance Technology: A Guide to Improving People, Process, and Performance describes each major category and component of the HPT Model in a practical, how-to manner. Using a handbook format, this book is designed to make the theory understandable and action-oriented. It offers commonsense interventions for improving workplace human behavior. Each chapter contains a description of one component of the HPT Model, followed by a case study to illustrate the component, and a job aid. The reader will finish the book energized by the belief: "Yes, I can do that!"

FIGURE I-I

HUMAN PERFORMANCE TECHNOLOGY (HPT) MODEL

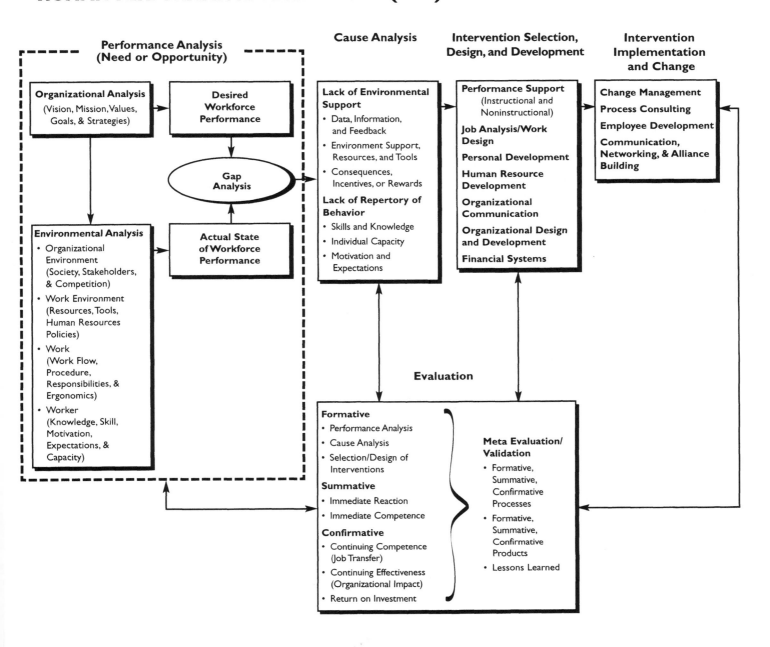

Readers new to the field may not be familiar with job aids. They are officially known as *performance support tools;* they provide highly organized information needed to support desired action. They may be paper-based, computer-based, cardboard, laminated, or spiral bound. They are intended to be convenient, easy-to-grab, easy-to-skim, easy-to-follow. According to Elsenheimer, job aids are well-suited for tasks with the following characteristics:[1]

- Low frequency—seldom happens, no need to memorize task
- High complexity—unrealistic to learn multitask steps, especially when in a particular order
- Frequently changing—quick updates are possible because people rely on the latest information
- Low budget—simple to develop and update in the beginning or as information changes
- High consequence of errors—used as a reminder to minimize errors

Summary

PT is an important and growing field because organizations recognize the value people provide (or can provide). There is increasing emphasis on human capital and maximizing the potential of people as a way to gain a competitive advantage.[2] *Fundamentals of Performance Technology: A Guide to Improving People, Process, and Performance* is an easy-to-read, easy-to-apply comprehensive explanation of the factors affecting workplace behavior. Using a commonsense approach and consistent structure, the book explains how to (1) diagnose workplace situations, (2) identify causes, (3) select doable, adequate interventions, (4) implement changes, and (5) evaluate results.

CHAPTER

2

THE HUMAN PERFORMANCE TECHNOLOGY MODEL

"THE GUYS DON'T LIKE MY EFFICIENCY IDEAS."

WHAT IS THE HPT MODEL?

The world has entered a new economic era, characterized by rapid change, heightened competitiveness, and unprecedented productivity challenges. More machines, improved computers, or reliance on cost-cutting alone will not increase competitiveness and improve productivity. Greater productivity will be achieved via one of the world's most critical resources: *people*.[1]

Performance technology (PT) improves productivity by improving employees' accomplishments. *PT is a systematic, comprehensive approach to improving job performance.* "Performance technology is a set of methods and procedures, and a strategy for solving problems, or realizing opportunities related to the performance of employees. It can be applied to individuals, small groups, and large organizations."[2]

In 1992, the International Society for Performance Improvement (ISPI), a professional association based in Washington, D.C., published the original HPT Model to impact performance on the job.[3] The original HPT Model was developed by Deterline and Rosenberg and published by ISPI to illustrate the steps needed to function as a PT practitioner and accomplish performance improvement in the workplace. The model defined performance analysis, cause analysis, and intervention selection and design. Intervention implementation and evaluation were identified but not defined.

Fundamentals of Performance Technology: A Guide to Improving People, Process, and Performance explains how to apply the HPT Model (Figure 2-1) in the workplace. The book's case studies provide real-world examples of how to implement the HPT Model. Its job aids give the reader helpful worksheets for applying the HPT Model easily and confidently. In addition, *Fundamentals of Performance Technology: A Guide to Improving People, Process, and Performance* expands the original HPT Model to cover the entire performance improvement process by defining intervention implementation and evaluation.

Our second book, *Performance Improvement Interventions*, will provide further assistance to PT practitioners as they strive to improve workplace performance. This book will more fully describe each intervention found in *Fundamentals of Performance Technology*, providing detailed information on how to implement the intervention. The job aids will expedite intervention application by helping the reader understand how to apply the change

ideas to each unique work situation. Additional case studies will illustrate how the intervention actually works within today's competitive organizational environment. *Performance Improvement Interventions* will be published in 2001.

Performance Analysis

PT practitioners begin by learning the expectations and requirements of the organization. This stage describes the desired situation and what is actually occurring. The outcome of performance analysis is an explanation of the gap, or difference, between the current and the hoped-for situation.

Cause Analysis

The second stage takes a deeper look at the organization and the individual to determine what actually caused the gap. Two types of factors impact human performance: organizational (also known as environmental) support and individual behavior. PT practitioners need to consider the information, data, and feedback that is provided to employees. Adequate environmental support includes sufficient resources, tools, and equipment to do the job well. Organizational incentives, rewards, and consequences have a significant impact. In other words, people need to have the pertinent information, equipment, and supplies, and work in an environment that encourages positive results.

In addition, employees need the capabilities to perform well. They need the right knowledge, skills, and attitudes to succeed. They need innate capacity, such as stamina or strength. Finally, they must have sufficient personal motivation and drive.

Intervention Selection and Design

After determining the gap and the cause(s) for it, PT practitioners must decide what to do to improve the condition. There are many possible options. However, it is necessary to design a comprehensive, holistic approach that covers all of the issues. That may mean selecting more than one approach.

Interventions should be selected based on the costs and benefits to the organization and the employees. Knowledge and skills can be improved through training and education

FIGURE 2-1

HUMAN PERFORMANCE TECHNOLOGY (HPT) MODEL

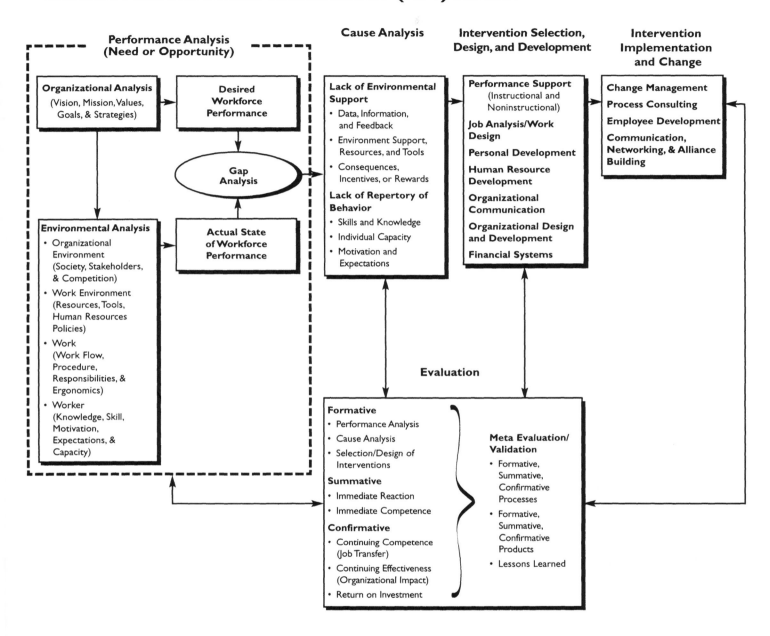

or job aids. Jobs can be redesigned to improve health, wellness, comfort, or ergonomics. Personal development includes coaching, mentoring, career development, effective supervision, and reliable, informative feedback. Assessment centers, competency testing, and performance appraisals provide the organizational metrics that help the organization compensate, reward, and evaluate people in a reliable manner. Organizational communication takes many forms, including networking and collaboration, knowledge management and capture, conflict resolution, and grievance and suggestion systems. Finally,

organizations can improve their culture, increase their appreciation of diversity, build effective teams to solve problems, look to other organizations for benchmarks, and make strategic plans for the future.

Intervention Implementation and Change

Change implementation requires communication of plans and progress. PT practitioners need to network with various affected departments to ensure an accurate understanding of their expectations and concerns. Careful attention to resistance and fears helps contain problems. Problem solving should include setting benchmarks to create realistic targets. Process consulting may be beneficial if the improvement involves extensive redesign of processes. Ongoing support for employee development enables people to retain competitiveness and to prepare for the organization's future.

Evaluation

Measuring and reporting results is critical for maintaining the confidence of PT practitioners. Interventions should be measured at the onset of implementation and throughout the improvement effort to ensure that intended results are occurring.

Basis of the Technology

PT is called a technology because practitioners are careful, methodical, and observant. "Technology represents intelligence systematically applied to the problem";[4] in other words, technology applies scientific and technical

advances. The model and practice of PT are based on the writings of many behavioral experts. Some of the leading PT experts and their contributions are highlighted in Table 2-1 to provide examples of the scientific foundation and evolution of PT.

Thomas Gilbert

Thomas Gilbert established much of the conceptual framework for performance technology. He defined *worthy performance* as behavior valued for its accomplishment. Worth is determined by dividing value by cost (W=V/C).

Gilbert's Behavior Engineering Model (Table 2-2) consists of six basic influences on human behavior that impact performance improvement. They are grouped under two different areas: environment—data (production standards), instruments (equipment), and incentives (rewards); and repertory—knowledge (the "know how" to perform), capacity (physical and intellectual ability), and motives (willingness to work for the incentives). The HPT

TABLE 2-1

PT SCIENTIFIC FOUNDATION AND EVOLUTION

Expert	PT Aspect
Thomas Gilbert	Worthy Performance
Geary Rummler	Components of Performance
Robert Mager	Objectives
Joe Harless	Front-end Analysis
Dale Brethower	Performance-based Instruction

TABLE 2-2

GILBERT'S BEHAVIOR ENGINEERING MODEL: OVERVIEW

	Information	Instrumentation	Motivation
Environmental Support	Data	Instruments	Incentives
Person's Repertory of Behavior	Knowledge	Capacity	Motives

Model's cause analysis is based on Gilbert's Behavior Engineering Model.[5]

In addition, Gilbert's Performance Matrix contained six vantage points (or outlooks): logistical, tactical, strategic, policy, cultural, and philosophical. Gilbert believed it unwise to define change in terms of desired behavior, preferring instead to describe it in terms of performance outcomes.

Geary Rummler

Geary A. Rummler defined the five components of a performance system. His work helped PT practitioners view the components of individual performance as much more than behavior and outcomes. He stressed the interrelationship of the individual employee and the organization.

Rummler's five components of a performance system are as follows:[6]
1. Job situation (the occasion of the performance)
2. Performer (the worker)
3. Response (the action or decision that occurs)
4. Consequence (may be reward, punishment, or nonexistent consequences)
5. Feedback (information about whether the response was adequate or inadequate)

Later, Rummler and Alan P. Brache described the cumulative, collective impact of performance variables based on Level—Organization, Process, or Job/Performer—and Performance Needs—Goals, Design, and Management. Rummler and Brache emphasized the importance of managing the interrelationships between departments and processes, the "white space on the organizational chart." They saw creating harmony and reducing tension as critical to developing departments that are "centers of excellence."[7]

Robert Mager

Robert Mager provided the concept of objectives as a consistent framework for describing desired outcomes. *Objectives* are statements that are precise and clear descriptions of performance (what the learner or worker is able to do), conditions (important circumstances under which the performance is expected to occur), and criterion (the quality or level of performance that will be considered acceptable). Mager helped PT practitioners define desired performance using common terminology.
For example,

> Given a DC motor of ten horsepower or less that contains a single malfunction, and given a kit of tools and references, be able to repair the motor. The motor must be repaired within 45 minutes and must operate to within 5 percent of factory specifications.[8]

Joe Harless

Joe Harless claimed that the most important job of a trainer, or PT practitioner, is to determine what problem needs to be solved.[9] Front-end Analysis (FEA) describes the performance indicator needing improvement, identifies behavioral causes (caused by people) and non-behavioral causes (not caused by people), and prioritizes possible solutions to overcome the deficit. Harless challenged trainers (and later PT practitioners) to spend time adequately understanding the problem. In 1975, training was the most frequent performance improvement solution, and Harless cautioned that only behavioral problems would benefit from training, and even then only if lack of knowledge or skill was the cause. Harless emphasized looking for multiple remedies, not simple, one-shot solutions.

Dale Brethower

More recently, Dale Brethower challenges PT practitioners to focus on the job when designing instruction to link training directly to business results. *Performance-based Instruction* "uses joblike materials and procedures to help learners become capable of excellent performance."[10] It is an intervention format that applies to instruction, facilitation, coaching, on-the-job training, teambuilding, or performance support/job aids. Brethower advocates three basic steps: guided observation, in which learners experience examples or demonstrations; guided practice, in which learners practice specific processes that accomplish specific results; and demonstration of mastery, in which students demonstrate their competency in performing tasks, thereby generating the desired products or services. Brethower's approach provides realistic situations and procedures to help students quickly achieve excellent performance.

People Orientation

Performance technology is *people-oriented*, meaning that practitioners typically share a set of common beliefs:
- People are important.
- Appropriate PT solutions are beneficial for people and are future-oriented.
- PT approaches to analysis, design, implementation, and evaluation need to be multidimensional.
- PT practitioners work in a manner that is team-oriented and interdependent.

People Are Important

PT practitioners are committed to people—their capabilities and their potential. People provide the core energy of organizations. Equipment and financial reserves are important, but people are its heart and soul. They purchase, operate, and maintain the equipment; they budget, account for, and report the financial reserves. People are behind everything that happens.

Positive and Future-oriented

PT practitioners have a positive outlook and are oriented to the future. They believe it is possible to improve situations and look for solutions that are beneficial for people, no matter how complex the problem, how great the hurdle to overcome, or how discouraging the present situation.

Multidimensional Approaches

PT practitioners are committed to adopting comprehensive interventions that include many of the major factors identified in the PT cause analysis model. Rather than rushing in with interventions based only on gap analysis, PT practitioners first search for causes. Reducing gaps often provides only temporary relief, but eliminating causes can fix real problems.

Equally important to solving problems is getting the commitment from senior management and other stakeholders to support the interventions. Through networking, communication, and alliance building, PT practitioners implement effective interventions based on strategic planning and results-oriented feedback.

Team-oriented and Interdependent

PT practitioners accomplish performance improvement and change through groups or teams. PT practitioners rely on senior management to articulate organizational needs, to support analysis, and to sponsor interventions and follow-up evaluation. Comprehensive intervention designs usually include many specialized features, such as compensation, work environment, motivation, and skill development. Specialists in compensation, selection, or job design need to work with PT practitioners to craft communication plans, intervention timelines, and follow-up strategies to achieve desired changes.

The Challenge

Performance technology challenges practitioners to be thoughtful, observant, knowledgeable, systematic, hopeful, comprehensive, people-oriented, and scientific. PT is a rewarding approach to performance improvement, but, due to its complexity, it is also challenging and demanding.

Organizational Implementation

PT practitioners adapt the generic HPT Model to the unique requirements of their own internal organization.

Modifying the HPT Model and the job aids into unique tools strengthens performance outcomes. PT practitioners need to adapt to the mission, strategic direction, and culture of each organization. Visteon Automotive Systems, an enterprise of Ford Motor Company, adapted the generic HPT Model into a standardized and easy-to-use set of procedures for assisting internal customers. They also developed a tool kit binder of job aids and instruments designed to make Visteon's performance improvements consistent and effective.

Case Study: Visteon Automotive Systems Education, Training, and Development Performance Improvement Tool Kit

Background

Visteon Automotive Systems is an enterprise of the Ford Motor Company and provides integrated systems and component solutions to Automotive Original Equipment Manufacturers. Visteon's mission is to be the best supplier of automotive systems and to create new opportunities for its employees, customers, and the industry. Based in Dearborn, Michigan, Visteon employs more than 80,000 hourly and salaried employees. Visteon's 82 manufacturing and production facilities in 21 countries deliver uniform product quality and service to meet their customers' needs worldwide. One of the major challenges Visteon faces is transforming from a cost to a profit center, with its main objective to grow non-Ford business by 20 percent during the next three years.

Situation

Visteon Education, Training, & Development (ET&D) plays a critical role in shaping performance to meet Visteon's business plan objectives relative to quality, cost, and efficiency. Although Visteon is familiar with conventional training interventions, the internal customer base needs to understand the variety of potential performance interventions that could help them achieve their organizational goals. A decentralized approach to training programs within the organization resulted in inconsistent customer engagement and dissimilar return-on-investment (ROI) outcome measurement practices throughout Visteon.

ET&D is required to constantly demonstrate the consistent value they add to the organization. One way to accomplish this is to measure their impact on the bottomline through cost-benefit analysis and a solid ROI calculation. Satisfied customer testimonials, although meaningful, are not accepted as an adequate ROI measure.

A review of current company training procedures determined that there were some isolated cases in which ROI calculation for training initiatives is currently in use. There is no evidence of any consistent use of the ROI calculation process for PT initiatives. Training and development managers in Visteon were interviewed to better understand the organizational need for a practical PT intervention process. They also provided input for an ROI calculation that would identify both tangible and intangible benefits from an implemented PT intervention.

Intervention

ET&D's findings indicated the need for a standardized and easy-to-use HPT Model for internal customers. The Visteon Education, Training, & Development Performance Improvement Tool Kit binder was developed to provide instruments for the PT practitioner to:

- Identify performance issues and opportunities.
- Determine the cause(s) of the performance issues/opportunities.
- Isolate the most appropriate performance improvement intervention.
- Converge to an appropriate measure of intervention success.
- Determine tangible and intangible benefits of the performance improvement intervention.
- Calculate an ROI from a cost-benefit analysis.
- Evaluate the impact of the intervention on employee performance.

The main purpose of the tool kit binder was to offer a consistent and uniform service to internal customers while instilling a professional discipline for all PT practitioners at Visteon. The tool kit also provided both practitioner and customer with two models: a seven-step performance improvement process and a five-step ROI process. These visuals were a key marketing piece for ET&D because they helped educate customers on what performance improvement professionals do and the beneficial results they can deliver to organizations.

The tool kit binder was structured in an easy-to-use format, divided into seven sections based on each step of the performance improvement process. Each step contained specific job aids and tools. There was also a brief purpose statement at the beginning of each section indicating how each tool was to function as a job aid to practitioners. Tools, which were self-explanatory and menu-driven whenever possible, included a project status report, a project scope analysis, an intervention project plan, an intervention checklist, intervention evaluation forms, and an ROI worksheet. ET&D consultants (PT practitioners) were able to access these job aids and forms on the shared drive of the Visteon local area network.

ET&D performance consultants (PT practitioners) piloted these instruments with customers in a variety of performance improvement scenarios. The entire process was reviewed at the initial project scope meeting between the consultants and the customer.

The feedback from customers was systematically analyzed at weekly staff meetings to aid process refinement and redesign. Initial customer feedback indicated the tool kit was extremely favorable. Their suggestions were incorporated to improve the overall quality of the tool kit.

Lessons Learned

1. A consistent, disciplined approach to performance improvement should be implemented by PT practitioners when working with customers. Using a consistent process such as the Performance Improvement Tool Kit demonstrates the PT practitioner's ability to effectively assess and analyze the situation; develop, implement, and evaluate an intervention; and measure its impact the organization's bottom line.

2. The value-added by performance improvement interventions can be determined in terms of tangible and intangible benefits. Follow-up is critical to determining the success and the value of an intervention. The evaluation instruments in the tool kit provide a consistent approach to calculating the ROI for a performance improvement intervention.

3. It is important to educate the customer on the benefits that PT interventions can deliver within organizations. Customers need to understand how and why performance improvement interventions can help their organizations improve employee performance and impact the bottom line.

4. Organizations need a practical and useful PT process to help them understand why people do what they do. PT is focused on people and improving performance and provides insights into why people do what they do. Organizations that use a uniform and practical PT process, such as the tool kit, improve employee performance and, in turn, improve customer satisfaction.

The Visteon case study was coauthored by Don Blum, Division Manager, Visteon Education, Training, & Development, Jonathan Campbell, and Michelle Goad, Visteon Education, Training, & Development Performance Consultants. Used with permission.

JOB AID 2-1: SITUATIONAL ANALYSIS

The performance technologist and the department requesting performance improvement assistance should discuss the following topics to begin a performance technology (PT) effort. There should be overall agreement between the requesting department and the performance technologist before the intervention project begins.

Statement of the Problem: Describe the performance problem that seems to require an intervention.
Work Environment: Define culture, department responsibilities, or inputs/outputs. Describe all factors that may influence performance.
Target Audience: Describe employees involved by job roles, estimated current performance level, and estimated required performance level.
Sponsor: Describe champion, who is the senior-level person committed to the performance improvement and will stand behind the effort if a setback or problem arises. (Determine if there is strong enough commitment and if the sponsor is at the appropriate level.)
Performance Improvement Goal: Write overall anticipated benefits and changes to individuals.
Measures of Success: Write anticipated benefits and changes to organization and department.

IS PT JUST A PASSING BANDWAGON?

People are the most important resource for the knowledge era; people are the fundamental determinants of economic growth and productivity.[1] These concepts are not new. But PT is a relatively new and dynamic approach for putting this concept into practice. Human resources and training and development survey results indicate that more and more senior managers are committed to people as their most important resource.[2]

However, there is skepticism regarding people issues in the business sector. Frequently, people-oriented initiatives are viewed as passing bandwagons. They are colorfully and convincingly presented to workers and enthusiastically supported by senior management. Then they are hastily replaced by a different bandwagon initiative when workplace improvements are not quickly achieved. Will PT become a passing bandwagon, like the bandwagons that came to town and left with the circus? Can PT maintain its enthusiastic supporters? Does PT stand up to application in the workplace?

Performance technology is a systematic, comprehensive, and analytical approach. It links many factors together to generate solutions and is well-suited for the people-oriented, team-based, knowledge era. PT is key to explaining why people do what they do.

Teams

The sports arena provides an appropriate analogy to PT. Most sports teams have a long tradition of strategically selecting players and planning competitive plays. Football players, for example, study the strengths and weaknesses of opponents and practice their assignments accordingly. Coaches motivate players to win by giving feedback and encouraging team playing. As Casey Stengel, the legendary manager of baseball's New York Yankees, often remarked, "Finding good players is easy; getting them to play together is the hard part."[3]

Businesses and other organizations, like sports teams, need to recognize the strengths, weaknesses, and interdependencies of their workforce to ensure that workers "play together" effectively in support of business objectives.

Knowledge Era

Today's knowledge era organizations are creating team cultures that are dependent on contributions by all team members. Fisher and Fisher predict that most future work will be mental and team-based.[4] Individuals will bring their specialized knowledge and skills to teams. Teams will often be virtual, and their membership will be constantly shifting as teams members accomplish their task and move on to another assignment. Team members may never physically meet their coworkers.

In this knowledge era, organizations need to value and reward the sharing of information. According to Millman, "Intensely competitive or territorial organizations, in which personnel tend to hoard all information, will achieve less success than those companies in which top management encourages an open, cooperative workplace."[5] Organizations need to encourage information exchange and ensure that employees do not lose power when they share knowledge.

Clearly, the trend towards valuing people and knowledge requires a paradigm shift. PT provides such a methodology. PT can be sustained because people and their knowledge truly are the organization's most valuable resource.

Human Resources Trends

Understanding human resource (HR) trends is critical to analyzing organizations and employees, determining causes of problems, designing interventions, and evaluating results. By studying staffing, training, performance, outsourcing, and various other trends, PT practitioners are able to predict future directions and make better decisions about performance issues. Change interventions are usually difficult to execute and often meet with resistance because people do not understand the underlying rationale.

Human Resource Survey

The Society for Human Resource Management (SHRM) and AON Consulting surveyed human resources leadership and jointly published *The 1997 Survey of Human Resources Trends Report*.[6] Survey responses included more than 1,700 HR professionals across the U.S. More than 60 percent of the survey participants held vice president or director of human resources titles. More than 20 million U.S. workers are employed by the organizations that employ the survey participants.

The SHRM/AON survey summarized many people-oriented trends. Change management and strategic planning initiatives are rapidly increasing in importance. Organizational change efforts involving senior management are making a major contribution to organizational effectiveness. AON Consulting also found that productivity expectations have increased more than quality expectations.[7]

Staffing and Selection

Selection of people is important to successful organizations. Finding desirable candidates is the number one employment challenge, and retaining desirable employees ranks second.[8] Staff turnover is still considered the greatest HR worry. The diminished applicant pool is a concern. Fewer applicants have the necessary knowledge, skills, and positive attitude to work effectively. In other words, job-specific skills are more readily found in job seekers than are desirable work attitudes.

In the applicant pool, negative work attitudes are considered to be a more serious deficiency than work aptitudes and skills by a ratio of 56 percent to 41 percent. As illustrated in Table 2-3, nonmanagement applicants' greatest weaknesses are in (1) dealing with change, (2) problem solving and reasoning, (3) creativity and innovation, (4) communications, (5) basic skills, and (6) interpersonal and team skills. Management applicants' weakest areas are (1) change facilitation, (2) leadership, (3) communications, (4) interpersonal and team skills, and (5) creativity and innovation.

Well-designed selection procedures increase an organization's hiring success rate and can include validated skills tests, structured applications, and behavioral interviews.

Training and Development

More money and other resources are available for developing and training people.[9] Training budgets have increased by an average of 45 percent in the last three years. However, documenting the value of training with measurable results continues to be the training staff's greatest challenge. As a result, calculating ROI will continue to be a high priority.

Performance Management

Satisfaction with performance management, such as performance appraisal and career development, has greatly increased but still remains a problem. Employees believe annual appraisals are unfair if they are evaluated by only their managers. However, "full-circle" or 360° feedback increased employee confidence. Full-circle or 360° feedback is a multirater process that includes opinions of managers, peers, customers, as well as a self-appraisal. Currently, these multirater processes are most commonly used for executives, managers, and supervisors. There is growing interest in extending the multirater process to professional, technical, and sales workers.

Career Development

Career development is important for helping employees prepare for future job opportunities.[10] Job markets change rapidly, and it is difficult for people to know how to plan their careers. Career development specialists help people analyze their interests and skills and match their strengths with the desired career. Competency modeling helps people determine the skills needed for particular careers. Competency modeling describes jobs based on the

TABLE 2-3

JOB APPLICANT WEAKNESSES

Nonmanagement	Management
Dealing with change	Change facilitation
Problem solving and reasoning	Leadership
Creativity and innovation	Communications
Communications	Interpersonal and team skills
Basic skills	Creativity and innovation
Interpersonal and team skills	

knowledge, skills, and abilities necessary and prioritizes each competency relative to potential for job success. Career development specialists also help people create career plans to reach their goals.

Information Technology

Information technology and computer processing are primarily used for managing payroll, maintaining training histories, and tracking job applicants. Computer software will increase employee access to HR information and help managers and employees prepare educational plans as a part of career development and performance management. Computer usage is expected to improve the speed of HR services.

Outsourcing

Outsourcing is common in HR departments, especially in organizations of 3,000 or more employees. Nonstrategic functions, such as wellness programs, reference checking, and benefits and pension administration are the most frequently outsourced. Organizations with 10,000 or more employees are likely to outsource recruiting, pre-employment testing, applicant screening, interviewing, and equal employment opportunity (EEO) tracking as well. In other words, most operational, nonstrategic HR functions are suitable for outsourcing.

International

The human resource function is expected to grow outside the U.S. more than within the U.S.[11] Pre-assignment visits to foreign countries, language training, health and drug screening, and realistic job previews are the most common expatriate HR services.

HR Trends Summary

HR will continue to be critical to organizations, and its value will become more strategic. Heightened concern about knowledge and skills competencies will drive organizations to increase competency modeling, training, and development and to further improve career management. Information technology will facilitate the integration of human resources with other resources within the organization.

Training and Development Trends

Performance technology is broad in scope and includes many factors considered to be part of human resources. One of the most common interventions is training and development. As a result, PT practitioners need to be familiar with training and development trends.

The American Society for Training and Development (ASTD) conducts ongoing benchmarking studies and researches government publications, professional journals, and other research-oriented sources to track training, development, and performance improvement trends.[12] ASTD publishes well-respected research, which has a significant influence on curriculum planning, budgeting, and future directions. ASTD research guides PT practitioners as they set direction, plan interventions, and secure support.

Traditionally, training and development was believed to be the most useful method for performance improvement. Recently, the training field has broadened its approach to link the many aspects of performance. Seasoned trainers are transitioning to performance consultants.[13] In the past, training was often not valued because it focused on information and not on job knowledge and skills transfer. In fact, training unsupported by management is usually of little benefit. Trainers and performance consultants work to ensure that training is supported.[14]

Skills Requirements

Demand for computer and other job-specific skills is increasing. According to a 1993 report from the U.S. Bureau of Census, workplace use of computers has nearly doubled from 25 percent to 46 percent in 15 years.[15] As a result, skill training, in general, is dramatically increasing in importance. "Just to keep even each worker will need to accumulate learning equivalent to 30 credit hours of [higher education] instruction every seven years."[16]

Workforce Diversity

Organizational cultures are becoming more diverse. The U.S. Department of Labor estimates that the percentage of women, older workers, and Asian and Hispanic workers will continue to rise until the year 2005.[17] There will be more diverse ideas within organizational cultures and a shifting from traditional organizational norms. For example, benefits and job design may need to be more flexible to allow job sharing for working mothers, elder caregivers, or seniors.

Corporate Restructuring

According to Bassi, Cheney, and Van Buren, businesses will continue to restructure.[18] Continued downsizing, the growth of small businesses, and the lack of job security will all contribute to lower morale and dissatisfaction. This leads to symptoms of stress and anxiety, particularly about career development.

For example, restructuring has led to multiskill jobs with employees taking on tasks previously assigned to several workers. Small businesses tend to have more generalists and fewer specialists. In addition, "virtual" organizations, in which employees do not go to a central, physical location considered "company property," are becoming commonplace. Many employees meet via computer in cyberspace, receive job assignments through e-mail or overnight package express, and submit reports and evidence of work via cyberspace.

Performance Improvement

The demand for increased productivity and improved job performance will likely cause a shift away from traditional training or skill development. Future emphasis will be on "learning events" using emerging learning technologies and other training efficiencies. Use of distance learning, such as multimedia software, videoconferencing, and Web-based solutions will increase. Learning will be "just-in-time" and "just enough" because it is readily available on CD-ROM, the Internet, or intranet. Videoconferences give the feeling of face-to-face contact while reducing travel costs and time away from the job. Organizations will become learning organizations in which opportunities for growth are ubiquitous and part of the job.[19]

Results Orientation

Another important trend in training and development is a results orientation. PT practitioners, like training and development specialists, will need to track costs and benefits to prove value. Benchmarking will be useful for establishing standards and making comparisons.

PT as a Profession—Not Just a Passing Bandwagon

In summary, trend analysis underscores the importance of people to the organization. These same trends emphasize the changing nature of people services. High levels of skills and abilities will be critical for the knowledge era. Both SHRM/AON and ASTD research reports make strong cases that performance technology is not just a passing bandwagon.[20] PT will not "leave town with the next circus train."

PT Within Individual Organizations— Not Just Another Bandwagon Either

Based on national surveys and research,[21] commitment to people is becoming stronger. However, each organization has a unique culture, processes, products and/or services, and external and internal customers. As a result, generalizations regarding people issues need to be revalidated in each organization.

PT practitioners need to track internal and external performance indicators and to analyze their own data. Data gathering and analysis is difficult because workplace performance outcomes are hard to define and the data are difficult to secure.[22] For example, what should be measured to determine improvements in management leadership? What outcomes should document satisfactory communication? Table 2-4 illustrates sample performance outcome indicators.

Demonstrating results through effective reporting communicates the value-added advantage of PT efforts. Communicating results encourages the commitment to not let PT become a passing bandwagon. Readily understood graphs,

TABLE 2-4

SAMPLE PERFORMANCE OUTCOME INDICATORS

Management Leadership	Communications
% employees mentored/coached	% employees submit suggestions
% employees complete developmental plan	% employees receive performance appraisal
% employees on special assignments	Articles submitted to organizational newsletter
% successful improvement projects	Effective process for problem solving
Cultural survey results	Cultural survey results

charts, and explanations help management and employees realize the benefit of people-oriented services.

For instance, in the area of training, the Organisation for Economic Co-operation and Development reported that time spent in training beyond high school leads to increased wages.[23] In addition, the U.S. Department of Labor also found that training attendance leads to increased wages, especially if the training is general because the learning can be transferred from job assignment to job assignment.[24] It is clear that performance technology is not a passing bandwagon within individual organizations either. PT will not be "leaving town" soon, like the bandwagons that used to leave with the circus posters and the big-tent entertainers. However, PT efforts involving training need to be measured both with numbers (quantitatively) and with success stories (qualitatively) to convey value and help employees and management make better decisions.

Case Study: Health Alliance Plan's Human Resource Effectiveness Report

Health Alliance Plan (HAP) is a well-respected health maintenance organization associated with Henry Ford Health Systems, based in Detroit, Michigan. It provides primarily employee-based health services to large manufacturing companies, nonprofit organizations, and small companies. HAP's service area focuses on southeastern Michigan, northern Ohio, and greater Flint. The National Committee for Quality Assurance awarded HAP three-year full accreditation status. HAP was rated the number-one plan in the state of Michigan and number 17 nationwide.

Situation

In the 1980s, HAP's Department of Human Resources (HR) was not respected for its contributions to the organization. Executives and employees alike were not familiar with the value added by HR. *The Human Resources Effectiveness Report* was started as an effort to "shine the light" on the people aspects of the organization. The report was designed to market and educate employees about HR and, as a result, to improve the performance of the workforce.

The effectiveness report was also created to demonstrate that HR initiatives were *not just a passing bandwagon*, but added permanent value that improved year-after-year. By measuring HR services and showing year over year trends, HR developed a closer working relationship with other divisions, such as operations, marketing, financial, information systems, and executive/

legal. This enabled other divisions to see how their HR partnership initiatives impact the effectiveness report findings. Each division can now compare its statistics with those of the other divisions. The report portrays an "open book" approach that is designed to support decision making and planning.

Intervention

HR's goals were to gain respect and to encourage partnerships between the other divisions and HR. To accomplish these two goals, Vice President of Human Resources Don Davis decided to initiate an effectiveness report to illustrate HR activities and to demonstrate measurable value. In PT terms, Davis selected organizational communication as the intervention to educate, market, and demonstrate HR's worth. The effectiveness report contained extensive graphics, particularly bar charts, pie charts, and tables, to illustrate relationships among divisions and to show changes from year to year. In addition the report provided information for process improvements, while its openness encouraged suggestions from the divisions, creating a dialogue.

For example, the report's turnover section contained tables regarding reasons for leaving based on exit interviews of non-exempt and exempt employees. Reasons included family responsibilities, relocation, management, advancement, career change, and salary.[25] Davis stated that before the report managers usually believed that salary was the primary reason for leaving. Armed with actual knowledge about voluntary separations, managers realized that there are many reasons. Due to exit interview findings, HR now collaborates with divisions to create career opportunities and the flexibility to accommodate family responsibilities.

Results

Overall, the people-oriented improvements were remarkable, and they cut across the divisions. For example:
- Separations and new hires went down.
- Promotions went up.
- Recruitment advertisement costs were cut.[26]

In addition, the effectiveness report provided comparisons of HAP's data with Saratoga Institute's national trend data for both the health care and insurance industries.[27] Comparative benchmark data improved confidence and strengthened decisionmaking.[28]

Davis believes that HR's favorable score on the employee (internal customer) satisfaction survey of 87 percent is a strong indicator of success for the effectiveness report. In addition, HR has been able to redefine its role from functional administrator to collaborative partner.

Lessons Learned

1. The report is considered by many to be an example of HR best practice.
   Eastern Michigan University/Arbor Group and the City of Detroit honored HAP's Department of Human Resources with two separate awards for excellence based on their effectiveness report.

2. Published information can be a valued asset.
   HAP's HR experienced increased respect by preparing and distributing the annual Human Resources Effectiveness Report.

3. Findings enabled HR to collaborate as consultants and partners to the other divisions. The tables, charts, and graphs serve as useful comparisons for planning and decision-making.

4. The report narrative, such as exit interview summaries, helped managers understand better why HAP people do what they do.

The HAP case study was based on an interview with Don Davis, Vice President of Human Resources, Health Alliance Plan (HAP) on November 23, 1998. Case study written by Darlene Van Tiem, Ph.D. Used with permission.

JOB AID 2-2: ORGANIZATIONAL PT EFFECTIVENESS MEASUREMENT

Intervention Data		Value to Organization
Intervention	*Data Source*	*Measurement and Analysis of Data*
Appraisal 360° feedback, educational objective		
Career Development Inventories, counseling		
Coaching On-the-job, formal mentoring program		
Culture Change Labor relations, grievances, culture survey		
Compensation Benefits, medical and family leaves, retirement plans		
Documentation References, guidelines, pocket guides		
Environment Accommodations for diversity		
Engineering Working conditions, on-the-job injuries		
Health/Wellness Employee assistance, unemployment		
Information Systems Human resources information systems, call centers, exit interviews		

JOB AID 2-2: ORGANIZATIONAL PT EFFECTIVENESS MEASUREMENT *continued*

Intervention Data		Value to Organization
Intervention	*Data Source*	*Measurement and Analysis of Data*
Job Aids Reminders, notices, directories, kiosks		
Job/Work Design Suggestion plan, incentive program		
Leadership Succession plans		
Organizational Design Benchmarking		
Electronic Performance Support Computer help		
Reengineering Automating, telecommuting		
Staffing Promotions, transfers, new hires, separations		
Supervision Absences, tardiness, disciplinary actions		
Team-building Outdoor adventure		
Training and Education Tuition assistance		
Other Awards and recognition, litigation avoidance		

CHAPTER

3

PERFORMANCE ANALYSIS

"YOU'RE BLOWING THROUGH THE WRONG END."

INTRODUCTION TO PERFORMANCE ANALYSIS

Performance analysis is the first step in the HPT Model (see Figure 3-1). There is no possibility of a chicken-or-egg paradox when it comes to performance analysis. Without first identifying and clarifying the problem or performance gap, it is unsound (and certainly unsystematic) to state the cause and select or design a solution. This chapter will provide the reader with an overview of performance analysis.

One way to view performance analysis is to picture "the anatomy of performance."[1] The anatomy of performance (see Table 3-1) contains nine performance variables—three levels of performance and three performance needs for each level. The nine variables provide "an organization x-ray that depicts the three critical interdependent Levels of Performance. The overall performance of an organization (how well it meets the expectations of its customers)

FIGURE 3-1

HPT MODEL: PERFORMANCE ANALYSIS PHASE

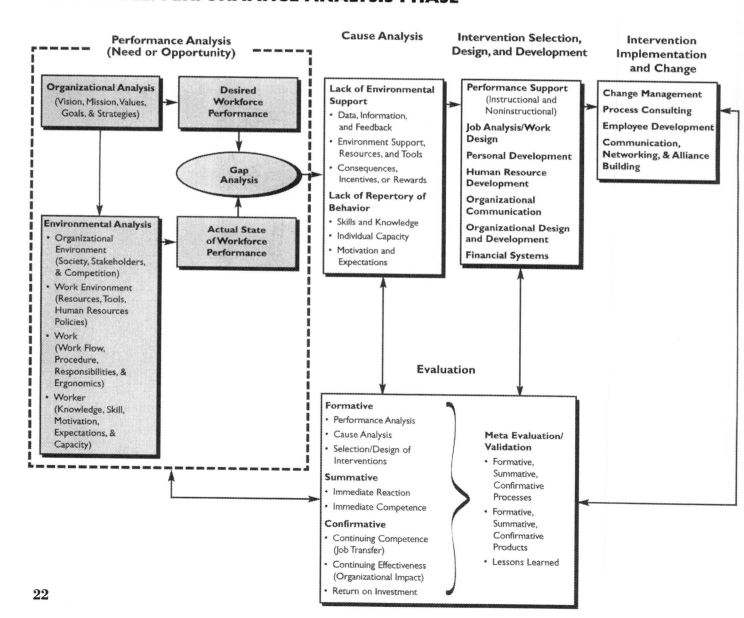

is the result of goals, structures and management actions at all three Levels of Performance."[2]

The definition of the three performance needs is as follows:
- Goals—Specific standards that reflect customers' expectations for product and service quality, quantity, timeliness, and cost.
- Design—The structure of the organization, process, or job, configured to efficiently meet the goals.
- Management—Practices that ensure the goals are current and being achieved.[3]

The organizational analysis sections of this chapter will focus on the first performance need: organization goals. Organization design and management practices are covered in the environmental analysis section, while goals, design, and management, as they apply to the job and the performer, are covered in the section on gap analysis.

Definition and Scope

"Performance analysis is the process of identifying the organization's performance requirements and comparing them to its objectives and capabilities."[4] Performance analysis also examines directions and drivers. "During performance analysis, we seek two broad kinds of information that serve as umbrellas for many concerns and considerations. First, we seek the performance and perspectives that the organization and its leaders are trying to put in place. Let's call them *directions*.... We also seek information about performance *drivers*, the factors that are now blocking or aiding performance or those that might do so in the future.... The quest for directions sketches out the scope of the effort, the analysis of drivers

determines what needs to be done to successfully develop performance, people and the organization."[5]

In the HPT Model, performance analysis focuses on three areas:
- Desired performance state
- Actual performance state
- Gaps between desired and actual performance

Because performance does not occur in a vacuum, the organization and the environment have a considerable impact on both the performance and the performer. This is why a comprehensive performance analysis also focuses on the:
- Vision, mission, values, goals, and strategies of the organization—*directions* that particularly impact the desired state of performance.
- Internal and external environment—organization, competition, work, performer—*drivers* that particularly affect the actual performance state.

Organizational directions have a significant impact on the performance standards that are used to determine desired or optimal performance. Environmental drivers significantly affect actual performance.

Purpose

The purpose of a performance analysis is to identify and measure the gap between desired or optimal performance and actual performance.[6] In broader terms, the purpose of performance analysis is to establish what should be (desired or optimal performance), to identify what is (actual performance), and to identify the gap between the two.

TABLE 3-1

ANATOMY OF PERFORMANCE

Performance Levels	*Three Performance Needs That Determine Overall Performance at Each Performance Level...*		
	Goals	Design	Management
Organization Level	Organization Goals	Organization Design	Organization Management
Process Level	Process Goals	Process Design	Process Management
Job/Performer Level	Job/Performer Goals	Job Design	Job/Performer Management

Performance analysis is the linchpin for the whole performance improvement system. It is "systematic and thorough workplace diagnosis and documentation (that provides) the true basis for improving performance at the organizational, process, and worker levels."[7]

Techniques

This segment of the introduction to performance analysis suggests that a complete performance analysis should include the following five techniques:[8]
- Extant data analysis
- Needs analysis
- Knowledge task analysis
- Procedural task analysis
- Systems task analysis

Extant Data Analysis

Extant data analysis focuses on accomplishments or performance outcomes that are documented in various company records such as sales reports, customer surveys, safety reports, quality control documentation, etc. Analysis of existing data enables the PT practitioner to make inferences about the actual performance.

Needs Analysis

According to Allison Rossett, needs assessment is "the systematic effort that we make to gather opinions and ideas from a variety of sources on performance problems...."[9] The sources may include performers, stakeholders, customers, management, subject matter experts, etc. Needs analysis seeks opinions and ideas about what *should* be happening, what *is* happening, how the sources *feel* about what is or is not happening, and what is *causing* the problem. The resulting data is always subjective; however it may illuminate *why* a desired performance is occurring or not occurring and *what* needs to happen to reach or to maintain the desired performance.

Knowledge Task Analysis

During knowledge task analysis, the analyst searches for detailed information about what the performer needs to know (the invisible part of performance) to successfully complete a specific job or task. The analyst collects and analyzes information from the literature of the performance field, subject matter experts, and expert performers to uncover the body of knowledge "that, if mastered, would contribute to or enhance work behavior."[10]

Identifying and synthesizing the invisible details of optimal performance ensures that the complete performance picture is in place when it comes time to compare desired

performance state with actual performance state to determine whether or not there is a performance gap.

Procedural Task Analysis

Procedural task analysis focuses on the visible details of optimal performance, "documenting people-thing workplace expertise in terms of precisely what people are required to know and be able to do to perform the task."[11] The term *people-thing* refers to the interaction between the performer and the object of the performance. An example of documenting people-thing expertise is a task analysis that examines what the performer (people) needs to know and be able to do to fill out a form (thing). The result of procedural analysis is a document containing "cookbook-style, step-by-step procedures."[12] The limitation of procedural task analysis is that it frequently focuses on tasks conducted under normal conditions and does not take into account what is required for optimal performance under abnormal conditions.

Systems Task Analysis

The last technique, systems task analysis, picks up where procedural task analysis ends by focusing on the "expertise workers must have to respond effectively to abnormal conditions."[13] Systems task analysis provides a series of snapshots that, if taken collectively, provide a composite of the total performance system:
- System overview (description, flow, components, and purpose)
- Process analysis
- Troubleshooting analysis

"Systems analysis can help develop a more accurate picture and understanding of the selected system, the connections among subsystems, and the expertise required of those connections and handoffs from one expert worker to another."[14]

When To Use What

Linking analysis techniques to a particular situation is often difficult and requires a knowledge of why the analyst is conducting the analysis (see Table 3-2).

Once purpose and techniques are determined and matched, "It is how the analysis phase is carried out...that determines whether performance improvement efforts support major business processes or are simply a series of activities."[15]

Tools

Every PT practitioner should have knowledge of and skill in the following data collection tools: interviews, group processes (brainstorming, focus groups, etc.), observation, and surveys. Plug the tools into Table 3-3 below, and it becomes a virtual performance analysis job aid!

Surveys, group processes, and interviews are tools that the PT practitioner can adapt to support all the techniques except extant data analysis, which requires a special set of quantitative and qualitative data analysis tools. Surveys, group processes, and interviews are also well-suited to

analyzing the desired and actual performance states, the organization, and the environment. Observation is best suited to procedural analysis and systems analysis. When to use which technique is determined by organizational climate and resource availability (time, money, and skilled personnel).

The tools and techniques for performance analysis will be discussed in greater detail in the following sections.

TABLE 3-2

LINKING ANALYSIS TECHNIQUES TO PURPOSE

Use This Technique...	To Find Out About...			
	Desired State	Actual State	Organization	Environment
Extant Data Analysis		X	X	X
Needs Analysis	X	X	X	X
Knowledge Task Analysis	X	X		
Procedural Task Analysis	X	X		
Systems Task Analysis	X	X		

TABLE 3-3

ANALYSIS TECHNIQUES, PURPOSES, AND TOOLS

Analysis Techniques

Purposes	Extant Data Analysis	Needs Analysis	Knowledge Task Analysis	Procedural Task Analysis	Systems Task Analysis	
Desired State	N/A	Surveys Group Interviews	Interviews Surveys Group	Observation Interviews Group	Interviews Observation Group	T o o l s
Actual State	Qualitative and Quantitative Analysis Tools	Surveys Group Interviews	Interviews Surveys Group	Observation Interviews Group	Observation Interviews Group	
Organization	Qualitative and Quantitative Analysis Tools	Surveys Group Interviews	N/A	N/A	N/A	
Environment	Qualitative and Quantitative Analysis Tools	Surveys Group Interviews	N/A	N/A	N/A	

ORGANIZATIONAL ANALYSIS

The following definition of performance analysis appeared in the introduction to this section, "Performance analysis is the process of identifying the organization's performance requirements and comparing them to its objectives and capabilities."[1] The HPT Model looks into the heart of the organization—its vision, mission, values, goals, and strategies—as the first step in the performance analysis process. "Proper strategic alignment of these organizational components is essential to facilitating an optimal performance environment."[2]

Definition

Organizational analysis is an examination of the stuff that strategic plans are made of—organizational vision, mission, values, goals, and strategies (see Table 3-4). There are two major roadblocks to organizational analysis:

1. Organizations vary in which words they use to communicate their strategic plan. For example, one organization developed a mission statement, goals, and strategies, but the organization's leaders did not feel that they needed to define their vision or values.
2. Individual members of an organization vary in how they define the words that the organization has selected. For example, three strategic planners were

TABLE 3-4

ORGANIZATIONAL ANALYSIS COMPONENT OF THE HPT MODEL

- Vision
- Mission
- Values
- Goals
- Strategies

asked to define vision, mission, and goals.[3] Their responses are listed in Table 3-5 below.

In the long run, however, words are less important than actions. What is really important is that (1) the organization defines itself using three "ingredients:" an end state, activities or strategies to reach the end state, and reasons for making the trip; and (2) the leaders and the employees understand and agree on these definitions.[4] As part of an organizational analysis, the PT practitioner may also examine the customer's current or future needs and expectations.

TABLE 3-5

VARIOUS STRATEGIC PLANNING DEFINITIONS

Term	Respondent	Definitions...
Vision	#1	Overall future direction (like north on a compass)
	#2	Where we want to be when we grow up (the picture of success)
	#3	Desired destination
Mission	#1	Focus (like a U.S. map of the Midwest)
	#2	Reason for being; purpose
	#3	How we are going to get there
Goals	#1	Instructions on how to get there (directions)
	#2	Milestones to achieve along the way
	#3	Steps we will take now to support our mission and vision (the to-do list)

Purpose, Timing, and Scope

The purpose of the organizational analysis is to seek directions, "the performance and perspectives that the organization and its leaders are trying to put in place."[5] Directions need to be identified before conducting a gap analysis because they will set the standards for desired or optimal performance.

The major factors that set the direction for the organization—vision, mission, values, goals, and strategies—are often found in the organization's strategic plan. The PT practitioner may also need to analyze such factors as:

- Organizational structure
- Centrally controlled systems
- Corporate strategies
- Key policies
- Business values
- Corporate culture[6]

Conducting an Organizational Analysis

The PT practitioner usually begins an organizational analysis by reviewing existing documents such as the organization's strategic plan, history, bylaws, board meeting minutes, annual reports, new employee orientation material, etc. Then the PT practitioner should try to gather feelings and opinions from as many internal and external stakeholders as possible.

One major but often ignored stakeholder is the customer. Leaders of successful organizations use information on present and future customer requirements and expectations to help them set the course or direction for their organization. Figure 3-2[7] illustrates how input from the customer helps to establish the desired performance state as a foundation for performance gap analysis.

Tools

Time, cost, the culture of the organization, and the availability of resources are the prime considerations when selecting tools for conducting an organizational analysis. Since it is extremely important to gather both facts and perceptions when analyzing an organization, the major analysis tools are extant data analysis, interviews, surveys, and group processes.

Interviews are probably the most helpful tool for accessing both fact and perception. The following three strategies are particularly appropriate for interviews conducted during an organizational analysis:

1. Let the flow of the other person's thoughts and ideas lead the conversation so that (the interviewer's) questions clarify, confirm, and guide rather than drive.
2. Always ask questions about purposes, goals, objectives, priorities, or dreams. Not only does that help define success, it also uncovers problems that are almost always there, such as conflicting goals and priorities or a lack of consensus or clarity.
3. A useful question is, Who else should I talk to? This enables the interviewer to find the key players, the opinion leaders, the technical experts, and the potential saboteurs. It also ensures that the analysis will be open and provides the basis for setting up an interview.[8]

Group processes such as brainstorming sessions, focus groups, and consensus activities, are also helpful tools for generating or prioritizing input from stakeholders.[9] The

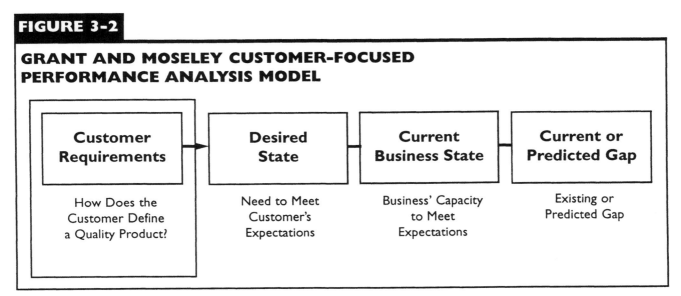

FIGURE 3-2

GRANT AND MOSELEY CUSTOMER-FOCUSED PERFORMANCE ANALYSIS MODEL

Customer Requirements	Desired State	Current Business State	Current or Predicted Gap
How Does the Customer Define a Quality Product?	Need to Meet Customer's Expectations	Business' Capacity to Meet Expectations	Existing or Predicted Gap

case study at the end of this section describes a group-process approach to organizational analysis.

Surveys are more anonymous than interviews and may also generate facts and perceptions about the directions established by the organization. The job aid at the end of this section contains a sample survey that may also be used as the script for interviewing internal and external stakeholders.

Case Study: Statewide Professional Organization

Situation

The executive board of a statewide professional organization decided to redefine the organization due to decreased membership and feedback from members that the organization did not meet their needs or expectations. The organization's membership included professionals from the health services and social science fields (60 percent), volunteers (10 percent), and students (20 percent) who shared a desire to help a specific population of disadvantaged adults. The organization produced five newsletters and held two membership meetings per 10-month membership cycle.

The executive board was elected annually by the membership. No students or volunteers were represented on the board. The executive board met once per month to plan the membership meetings and the newsletter. At the final board meeting of the year, the board set annual goals for the next year and selected topics or formats for the two membership meetings and the newsletters.

The organization did not have vision, mission, values, or goals statements. The president-elect suggested calling upon an outside consultant to conduct a strategic planning session just before the board recessed for the summer. The board unanimously agreed.

Organizational Analysis

To gain some insights into the desired and actual performance of the organization, the consultant reviewed documentation that included a history of the organization, board meeting minutes, membership material, feedback from membership meetings, and committee reports. The consultant then developed an agenda and materials for a one-day strategic planning session during which she would partner with the board members to develop strategic direction for the organization.

After the consultant was introduced to the board, she made a brief presentation on strategic planning. Then the board members completed a matching test similar to the one in the sample job aid at the end of this section. The purposes of the activity were to:
- Provide an opportunity for individual board members to focus on and define the terms vision, mission, values, goals, objectives, and strategies.
- Reach consensus on the definitions.
- Reach consensus on which terms to focus on during the strategic planning session, given the one-day time constraint.

The board decided to focus on producing vision, mission, values, and goals statements and, if time permitted, to brainstorm strategies for the following membership year to reach the goals.

The board then formed three subgroups of four members each. The subgroups participated in an activity designed to develop a vision statement for the organization based on past and present realities (the history of the organization) and future trends. Each subgroup wrote its vision statement on a white board. Then the entire board discussed the three statements and selected one statement for the organization.

The same procedure was repeated for developing mission and values statements.

Results

Although the board outwardly appeared to reach consensus on the vision, mission, and values statements, when it came time to brainstorm goals to support the broader statements, it soon became obvious that the board members were not in agreement about the organization's mission. The major problem involved the organization's desire or ability to meet the needs of members who were students or volunteers in the field. The board members brainstormed a set of tentative goals based on the mission statement they had chosen. Then the board members agreed to individually review the vision, mission, values, and goal statements, and hold a special meeting at one of the board member's summer home. During that meeting they would finalize the mission and goals statements and develop strategies for the upcoming membership year that would align with the new strategic plan. The board also agreed to introduce the strategic plan to the membership at the September general meeting and to seek membership approval for the plan.

Lessons Learned

1. Time, money, and the availability of human and other resources were generally perceived as major drivers or causes of organizational performance, yet unacknowledged personal agendas were having an even stronger impact on the organization's future.

2. Buy-in from the board and the membership was extremely important if the organization was to remain viable. However, buy-in could not be rushed, despite the pressure to save the organization from imminent atrophy and possible extinction.

3. It was difficult to determine how far apart the board and the membership were in terms of strategic direction. Involving the membership was an important next step.

4. The whole effort would collapse if the board failed to keep up the momentum that was achieved during the strategic planning session or if they failed to create a strategic plan that would set the course for "what should be."

This case study was written by Joan Conway Dessinger, Ed.D., The Lake Group. Used with permission.

JOB AID 3-1: ORGANIZATIONAL ANALYSIS SURVEY

Select the terms or sections of this job aid that are appropriate for the organization you are analyzing. Use the selected sections as a survey instrument or as a group discussion guide. The target audience may include all levels of management, workers, external stakeholders, competitors, or customers. The goal is to identify both facts and perceptions from a broad range of internal and external stakeholders. This will help determine whether or not the organization's vision, mission, values, goals, or strategies are aligned with the desired and actual performance state.

Defining Organizational Analysis Terms

Pick the definition from Column A that you feel *best* matches the term in Column B and write the number in the parentheses ( ) next to the term:

Column A: Definitions	Column B: Terms
1. The reasons for making the trip	A. ( ) Vision
2. Our principles and standards	B. ( ) Mission
3. Our reason for being	C. ( ) Values
4. What we do	D. ( ) Goals
5. The end state to be achieved	E. ( ) Objectives
6. Our notion of success	F. ( ) Strategies
7. Milestones along the way	
8. The means to be used	
9. The path to be taken	
10. Who we are	

Vision

What is the organization's vision?

Is the vision clearly defined?   ___ Yes ___ No

Is the vision adequately communicated to all stakeholders?   ___ Yes ___ No

Does the vision make sense in terms of internal strengths and weaknesses?   ___ Yes ___ No

Does the vision make sense in terms of external threats and opportunities?   ___ Yes ___ No

Mission

What is the organization's mission?

JOB AID 3-1: ORGANIZATIONAL ANALYSIS SURVEY *continued*

Is the mission clearly defined? ___ Yes ___ No

Is the mission adequately communicated to all stakeholders? ___ Yes ___ No

Does the mission make sense in terms of internal strengths and weaknesses? ___ Yes ___ No

Does the mission make sense in terms of external threats and opportunities? ___ Yes ___ No

Values

What are the organization's values?

Are the values clearly defined? ___ Yes ___ No

Are the values adequately communicated to all stakeholders? ___ Yes ___ No

Do the values match the mission and vision? ___ Yes ___ No

Do the values make sense in terms of internal strengths and weaknesses? ___ Yes ___ No

Do the values make sense in terms of external threats and opportunities? ___ Yes ___ No

Goals

What are the organization's goals?
- Products and services:

- Customers and markets:

- Competitive advantage:

- Product and market priorities:

Are each of the goals clearly defined? ___ Yes ___ No

Are each of the goals adequately communicated to all stakeholders? ___ Yes ___ No

Do each of the goals match the mission, vision, and values? ___ Yes ___ No

Do each of the goals make sense in terms of internal strengths and weaknesses? ___ Yes ___ No

Do each of the goals make sense in terms of external threats and opportunities? ___ Yes ___ No

JOB AID 3-1: ORGANIZATIONAL ANALYSIS SURVEY *continued*

Strategies

What are the organization's strategies for meeting its goals?

• Products and services (What are we going to do?):

• Customers and markets (Whom will we do it for?):

• Competitive advantage(s) (Why will the customer buy from us?):

• Product and market priorities (Where will we place our emphasis?):

Are each of the strategies clearly defined? ___ Yes ___ No

Are each of the strategies adequately communicated to all stakeholders? ___ Yes ___ No

Do each of the strategies match the mission, vision, values, and goals? ___ Yes ___ No

Do each of the strategies make sense in terms of internal strengths and weaknesses? ___ Yes ___ No

Do each of the strategies make sense in terms of external threats and opportunities? ___ Yes ___ No

This job aid is based on the work of Rummler and Brache[10] and Nickols.[11]

ISPI © 2000 Permission granted for unlimited duplication for noncommercial use.

ENVIRONMENTAL ANALYSIS

Performance does not occur in a vacuum. Performance technology "recognizes individual and organizational realities when solving on-the-job performance problems."[1] Part of the organizational reality is the environmental support provided by the organization, the work environment, the work, and the worker. Environmental support has the potential to sustain actual performance or raise actual performance to the desired or optimal level.

Definition and Scope

Environmental analysis is a process used to identify and prioritize the realities that support actual performance. The performance analysis section of the original HPT Model focused on the environmental support from the work, organizational, and competitive environments. Further efforts from the field (see Figure 3-3) made it possible to expand the work component of the HPT Model to include the work environment, the work, and the worker.[2]

Purpose and Timing

The purpose of environmental analysis is *not* to identify problems, but to assess what is actually happening, both outside and inside the organization, that might help to explain why people do what they do.[3] The enhanced HPT Model (see Table 3-6) helps to focus the environmental analysis as follows:

1. Organizational environment analysis focuses on how the organization's external stakeholders (customers, suppliers, distributors, stockholders, regulators, etc.) and competition (the industry area within which the organization functions, for example, manufacturing, health care, education, retail, etc.) influence performance.

2. Work environment analysis focuses on what is happening inside the organization to support performance (resource allocation, tools, policies for recruiting and hiring, feedback, and consequences of performance or nonperformance).

3. Work analysis focuses on what is happening at the job design level (processes).

4. Worker analysis focuses on what is happening with the workers (knowledge, skills, capacity, motivation, and expectations).

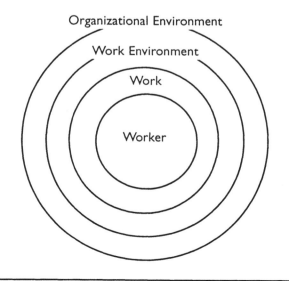

FIGURE 3-3

ROTHWELL'S ENVIRONMENTS OF HUMAN PERFORMANCE

Organizational Environment
Work Environment
Work
Worker

TABLE 3-6

ENVIRONMENTAL ANALYSIS COMPONENT OF THE HPT MODEL

Organizational Environment (external performance support)
- Stakeholders
- Competition

Work Environment (internal performance support)
- Resources and tools
- Policies and recruitment, hiring, feedback, consequences

Work (job design and performance support)
- Work flow
- Procedures
- Responsibilities
- Ergonomics

Worker (individual performance support)
- Knowledge
- Skill
- Motivation
- Expectations
- Capacity or ability

Environmental analysis may take place before, during, or after performance gap analysis. Often it is an integral part of analyzing actual performance. For example, while observing a performer on the job, the PT practitioner may note that safety procedures are clearly posted on the job site (work environment level) or that the worker does not have the necessary skill or knowledge to perform the job (worker level).

Analyzing the Organizational Environment

During an organizational environmental analysis the PT practitioner determines who are the external stakeholders and which of these stakeholders are most critical to the success of the organization. The organization's external stakeholders may include customers, suppliers, distributors, stockholders, industry regulators, etc.

Then the PT practitioner may review existing documents, such as customer surveys, and use interviews, group processes, or surveys to discover "how well the organization is interacting with its external environment."[4] One strategy is to collect information from within and outside of the organization and compare the findings. For example, one manufacturer randomly monitored conversations between product service representatives and customers on a product hot line, then surveyed both the product service representatives and the customers to identify facts and perceptions about what was happening at both ends of the hot line.

Analysis of the constantly changing competitive challenges facing the organization should also be part of the organizational environment analysis. This analysis should include an ongoing review of documents that chronicle industry activity, input from customers and knowledgeable employees, or product comparisons. Interviewing or surveying customers, sales staff, and even competitors may provide important insights into the competitive environment.

Analyzing the Work Environment

Work environment analysis looks within the organization to discover what is happening at the organizational level (big picture) and what is happening at the department, work team, or job level. The people who can provide the answers will include representatives from all levels of management, supervision, and the workforce. Seeking

input "from groups likely to have unique perspectives, such as temporary workers, recently retired workers, or others who have intimate and recent firsthand knowledge of the organization" broadens the perspective of the analysis.[5] The information that is gathered during this phase of analysis should answer the following questions:

- What factors or practices within the organization have influenced how effectively and efficiently people perform their work?
- What factors or practices within the organization are most critical to achieving desired performance?

Open-ended questions are the best source of information, so surveys, interviews, or group processes are the analysis tools of choice.

Analyzing Work

Each job should be structured to enable the performers to achieve the desired goals. Work analysis concentrates on the job design and examines whether or not the job is structured to make it possible for the performer to achieve optimal performance. Effective and efficient job design includes the following:

- Allocation of responsibilities among jobs to support rather than hamper the achievement of desired results
- Logical sequence of job activities or work flow
- Job policies and procedures that are clearly defined, documented, and accessible to the worker
- Ergonomic design of the physical work space to minimize barriers to optimal performance.[6]

The PT practitioner may use interviews, surveys, or group processes to collect information from supervisors and workers. Observation and review of documents such as quality reports, cycle time studies, safety reports, etc. may also provide useful information.

Analyzing the Worker

At this level of analysis the PT practitioner looks at the performer to identify the performer's actual skills, knowledge, capacity, motivation, and expectations. To discover facts, opinions, or feelings, the PT practitioner may review personnel documents, observe performers, and use interviews, surveys, or group processes. In the following case study, the PT practitioner focuses on observing and interviewing the workers.

Case Study: Training Legend

The Internet is full of *urban legends*, stories that have circulated for years about alleged incidents that have occurred in one city or another. The following case study is based on a training legend that surfaces from time to time during conference sessions and in classroom discussions. Although there are several versions of this legend, the basic situation and the results of the analysis are the same for all of them.

Situation

A plant manager called the training department manager of a glass manufacturing company and said: "We need a training program for our product inspectors RIGHT NOW! When can you schedule a class?" The training department manager made an appointment for one of his performance consultants to visit with the plant manager.

Environmental Analysis

When the performance consultant arrived in the plant manager's office, the manager immediately prefaced his remarks by saying: "I know what I need, and I need it now. This problem is critical." He then proceeded to tick off the following points on his fingers:

- Customers are complaining to the sales representatives that the glassware shipped to their retail shops contain imperfections.
- The inspectors do not know how to inspect the glassware properly.
- The inspectors need to be trained NOW before more orders are lost.

The performance consultant was prepared to make a case for identifying the performance gap and analyzing the cause before selecting an intervention. Fortunately she remembered the information she had just acquired from a publisher's online website,[7] so the consultant responded, "I know this is a critical problem and time is very important. I want to make sure that we do the best we can during the little time that we have and that we don't make false starts. We want to customize the solution to meet your needs and the needs of your employees and customers. I'm going to move very fast on this, using information we already have in our organization. Let's begin by talking about what it is you think is happening. I want to understand how you see it."

The performance consultant then asked the following questions:
- Why do you want to move forward with this now?
- What indicators moved you to take action?
- If we are successful with this, what changes would appear?

- How do you think the inspectors and their supervisors feel about this situation?
- Are the inspectors and their supervisors ready to move forward on this?

The plant manager didn't know how to answer the last two questions, so he agreed to let the performance consultant observe the inspection process and talk to some of the inspectors and supervisors. He also agreed to let the performance consultant review the error data, read the customer complaint reports submitted by the sales representatives, talk to a sales representative and her dissatisfied customer, and visit the glass inspection work area.

Results

The performance consultant reviewed the documentation and talked to the sales representative and customer. She determined that over the past six months there was a 20 percent increase in the return of shipments due to imperfections in the glassware. She also determined that three customers had canceled large orders based on the continued shipment of imperfect products, and five more customers were threatening to do the same. They all cited that the only reason they had not canceled sooner was because the glass company had an established reputation for quality products and service to the customer.

When she visited the inspection area, the performance consultant was greeted with frustration and anger. The inspectors quickly pointed out that the lighting in the area was so bad that they were unable to see the glassware clearly in order to inspect it correctly. The shift supervisor showed her a stack of orders to the maintenance department requesting new lighting in the inspection area. Maintenance had replied that all their electrical engineers were tied up with construction of the new plant and that they would follow up on the request as soon as possible. The lighting problems had begun approximately six months before the visit from the performance consultant.

After listening to the inspectors and their supervisor and observing the inspection process, the performance consultant made an appointment with the maintenance department supervisor. The supervisor was aware of the requests from the inspection supervisors, but he had been informed that the new plant construction took precedence over department needs unless department needs were "significantly affecting life, limb, or production schedules."

The performance consultant prepared a report for the plant manager in which she listed the results of the environmental and the performance analyses. She recommended the following steps:
- Authorize maintenance to develop an interim solution to the lighting problem (in this case, replacing some fuses and

burned-out light bulbs) and monitor the lighting in the area until a lighting engineer was available to analyze the problem and develop a long-term solution.

- Monitor the quality inspection output for one month to determine if the quality improved with the lighting or the inspectors really needed additional training.
- Provide an incentive for customers to remain with the company during the transition period.
- Communicate biweekly with the inspectors, their supervisors, the sales representatives, and selected customers over the next six months to evaluate the effect of the intervention package.

Lessons Learned

1. Performance does not occur in a vacuum. Customer expectations, worker expectations, work environment, and organizational resource allocation all have an impact on actual performance.
2. Environmental analysis and performance gap analysis go hand-in-hand when identifying performance gaps.
3. Training is not always the intervention of choice.

This case study was written by Joan Conway Dessinger, Ed.D., The Lake Group. Used with permission.

JOB AID 3-2: WHAT IS HAPPENING?

At this level of analysis...	Some of the issues are...
1. Organizational Environment Level What is happening when the organization interacts with its external stakeholders and competition? • Customers • Suppliers • Distributors • Industry regulators • Stockholders • Special interest groups • Professional associations • Competitors • Other _____	• How does the organization interact with its external stakeholders? • Which interactions are most critical to the success of the organization? • What is the effect of competition on the organization, the work environment, the work, and the worker? • What does the organization need to do to stay competitive? • How do the various stakeholders define a quality product or service?
2. Work Environment Level What is happening inside the organization to support optimal performance? • Resources (time, money, staff, tools, materials, space) • Information • Policies and procedures • Other _____	• Does the performer have adequate resources to achieve optimal performance? • Does the performer have the information required to achieve optimal performance? • Do policies for recruiting, hiring, feedback, and consequences support optimal performance?
3. Work Level What is happening on the job? • Job design • Work flow • Job responsibilities • Other _____	• Is the job designed for optimal performance? • Does the work flow foster efficient completion of tasks? • Are job responsibilities clearly established?
4. Worker Level What is happening with the workers? • Skills • Knowledge • Motivation • Expectations • Capacity or ability	• Does the performer have the requisite knowledge or skills to achieve success? • Is the performer motivated to achieve? • Do the performer's expectations match the reality of the total performance environment? • Is the performer able to achieve success?

Based on Langdon (1995), Rothwell (1996b), Rummler and Brache (1995), and Grant and Moseley (1999).

GAP ANALYSIS

There is an old children's rhyme that goes something like this:

> Good, better, best
> Never let it rest
> 'Til your good is better
> And your better best.

Too often the implied focus of PT is the performance problem. "In fact, the technology can and should be used proactively to address new opportunities and to make that which is good even better."[1]

Analyzing the desired and actual performance states (gap analysis—see Table 3-7) is the last step in the performance analysis phase of the HPT Model, and the first step toward making a poor performance better and a good performance best. During this step all of the performance pieces come together. Gap analysis identifies the type of performance improvement opportunity that exists and paves the way for cause analysis and intervention selection or design.

Definitions and Scope

From the perspective of many leaders in the field, performance gap analysis is much like needs assessment. During a needs assessment, needs are often viewed as "gaps in results, consequences, or accomplishments" and needs assessment is defined as "a very valuable tool for

identifying where you are—the current results and consequences—and where you should be—the desired results and consequences"[2] (see Figure 3-4).

The two major differences between needs assessment and performance gap analysis are as follows:

1. Needs assessment tends to focus on knowledge, skills, and attitude; performance gap analysis "identifies any deficiency or proficiency affecting human performance."
2. Needs assessment tends to focus on the past and present; performance analysis also looks to the future.[3]

Performance gaps may also be viewed as performance improvement opportunities that provide a chance to:

- Improve the actual performance state when it does not measure up to the desired performance state, or
- Enhance or intensify the actual performance state when it is equal to or exceeds the desired performance state (innovation).

There are six potential gaps in performance: present positive, present neutral, present negative, future positive, future neutral, future negative.[4] Figure 3-5 illustrates the concept of the six gaps in terms of the HPT Model.

The PT practitioner should be aware of three yellow caution flags regarding positive and neutral gaps:

1. Decisionmakers and PT practitioners should not become complacent about positive gaps.
2. "Organizations that experience breakthrough improvements in productivity are sometimes able to distinguish themselves by applying innovation to a neutral gap."
3. The greatest opportunity for performance improvement may occur when future neutral gaps exist "because competitors tend to overlook them."[5]

Purpose and Timing

Within the framework of the HPT Model and the work cited above, the purpose of performance gap analysis is to identify present and future gaps between the desired performance state and the actual performance state. Along the way the analyst performs the following three tasks:

1. Identifies the gaps as positive, neutral, or negative.
2. Identifies the type of performance improvement opportunity offered by each gap.
3. Prioritizes the performance gaps according to how important (criticality) the gap is to meeting the goals of

TABLE 3-7

GAP ANALYSIS COMPONENT OF THE HPT MODEL

Desired Workforce Performance

↓

Gap

↑

Actual State of Workforce Performance

FIGURE 3-4

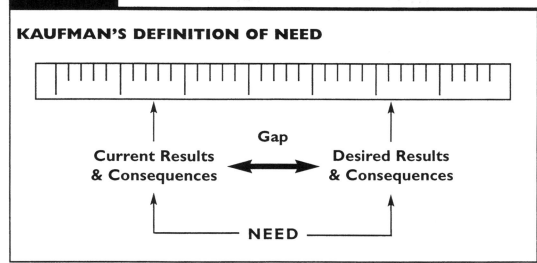

KAUFMAN'S DEFINITION OF NEED

FIGURE 3-5

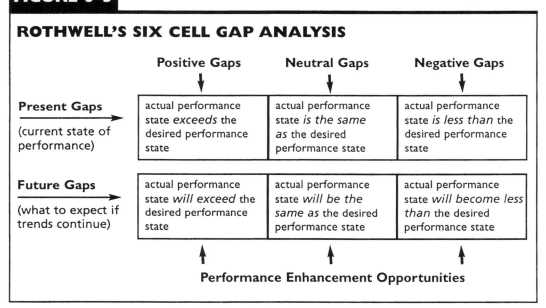

ROTHWELL'S SIX CELL GAP ANALYSIS

the organization, how difficult (complexity) it will be to resolve the gap, and how often (frequency) the gap occurs.

The proverbial horse-before-the-cart problem applies here. Performance gap analysis must occur before cause analysis, which in turn must occur before intervention selection and implementation. Performance gap analysis is truly the key to successful performance improvement or enhancement.

Conducting a Performance Gap Analysis

The systems approach to analyzing performance gaps includes three sequential steps:

1. Identify the gaps (present and future; positive, neutral or negative) between the actual performance state and the desired performance state.
2. Prioritize the gaps that are identified.
3. Analyze the causes.

The first two steps are discussed below. The third step, cause analysis, is examined in the next chapter.

Identifying the Performance Gaps

Identification of performance gaps may be approached by one or a combination of the following methods:[6]
• A single PT practitioner collects and analyzes information on the desired and actual performance states.

Data collection techniques may include reviewing pertinent records to discover present realities and future trends and examining opinions, feelings, and ideas from a variety of sources. The major tools available to the PT practitioner are surveys, interviews, and group processes such as brainstorming, focus groups, critical incident technique, etc.[7]

- A group of people (standing team, task force, committee, etc.) works together to collect and analyze information on the desired and actual performance states. If an PT practitioner is included in the group, he or she helps the group to organize and clarify issues, roles, and responsibilities and to keep focused on PT philosophy and strategies. The group may review pertinent records and examine individual and group feelings, opinions, and ideas. The major tool is an appropriate form of group process; however, the PT practitioner may wish to conduct surveys or interviews before, during, or after the life cycle of the group.

- The organization sends executives, middle managers, and supervisors on a retreat. The retreat environment promotes a high level of participation and encourages buy in. The PT practitioner plans and implements activities that encourage the participants to focus on the following issues:
  - the present and the future
  - the desired and the actual performance states
  - the resulting gaps and their relative importance in light of the organization's mission, strategy, and goals
  - the internal and external environment

  The techniques and tools to use during a retreat are the same as those indicated in the previous bulleted discussion.

- When the organization is massive and the stakes are high, a large-scale, short-term change effort may be the best method for analyzing performance gaps. This method involves stakeholders from inside and outside the organization—"Such gargantuan meetings are advantageous because they build a critical mass for change among many key decision makers at one time."[8] The purpose is to reach a general consensus among a broad base of stakeholders. The tools include both small group sessions and large plenary sessions. Once more, the participants may review existing data and probe opinions, feelings, and ideas using a variety of group processes. Surveys and interviews may prove helpful, particularly before and after the change effort.

- Using a Delphi group[9] to gather and validate information and to reach consensus might allow for wider participation, particularly if the Delphi is conducted on-line using e-mail or bulletin boards. A Delphi is useful for forecasting and prioritizing. During a Delphi, participants comment on questions or statements. The responses are then analyzed and synthesized and the respondents have another chance to comment or prioritize based on the results of the first round. The process may be continued until consensus is reached.

Prioritizing the Performance Gaps

Ideally, a group of people, preferably the stakeholders in the performance improvement effort, is involved in prioritizing the performance gaps. It is a crucial part of performance gap analysis because "...merely identifying a difference between what people are doing and what you would like them to be doing is not enough reason to take action."[10] In addition to the Delphi method discussed above, there are a number of process tools that help groups prioritize items and reach agreement or consensus on the results. As facilitator, the PT practitioner may provide a list of performance gaps or begin with a brainstorming session to generate the list.[11] Then the facilitator may use one or a combination of the following sorting tools to prioritize the gaps and to gain consensus:

- Nominal Group Technique[12]
- Priority Matrix (see the job aid at the end of this section)
- Consensus Survey[13]

Each of the above activities involves listing the performance analysis gaps (either in matrix form or on separate cards) and manipulating the list through several rounds, using criticality rating scales or physical sorting techniques. Using some form of the Priority Matrix (Job Aid 3-3) is the key to effective sorting and the attainment of consensus.

Case Study: University Development Center

The following case study has been adapted from an actual faculty consultation session at a university faculty development center. References to department and nationality have been changed to ensure client confidentiality. Faculty development specialists are experts in various course content areas and are exemplary performers.

Situation

The faculty development center director at a large urban university received a call from a department chair. According to the department chair, students, including department majors, were complaining directly to him about one of the department instructors. The complaints included the following:

- Unclear lectures
- Difficulty of the mathematics used in the course
- Poor English skills exhibited by the instructor
- Instructor's demeaning attitude toward the class

Of the 30 students originally enrolled in the course, 10 dropped out during the drop-add period.

Gap Analysis

The faculty development center director suggested that the instructor should call the faculty development specialist assigned to his content area. Shortly thereafter, the instructor made an appointment with the specialist for an initial interview and for a class observation. The specialist interviewed the instructor over the phone, reviewed student course evaluations and complaints made directly to the department chair, and observed the instructor during one of the course sessions.

The faculty development center uses the following criteria to describe desired performance in teaching:
- Content knowledge and organization
  - The instructor demonstrates a command of the course content.
  - The instructor provides a concise, meaningful organization of the course content.
- Presentation skills
  - The instructor interacts with the students in a positive, nonthreatening way.
  - The instructor's verbal and nonverbal communication with students creates an environment conducive to learning.
  - The instructor presents the content clearly.
- Use of instructional media
  - The instructional media support the educational goals.
  - The instructional media enhance the content.
  - The instructor demonstrates competency in the use of the selected media.

Results

The initial interview revealed that this instructor had been in the U.S. for five years. Before his current assignment, he had spent one semester as a teaching assistant at a research university, working with small groups of students. The instructor believed that he was teaching skillfully and that it was the students who were the source of the problem. He stated that he did not like his current students because they were unmotivated and had poor attitudes toward the class.

During both the initial interview and the class observation, the specialist noted English language communication problems, including the following:
- Monotone delivery (lack of enthusiasm and expressiveness)
- Soft, monotonous voice (difficult to hear in class)

- Intonation and articulation problems
- Generally low level of clear English speech patterns
- Limited conversational English vocabulary

The classroom observation established that the instructor, although knowledgeable about the content, did not organize the content well and demonstrated poor presentation skills and inappropriate use of media. Specifically, the specialist recorded the following observations:
- Knowledge and organization of content
  - The instructor seemed confident of his knowledge of the material.
  - The instructor did not present an overall organizational framework for the material (for example, transitions between formulas were inadequate).
- Presentation skills
  - The instructor referred to a diagram on the board as he explained how to approach a problem solution, and he summarized the material in conclusion. However, he did not attempt to reach out to students or to connect with their experiences by using concrete examples.
  - Periodically during class, the instructor stopped the lecture to ask, "Are there any questions?" However, he demonstrated limited understanding of the few questions he did allow and consistently ignored unsolicited student questions.
  - Students were hostile in their comments and body language toward the instructor during the class.
- Use of instructional media
  - The instructor wrote formulas and mathematical calculations on the board; however, he made multiple mistakes and would erase, start over, and erase again, in a very repetitive manner.
  - The instructor expended considerable effort on drawing and modifying diagrams on the board to supplement his explanations, however, he erased the formulas and notes on the chalkboard before students had a chance to copy or react to the visual material.

The faculty consultant sent the instructor a written report consisting of a general summary and some recommendations. The report suggested that the two major performance gaps were lack of communication (English) skills and lack of instructional skills. The instructor agreed to a series of sessions to improve his English skills as well as consultation sessions to polish his teaching skills.

Lessons Learned

1. Performance gap analysis identifies the gaps between optimal and actual performance. However, it is not possible to jump to a performance improvement solution without carefully considering the cause of the identified gaps, including possible environmental, experiential, or organizational causes.

2. In this case, the assumption was made that the performance problems were grounded in a lack of teaching experience and English language communication skills, both verbal and nonverbal. However, the collision between student and instructor expectations regarding course delivery and feedback may also be the effect of environmental, experiential, or organizational factors. Is the instructor basing his teaching style and expectations on his experience as a student? Are there cultural differences regarding education between the universities in his country and the university where he teaches?

3. Further analysis is required before a complete performance improvement package can be designed to meet the needs of the instructor, the students, the department, and the university's needs. Interviews with the department head and the students could be helpful. At the very least, the specialist needs to discuss the report and review the recommendations with the instructor.

This case study was written by Deborah Armstrong, MA. Used with permission.

JOB AID 3-3: SAMPLE PRIORITY MATRIX

Directions to the Participants: After considerable analysis, we have identified the following performance gaps within our organization. The gaps are listed in the first column. We are asking you to help us determine how critical each gap is to the attainment of our organization's strategic goals. Rank (✔) each gap on the Criticality Scale; then be prepared to compare your results with the rest of the group. Together we need to reach consensus on which gaps are the most critical and need to be resolved first.

Performance Gap	Low ←				Criticality Scale				→	High
	1	2	3	4	5	6	7	8	9	10

CHAPTER

CAUSE ANALYSIS

INTRODUCTION TO CAUSE ANALYSIS

C ause analysis is the second step in the HPT Model (Figure 4-1) and is based on Thomas F. Gilbert's Behavior Engineering Model[1] (see Table 4-1). Although thorough performance analysis yields valuable information about the organization, the environment, and performance gaps, a cause analysis will determine why the performance gap exists. This section of the chapter will provide the reader with an overview of cause analysis. The remaining sections will focus on six performance gap causes that are rooted in either the environment or the individual worker.

Definition and Scope

"Cause analysis is the process of determining the root cause(s) of past, present, or future performance gaps. It follows, but is integrally related to, performance

FIGURE 4-1

HPT MODEL: CAUSE ANALYSIS PHASE

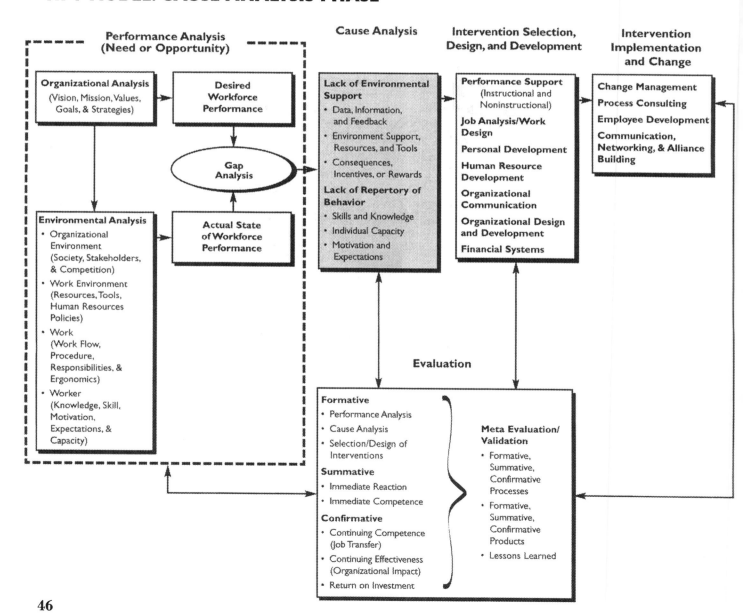

TABLE 4-1

GILBERT'S BEHAVIOR ENGINEERING MODEL

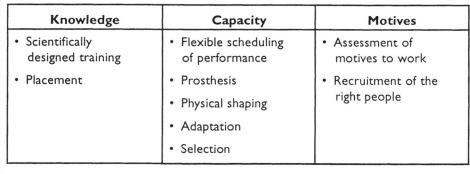

Information	*Instrumentation*	*Motivation*
Data	**Instruments**	**Incentives**
• Relevant and frequent feedback • Performance descriptions • Clear and relevant guides to performance	• Tools and materials of work to match human factors	• Financial incentives • Nonmonetary incentives • Career development opportunities
Knowledge	**Capacity**	**Motives**
• Scientifically designed training • Placement	• Flexible scheduling of performance • Prosthesis • Physical shaping • Adaptation • Selection	• Assessment of motives to work • Recruitment of the right people

 **Rooted in the Environment**

 **Rooted in the Individual Worker**

analysis."[2] Rosenberg sees cause analysis as the bridge between performance analysis and the appropriate intervention(s) that will eliminate the performance gap.[3] Using the roots-of-a-tree analogy, he tells us "to look under the performance gap to discover its roots ... select intervention(s) ... to both feed the high performance roots and eliminate the roots that caused the performance gap."[4]

Robinson and Robinson, in linking training to business needs, say that cause analysis "provides us with the data to respond to either of these two questions: What is causing an end-result and/or on-the-job performance deficiency? What might prevent newly learned skills from being transferred to the job?"[5]

Historically, theorists like Robert Mager, Peter Pipe, Thomas Gilbert, Geary Rummler, Alan Brache, and Joe Harless suggest that performance problems are essentially deficiencies of knowledge, skills, training, or a host of management deficiencies.[6] Allison Rossett identified four kinds of drivers (e.g., causes, barriers, or obstacles): lack of skill, knowledge, and information; flawed incentives, flawed environment; tools and processes; and lack of motivation.[7] She defined drivers as "everything that it takes to enable performance to 'grow.'"[8] Robinson and Robinson identified three major causes of performance

deficiencies: those due to the learner, those due to the manager (boss) of the learner, and those due to the organization.[9] Perhaps the most influential listing of performance gap causes comes from Gilbert's work on human competence, especially his Behavior Engineering Model, above.[10]

Rothwell and Dean have adapted the Behavior Engineering Model to guide the PT practitioner in the search for causes (see Table 4-2).[11,12] They focus on performance drivers, asking key performance questions and suggesting examples of performance deficiencies.

Conducting a Cause Analysis

Too often PT practitioners are overly confident in their diagnostic abilities, and they jump from performance analysis to intervention selection before thoroughly understanding the cause(s) of the performance gap. Symptoms are often disguised as causes. Without a solid understanding of cause analysis and how it affects work, workers, and workplace, the choice of interventions is flawed. Cause analysis determines why the performance gap exists and how it affects the unique mission, needs, wants, and desires of the organization. Once the cause of a performance problem is known, the PT practitioner can choose the appropriate intervention(s).

TABLE 4-2

BEHAVIOR ENGINEERING MODEL ADAPTATION

Performance Drivers (or Causes)	Performance Questions	Performance Deficiency Examples
• Data, information, feedback	• How well are people given data, information, feedback to perform when they are needed?	• Information not given on a timely basis • Lack of feedback mechanisms • Little documentation • Performance standards are nonexistent • Is data tied to performance?
• Environment support, resources, tools	• How well are people supported with resources, tools, equipment?	• Ergonomic deficiencies • Inadequate working conditions • Tools unavailable or not optimally arranged • Insufficient time to get things done
• Consequences, incentives, rewards	• How well do performers see the results or consequences of what they do? • How well are they rewarded or provided with incentives?	• Work unrelated to organization's mission and needs • Rewards not performance-based • Competing incentives • Poor performance rewarded
• Skills and knowledge	• How well do performers' knowledge and skills match performance requirements?	• Lack of knowledge, skills, training, education • Unable to maneuver in the system
• Individual capacity	• How well can people perform?	• Lack of aptitude, ability, physical or manual dexterity • Inadequate job analysis
• Motivation and expectation	• How well are people motivated to perform? Are expectations realistic?	• Boring and punishing performance system • Unrealistic payoffs

Techniques

The following steps can be used to conduct a cause analysis of a performance gap:

1. Identify the driver or cause of the performance gap.
2. Classify the driver or cause by determining where it originates within Rothwell's classification of the environment of human performance:[13]
   – Organizational environment
   – Work environment
   – Work
   – Worker
3. Prioritize the driver or cause according to high or low impact on the performance environment.
4. During cause analysis it is important to generate as many cause examples as possible. This gives the opportunity to look at many sides of the problem. If either skills or knowledge is identified as a cause, the example list may include these: employee has forgotten how to use the skill, doesn't have adequate information, lacks training in specific processes and procedures,

doesn't know the components of the system, etc. If consequences, incentives, and rewards are identified, the example list may read: poor performance is rewarded, no management planning exists, competing incentives send mixed messages, etc.

5. The PT practitioner should also verify causes and corresponding examples with clients. Ask who, what, when, where, and why questions, and involve them— clients may shed light on the topic and client support and buyin are necessary for the next phases of the HPT Model.

Tools

There are a variety of tools employed for conducting cause analysis. Table 4-3 illustrates cause analysis tools suggested by Rossett[14] and Rothwell.[15]

In addition to these tools, flowcharts, histograms, Pareto charts, and run charts are useful for identifying causes of performance gaps.[16]

TABLE 4-3	

CAUSE ANALYSIS TOOLS

Name of Tool	Brief Description
• Interview	• Structured or unstructured • Excellent for rapport building and follow-up questions • Questions can be open-ended or probing
• Observation	• Captures current skills and knowledge as well as context • Inferences about work are generated • Takes time to use effectively
• Surveys or Questionnaires	• Anonymous • Large numbers of people can be surveyed • Require clarity, effective directions, user-friendly questions, and skill in constructing
• Focus Groups	• Structure opportunities for soliciting information • Participants must be briefed and debriefed • Roles of facilitator and scribe are crucial
• Root Cause Analysis	• "Traces the causes and effects of accidents or other problems ... tends to be past oriented and focused only on pinpointing the causes of negative performance gaps."[17] • Chronology of events reported and recorded on paper • Relationship of one event to another becomes clear • Result is a wall-sized flowchart • Participants questioned to pinpoint root cause of problem[18]
• Fishbone Diagram	• Cause-and-effect diagram, used in total quality management • Past-oriented with focus on identifying negative performance gaps • All causes traced to people, policies/procedures, equipment, climate • Troubleshooting tool[19]
• Portfolio Analysis	• Financial management tool with focus on positive performance gaps • Develop grid • Make decisions based on likelihood of payoff • Great for stakeholder involvement[20]

LACK OF ENVIRONMENTAL SUPPORT

One cause of performance problems is a lack of environmental support. Environmental support includes those things that management provides and that the performer needs to perform effectively and efficiently. According to Gilbert, environmental performance support includes the following:[1]

- Information (data, information, and feedback)
- Instrumentation (environment support, resources, and tools)
- Motivation (consequences, incentives, and rewards)

A gap between the available environmental support components shown Table 4-4 and the performance support requirements or needs of the worker usually drives or causes a performance gap. This section will focus on how to analyze environmental support components (information, instrumentation, and motivation) to determine the cause of a performance gap.

Data, Information, and Feedback

How do data, information, and feedback support performance and relate to why people do what they do? According to Rossett, "A successful performer knows how to do what is expected and when it is appropriate to do it."[2] Part of this knowledge may come from schooling or past experience; however, complete, clear, unambiguous, and up-to-date data on performance expectations and information regarding correct procedures are required for successful on-the-job performance. The data or information must also be available and easily accessible to the performer. Data and information that are vital to successful performance may include organizational policies, job or task procedures, tolerance levels for machinery, customer requirements, or supplier concerns. "Lack of information is not identical to 'lack of timely information.' Instead, it means that performers receive no information and remain in the dark about changes affecting the organization."[3]

Performers also need frequent and timely feedback on the results of their performance:

> Lack of feedback on consequences means that performers are not being given feedback on the results of their work activities. They are performing in a vacuum ... No timely feedback means that the time lag is excessive between worker performance and feedback received about that performance. People do not know what they are responsible for doing or what results they should be achieving. Hence they are not accountable for what they do.[4]

Environment Support, Resources, and Tools

Environment support, resources, and tools are those things that management provides to support or assist the performer. Environment support may include ergonomic, health, wellness, and safety factors that have an impact on performance. For example, problems with such diverse factors as air quality, workspace, rest areas, lighting,

TABLE 4-4

GILBERT'S BEHAVIOR ENGINEERING MODEL: ENVIRONMENTAL SUPPORT

	Information	*Instrumentation*	*Motivation*
Environmental Support	Data Information Feedback	Work Environment Support Resources Tools	Consequences Incentives Rewards
Repertory of Behaviors	Skills Knowledge	Individual Capacity	Motivation Expectations

workload, hazardous material handling, work flow design, or workstation construction may cause performance gaps.

The term *resources* refers to the time, money, materials, and personnel allocated to the performance. Resources must be adequate and of sufficient quality to allow for successful accomplishment of the performance. Allocating inadequate resources or substituting poor quality resources may cause performance problems.

Tools are instruments required to complete the job, such as a computer and software for filling out tax forms or the correct equipment to attach a car part on the assembly line. Tools should be available, accessible, efficient, and safe.

How do environment support, resources, and tools support performers and cause people to do what they do? Sometimes employees do not have the environment support, resources, and tools they need to do their job—either what they need does not exist because the company has not made the investment, or what they need exists, but is not functioning properly.

Performing an appendectomy in a hospital operating suite is a routine procedure. The operating room has a sterile, controlled environment, state-of-the-art machinery and instruments, and qualified personnel. Emergency equipment and staff are on hand in case of complications. In contrast, performing an appendectomy in the wilderness without the appropriate facilities, machinery, tools, staff, or emergency backup would not be routine and could cause a gap between desired and actual performance.

Consequences, Incentives, or Rewards

Consequences are events or effects produced by a preceding act. For example, inappropriate lighting may cause eyestrain and prevent an employee from doing a stellar job.

Incentives are the stimuli that influence or encourage people to do their jobs. Incentives may be internal or external. Going the extra mile with a work task may be sufficient for one employee to earn merit, while another employee may need feedback from a supervisor. On the other hand, rewards are items given in return for services. Rewards may be monetary or nonmonetary. Gilbert lists three types of performance-based incentives: [5]
1. Monetary incentives
2. Nonmonetary incentives
3. Career development opportunities

Examples of monetary performance-based incentives include:
• Suggestion systems that offer money to employees whose suggestions are adopted

• Profit sharing
• Stock options
• Bonuses

Career development opportunities may be monetary or nonmonetary depending on whether the opportunities include tuition reimbursement or an increase in pay upon completion of a program.

Examples of nonmonetary performance-based incentives include the following:
• Teacher rewards a young child by placing a star on the child's paper to indicate a creative drawing
• Time off with pay
• Gifts
• Simple recognition awards or programs

Both monetary and nonmonetary incentives can contribute to increasing productivity and self-esteem. Assessing consequences, incentives, or rewards helps determine why people do what they do. Most employees perform tasks, react to their environment, and interact with colleagues based on perceptions of rewards for performance and consequences of actions. They maximize positive consequences, incentives, or rewards and minimize negative forces.

Analyzing Environmental Factors That Influence Performance

"It is one thing to acknowledge that the work environment can cause performance problems, but another to find out from *where* in the work environment the problem stems."[6] In addition to assessing consequences, incentives, and monetary or nonmonetary rewards, the PT practitioner should also assess whether the organization consciously or unconsciously supports a policy of *disincentives*. Rossett writes about companies "speaking with two voices" and cites two common examples of disincentives:

• One common problem is ignoring desired performance. When you ask a group of training professionals about the incentives for excellent performance, they'll often laugh. Too frequently, they perceive none. In fact, some contend that there is punishment associated with excellence, with the best people getting the thorniest clients or challenges.[7]
• Another typical problem with incentives is when they conflict, i.e., when the organization is rewarding behavior that crowds out the desired performance. This happens to customer service people who are often measured and applauded for the quantity of their contacts but exhorted to deliver high-quality, relationship and loyalty building interactions.[8]

Recognizing that the Behavior Engineering Model was not sufficient in itself to pinpoint the causes of performance gaps within the work environment, Tom Gilbert developed the PROBE model.[9] The model provides a series of questions that help the PT practitioner probe and assess the work environment for performance gap drivers or causes (Job Aid 4-1 at the end of this section).

Some of the answers to the questions in the PROBE model may be found in documentation from the performance gap analysis. In fact, seeking for answers during the gap analysis may save time and resources in the performance analysis process and shortcut the cause analysis process. If the answers are not available, the PT practitioner will need to interview or survey the performer(s).

Case Study: Kaizen Projection—Injection Molding Operation

Situation

The operation produces air bag covers for steering wheels. They are injection molded and have to meet tight tolerance standards due to their inclusion as part of a safety feature. A typical molding station consists of two molding machines; two bins of hard plastic frames, which are inserted into the mold machines and on which the rubber compound is molded; and a finishing/inspection/rework area. The performance improvement opportunity involved a redesign of the work area to achieve greater throughput. Prior to the intervention it took approximately five minutes to complete each step. A second opportunity involved reducing the number of people required to staff the station from three to two, one operator per machine and one person at the take off/inspection/rework area.

Intervention

The intervention was a week-long Kaizen project. Kaizen is the Japanese term for a process improvement exercise. A team of people, led by the Kaizen project operator, conducted time studies, discussed new ways of doing things, then redesigned the work area and processes to achieve the two objectives. Any new tooling or equipment requests would be presented to plant management by the team, and a decision would be made that day as to its viability. The physical layout of the work area was open, so work was rerouted to allow for a one-day shutdown of the cell for physical rearrangement.

The cell was completely redesigned to reduce the number of turns required by the machine operators. Also, the hard plastic frames, which were originally kept in a bin that the operator had to bend down to access, were relocated to "trees." The plastic frames now hung from the tree's "branches" so the operator could reach them without bending. The trees could be rotated to expose more frames.

Results

The results of the week-long Kaizen effort were as follows:

- There was a reduction of nearly two minutes to produce a part. This resulted in an increased capacity for output from 12 pieces per hour to 20. In other words, what once took one hour to produce could now be done in 40 minutes.
- The operators were able to use the extra time for doing finishing work, inspection, and rework. Because two people could now accomplish the work of three, the third person was reassigned.
- A six-week follow up determined that the improvements were not only maintained, but improved on by the operators. Operators commented that in spending more time with the product during the finishing work, inspections, and rework phases, they were getting a better feel for the process and could anticipate problems.

Lessons Learned

The most obvious lesson learned is that when employees are provided with the right equipment (in this case, the "tree"), the right environment (the redesigned work area), and the right resources, performance can be improved. The new equipment was inexpensive and the redesign required no additional floor space. In fact, the redesigned work area actually used less space and opened up a new aisle.

The second lesson may be even more important—involving employees in the change appeared to motivate them to employ other strategies for efficiency. Also, by involving the operator, who functioned as lead expert in the process, the Kaizen changes not only survived, but were improved on in the true spirit of continuous improvement.

The case study was contributed by Douglas Swiatkowski, M.Ed., Tenneco Automotive. Used with permission.

JOB AID 4-1: PROBING FOR ENVIRONMENTAL SUPPORT DRIVERS (OR CAUSES)

This job aid is an adaptation of Gilbert's PROBE Model.[10] Answers to the following questions help to establish the drivers or causes of performance gaps. Some of the answers may be found in documentation for the performance gap analysis. Other answers may require additional input from actual performer(s).

Category	Questions	Yes	No
Data	1. Are there sufficient, accessible data (or signals) to direct an experienced person to perform well?		
	2. Are they accurate?		
	3. Are they free of confusion and stimulus competition that slow performance and invite errors?		
	4. Are directions free of data glut, stripped down to the simplest form, and not buried in extraneous data?		
	5. Are they timely?		
	6. Are good models of behavior available?		
	7. Are clear and measurable performance standards communicated so that people know how well they are supposed to perform?		
	8. Do they accept the standards as reasonable?		
Feedback	1. Is work-related feedback provided describing results consistent with the standards and not just behavior?		
	2. Is it immediate and frequent enough to help employees remember what they did?		
	3. Is it selective and specific, limited to a few matters of importance and free of data glut and vague generalities?		
	4. Is it educational, positive, and constructive so that people learn something from it?		
Tools	1. Are the necessary implements usually on hand for doing the job?		
	2. Are they reliable and efficient?		
	3. Are they safe?		
Information	1. Are procedures efficient and designed to avoid unnecessary steps and wasted motion?		
	2. Are they based on sound methods rather than historical happenstance?		
	3. Are they appropriate to the job and skill level?		
	4. Are they free of boring and tiresome repetition?		

JOB AID 4-1: PROBING FOR ENVIRONMENTAL SUPPORT DRIVERS (OR CAUSES) *continued*

Category	Questions	Yes	No
Resources	1. Are adequate materials, supplies, and assistance usually available to do the job well?		
	2. Are they efficiently tailored to the job?		
	3. Do ambient conditions provide comfort and prevent unnecessary interference?		
Incentives	1. Is the pay for the job competitive?		
	2. Are there significant bonuses or raises based on good performance?		
	3. Does good performance have any relationship to career advancement?		
	4. Are there meaningful nonmonetary incentives (recognition and so on) for good performance based on results and not behavior?		
	5. Are they scheduled well, neither too frequently (lose meaning) nor too infrequently (becoming useless)?		
	6. Is there an absence of punishment for performing well?		
	7. Is there an absence of hidden incentives to perform poorly?		
	8. Is the balance of positive and negative incentive in favor of good performance?		

Dean, P.J. and Ripley, D.E. (Eds.), (1997). Performance Improvement Pathfinders: Models for Organizational Learning Systems, pp. 57–58. Washington, D.C.: The International Society for Performance Improvement. Used with permission.

ISPI © 2000 Permission granted for unlimited duplication for noncommercial use.

LACK OF REPERTORY OF BEHAVIOR

Another cause of performance problems is people's lack of repertory of behavior.[1] There are three factors that people bring to the performance picture. All three have an effect on performance in the workplace.

1. Information (skills and knowledge)
2. Instrumentation (individual capacity)
3. Motivation (motivation and expectations)

If a gap exists between desired and actual performance, and the gap is not caused by environmental support problems, the question is, "Could they do it if their lives depended on it?"[2] There are two possible responses to this question—yes or no. If the answer is "No," the PT practitioner should focus on determining the skills or knowledge deficiency that interferes with the accomplishment of the desired performance. If the answer is "Yes," the PT practitioner can rule out a skill or knowledge deficiency and focus on lack of individual capacity, motivation, or expectations (see Table 4-5).

Skills and Knowledge

If people "couldn't do it if their lives depended on it,"[3] the PT practitioner should suspect a skill or knowledge deficiency. People cannot be expected to perform to standards if they lack the required skills or knowledge. "It is not possible for people with the right motivation, performance standards, resource tools, support, capacity, and motives to be successful performers if they don't know how to perform."[4]

Analyzing Skills and Knowledge

Identifying the cause of a performance gap as lack of skills and knowledge isn't as simple as it sounds. Cause analysis, like performance analysis, "occurs at both the macro- and microlevels so the PT practitioner may understand both what the gaps (or causes) are and why they came to be."[5] First, the PT practitioner needs to discover what skills and knowledge are required for the desired performance. Documentation (job or task analysis, performance standards, etc.) from the performance gap analysis should provide this information.

Then, the PT practitioner needs to consider the following:[6]
- Did the employee once know how to perform as desired?
- Has the employee forgotten how to perform as desired?

Perhaps the employee possessed the necessary skills and knowledge at an earlier time, but the nature of the job has changed and she or he needs to be updated. Another possibility to examine is whether or not the employee possesses the necessary skills and knowledge, but has not had the opportunity to use them for some time because the need for the performance has changed. It is easy to forget skills and knowledge when they are not used.

There is another perspective on lack of knowledge and skills that requires examination—"(Maybe) there is just too much to know."[7] In today's information age employees

TABLE 4-5

GILBERT'S BEHAVIOR ENGINEERING MODEL: REPERTORY OF BEHAVIOR

	Information	*Instrumentation*	*Motivation*
Environmental Support	Data Information Feedback	Work Environment Support Resources Tools	Consequences Incentives Rewards
Repertory of Behaviors	Skills Knowledge	Individual Capacity	Motivation Expectations

are frequently inundated with documentation or updates until it may become "disinformation" [sic] or the employees just plain "tune it out."

Finally, the PT practitioner may want to look at the report from the environmental analysis. The workplace has to support the performer's knowledge and skills. "If you pit a trained employee against an environment that does not value the new skills and knowledge, the environment wins every time."[8]

Individual Capacity

Individual capacity is another component of people's repertory of behavior. Capacity "represents the individual's ability to perform the job. It is represented by a match or mismatch between the employee and the job requirement."[9] Individual capacity helps to match the right person to the right job. A mismatch, or employee selection error, can cause a performance gap.

Lack of ability means that a mistake was made during employee selection. An individual was hired, transferred, or promoted into a job that he or she lacked the ability to perform or to learn. In one organization, an employee was promoted to executive secretary. She was unable to type—and was also unable to learn how to type.[10]

Employee selection processes may also help to avoid a potential performance gap. A young man was interviewing for a job as a shoe salesman. The final question was, "Based on everything you have heard about this job, are there any areas that may be problematic?" Without delay, the young man replied, "I really despise people." Needless to say he was not hired. Even if he possessed the required skills and knowledge, the young man lacked the capacity or ability to accomplish the desired performance—selling shoes to people.

Analyzing Individual Capacity

To determine whether or not a lack of individual capacity is causing a performance gap, the PT practitioner needs to look at capacity from two perspectives:[11]

- Does the individual lack the capacity (ultimate limits to which an individual develops any function given appropriate training and environment) or ability (physical, mental, or social powers, inherited or acquired by an individual) to perform or learn?
- Do the organizational, workplace, and work environments support the individual's capacity to perform or learn?

First, the PT practitioner needs to review the performance gap analysis to discover what individual capacity or ability

is required to meet the desired performance requirements. The following questions may help to identify individual capacity requirements for a specific performance:

- Is it certain and proven that one must have special aptitudes, intelligence scores, verbal skills, manual dexterity, and so on, to perform in an acceptable, if not exemplary, manner?
- Is the proof so sound that there are virtually no exceptions?[12] The PT practitioner then looks at the employee to assess whether or not the individual's physical and mental capacity matches the performance requirements. A review of the gap analysis or personnel records, or an interview with the employee, may provide information on the performer's aptitude, intelligence, verbal skills, etc.

Finally, the PT practitioner may look at the organizational and environmental analyses to find out if the organization, workplace, and work environments support the individual's capacity or ability to perform and learn. For example, does either the organization or the environment:

- Offer flexible scheduling to accommodate people when they are at their sharpest?
- Consider the difficulty level and individual capacity when selecting someone to perform a task?
- Provide response aids, e.g., large-print job aids for older workers, to determine whether lack of individual capacity is causing a performance gap?[13]

Motivation and Expectations

Motivation comes from within. The performer encourages himself or herself to succeed. Expectation also comes from within the performer. The performer expects or believes that certain conditions or resources are required to accomplish a given task. If the employee is not motivated to perform, or feels that his or her expectations have not been met, there is a good chance that there will be a gap between desired and actual performance.

Using the model on the first page of this section, it is possible to make an important connection between the performer's motivation and expectations and environmental support factors:

It was Gilbert's contention that motivation, the third factor related to the individual, will be high if all the other five cells, especially those related to work environment, are provided. Thus he believed that evidence of low motivation is a red flag to look for deficiencies in information, resources, or incentives. In communicating this concept, he stressed that factors in the work environment will not directly motivate employees. Rather, by dealing with these work environment factors, the organization can create an environment within which the employees' own intrinsic motivation can flourish.[14]

Analyzing Motivation and Expectations

It is difficult at best to determine what motivates an individual to accomplish peak performance. It is almost as difficult to discover a performer's expectations. Perhaps the first step is to ask, "Is the performance system inherently so dull, unrewarding, or punishing that people must have special motives to succeed in it, even when the incentives provided are excellent?"[15] The organizational, environmental, and gap analyses should shed some light on the nature of the performance system in which the performer is functioning. The same documents should uncover what expectations the performer might have given optimal work environment.

The PT practitioner may also want to interview the supervisor, manager, coworkers, and performer or observe the performer in action. However, these methods are less than scientific and rely on self-reporting (performer) or perceptions (supervisor, manager, coworkers).

There are some instruments on the market that deal with motivation and expectations. Major publishers of HRD resources usually list the instruments in their catalogs. Despite the fact that the instruments may or may not be valid and reliable, they can prove useful in uncovering intrinsic feelings or concerns that are not evident in overt performance.

Case Study: Matching Capacity With Job Requirements

This case study features a manufacturer of plastic exterior trim parts for the automotive industry. The company is a multinational organization with sales of more than $1 billion and approximately 13,000 employees worldwide.

Situation

The company was experiencing a substantial turnover in its manufacturing facilities in North America and, to a lesser extent, in Europe. The work is semi-skilled, and there is a three-month learning curve before a new person is considered established and efficient. Due to extremely rapid growth, most of the manufacturing plants were in a hiring mode. However, with a tight labor market, the human resources professionals found it difficult to match positions with the right people.

Cause Analysis

Rather than focus on the tight market, corporate human resources chose to look at why people were leaving. One of the common answers was that the people just did not like the work, which at times was tedious and physically demanding. Corporate human resources met with the human resources managers from the North American plants to brainstorm possible solutions to the problem. It was suggested that perhaps the plant human resources staff was simply hiring the wrong people for the job, which required a certain capacity for repetitive motion in an uncomfortable environment.

The cause analysis for this situation was a two-step process. With the help of a physician and an occupational therapist, a study was done on the jobs performed on the floor. A physical profile was created for each job that highlighted the unique demands each placed on the human body. A battery of tests was developed that enabled HR staff to test prospective applicants' capacity for the physical demands of the job. After applicants passed the physical, they moved on to the simulations.

Designed and developed with the help of the physician and occupational therapist, simulations modeled real work conditions and took place on the plant floor. For a full shift, applicants would perform the tasks in the duplicated environment. If hired, they would spend the first week of their employment in this area for "job toughening." For that week they would perform the simulations to condition the muscles that their job would require. During this time they were also instructed on how to avoid injury, recognize the onset of fatigue or other physical problems, and cope with stress.

Results

The piloted program was housed at one of the company's plants for six months. In that time many applicants demonstrated diminished capacities for the jobs they originally sought. Many of them found employment in different positions, which better matched their capacity profile. Although measurable numbers are yet to be verified, not a single individual who went through the process has left the company. Of these people, none has missed time due to injury. Another sign of the pilot program's success has been the number of current employees requesting to go through the one-week job toughening program. The plan is to roll the program out in a few plants at a time while tracking turnover and injury costs. Projections are that if the other plants experience results similar to the pilot, within a year's time all costs associated with implementing the plan will be recouped and the program will begin generating measurable savings.

Lessons Learned

What does this example tell us about individual capacity? It reveals a few things:

1. It appears that when a person's capacity and job are matched, they seem to be happier and stay with the company.

2. The job-toughening experience seems to show that capacity can be extended or enhanced with exercises.

3. There have been no injury claims from the employees who went through the program for capacity diagnoses, job toughening, and training about the management of fatigue.

The case study was developed by Douglas Swiatkowski, M.Ed., Tenneco Automotive. Used with permission.

JOB AID 4-2: PROBING FOR PEOPLE'S REPERTORY OF BEHAVIOR DRIVERS (OR CAUSES)

This job aid is an adaptation of Gilbert's PROBE Model.[16,17] Answers to the following questions help to establish the drivers or causes of performance gaps. Some of the answers may be found in documentation for the performance gap analysis. Other answers may require additional input from actual performer(s).

Category	Questions	Yes	No
Knowledge and Training	1. Do people understand the consequences of both good and poor performance?		
	2. Do they grasp the essentials of performance? Do they get the big picture?		
	3. Do they have the technical concepts to perform well?		
	4. Do they have sufficient basic skills such as reading?		
	5. Do they have sufficient specialized skills?		
	6. Do they always have the skills after initial training?		
	7. Are good job aids available?		
Capacity	1. Do the incumbents have the basic capacity to learn the necessary perceptual discriminations with accuracy and speed?		
	2. Are they free of emotional limitations that would interfere with performance?		
	3. Do they have sufficient strength and dexterity to learn to do the job well?		
Motives	1. Do incumbents seem to have the desire to perform well when they enter the job?		
	2. Do their motives endure? Is the turnover low?		

Dean, P.J. and Ripley, D.E. (Eds.), (1997). Performance Improvement Pathfinders: Models for Organizational Learning Systems, pp. 57–58. Washington, D.C.: The International Society for Performance Improvement. Used with permission.

ISPI © 2000 Permission granted for unlimited duplication for noncommercial use.

CHAPTER

5

INTERVENTION SELECTION AND DESIGN

"CAN'T WE JUST HAVE A REGULAR JOB
INTERVIEW?"

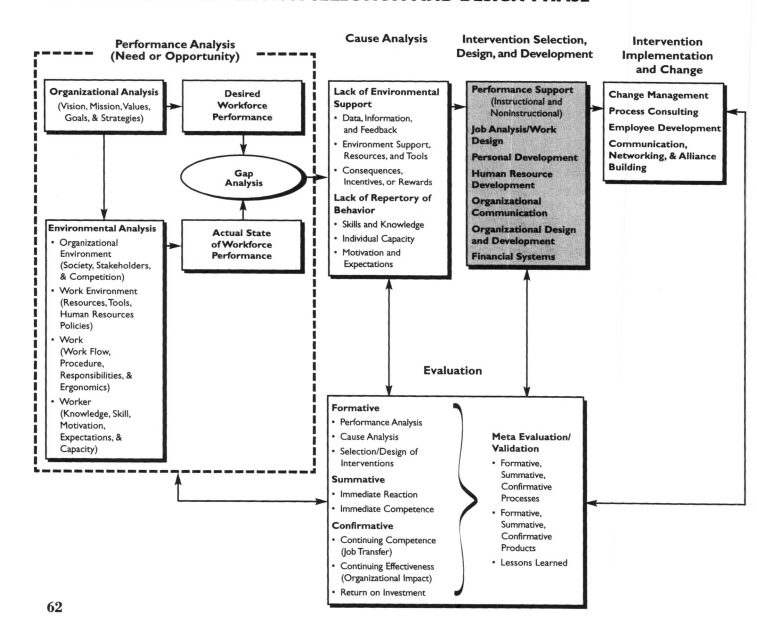

Introduction to Intervention Selection and Design

The organizational scan of your performance environment is completed. The conditions, circumstances, and influences of the performance outcome have been considered. The intra- and interworkings of the organization have been meticulously studied. The performance environment and the gap between actual and optimal performance have been analyzed. An extensive cause analysis has been generated. The next phase of the HPT Model—Intervention Selection and Design—will help to address performance concerns (see Figure 5-1).

Definition and Scope

Interventions are deliberate, conscious acts that facilitate change in performance. Rothwell sees interventions as change efforts that are long-term, evolutionary, and

FIGURE 5-1

HPT MODEL: INTERVENTION SELECTION AND DESIGN PHASE

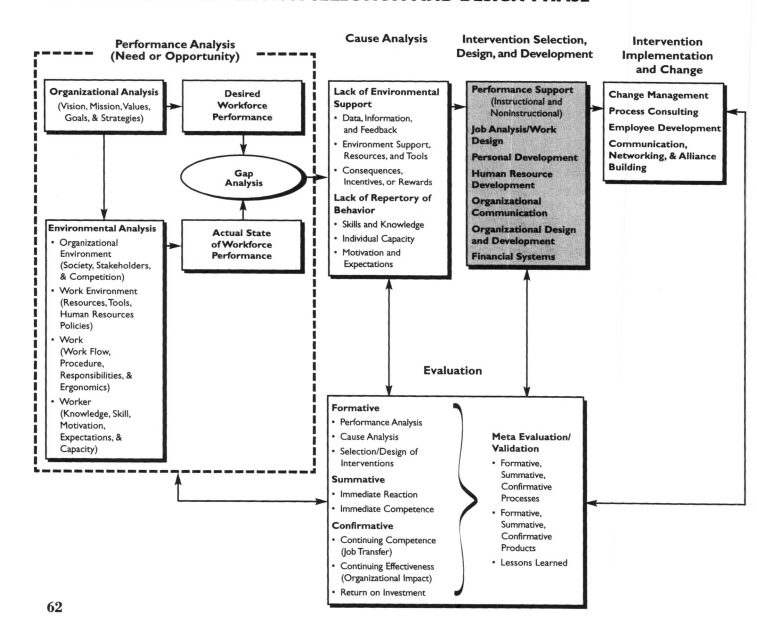

progressive.[1] A well-known consulting agency sees them as "conscious planned actions designed to affect human performance."[2] Interventions are targeted to organizations, departments, work groups, and individuals. The late Clay Carr defined interventions as "the kinds of things you can do to bring about changes in job performance."[3] However they are defined, they run the gamut from large-scale organizational change efforts that affect entire organizational systems at local, national, and global levels to modest ergonomic efforts that provide comfort from Repetitive Stress Syndrome. Even job aids, which remind, aid, or assist workers to evaluate and do work, are unique kinds of interventions (see Table 5-1).

Potential Problems With Interventions

The PT practitioner must select the interventions that work best according to the problems identified. The interventions

TABLE 5-1

LIST OF INTERVENTIONS

Performance Support	**Human Resource Development**
• Instructional 　Learning Organization 　Action Learning 　Self-Directed Learning 　Training 　Knowledge Capture and Management 　Education 　Interactive Technologies 　　Distance Learning 　　Telecommunications 　　Satellite Technology • Noninstructional 　Job Aids 　Electronic Performance Support Systems 　Documentation (Job Specification) and Standards	• Selection and Staffing • Compensation and Benefits • Literacy • Retirement Planning • Health and Wellness • Motivation (Incentives and Rewards) • Performance Appraisals • Assessment Centers and Competency Testing • Succession Planning and Career Pathing • Leadership and Executive Development • Management and Supervisory Development
Job Analysis/Work Design	**Organizational Communication**
• Job Specifications • Job Rotation • Job Enlargement • Work Methods • Quality (Control, Management, and Assurance) • Continuous Improvement • Value Engineering • Interface Design • Ergonomics • Preventive Maintenance • Safety Engineering	• Networking and Collaboration • Information Systems • Suggestion and Grievance Systems • Conflict Resolution
	Organizational Design and Development
Personal Development	• Strategic Planning and Management • Environmental Scanning • Globalization • Benchmarking • Reengineering, Realignment, Restructuring • Teambuilding Strategies • Problemsolving and Decisionmaking • Culture and Diversity • Ethics • Spirituality in the Workplace
• Mentoring and Coaching • Career Development • Career Assessment • Feedback	
	Financial Systems
	• Financial Forecasting • Capital Investment and Spending • Cash Flow Analysis • Mergers, Acquisitions, and Joint Ventures
	Other Interventions

Developed by Darlene Van Tiem, James Moseley, and Joan Dessinger.
Sources: Gayeski, Hutchinson and Stein, Stolovitch and Keeps, Hale, and Whiteside and Langdon.

selected will flow smoothly from detailed performance and cause analyses. The practitioner's repertoire should include basic instructional and noninstructional interventions. Although practitioners are not expected to be experts in all categories and subcategories of interventions, they are expected to know where to locate information about interventions. The PT practitioner needs to be able to communicate to all constituents a basic knowledge and understanding of a variety of interventions, especially those in the areas of training, human resources, finances, marketing, organizational design, labor relations, etc.

Successful Interventions

Spitzer lists the following criteria for successful interventions.

1. Design should be based on a comprehensive understanding of the situation. This is where previous performance and cause analyses come together.
2. Interventions should be carefully targeted. Target the right people, in the right setting, and at the right time.
3. An intervention should have a sponsor. A sponsor is someone who will champion the activity.
4. Interventions should be designed with a team approach. The ability to draw upon expertise from all areas of the organization is vital to successful intervention selection.
5. Intervention design should be cost-sensitive.
6. Interventions should be designed on the basis of comprehensive, prioritized requirements, based on what is most important to both the individual and the organization.
7. A variety of intervention options should be investigated because the creation of a new intervention can be costly.
8. Interventions should be sufficiently powerful. Consider long-term versus short-term effectiveness. Use multiple strategies to effect change.
9. Interventions should be sustainable. Thought must be given to institutionalizing the intervention over time. To really be successful, the intervention must become ingrained in the organization's culture.

10. Interventions should be designed with viability of development and implementation in mind. An intervention needs human resources and organizational support.
11. Interventions should be designed using an iterative approach. This occurs during the formative evaluation stage (discussed under the evaluation component of the HPT Model) when multiple revisions will generate interventions to fit the organization.[4,5]

Practical Guidelines

This section outlines suggestions based on actual consulting experiences.

- Conduct thorough performance and cause analyses before considering interventions.
- Remain focused on a solution for performance problems rather than on a specific intervention.
- An intervention applied to one performance setting may not work in another setting.
- Think outside the box. Consider noninstructional interventions too, especially those which are less frequently used.
- Performance problems have many solutions as well as appropriate and timely interventions to address them.
- Consider using two or more interventions to address a performance problem.
- Establish an appropriate set of criteria for evaluating interventions. Justify the use of particular interventions in a variety of settings. An evaluation of the interventions should be ongoing to determine their appropriateness (see chapters on performance and cause analysis).

Subsequent sections will provide an overview of intervention categories, case studies, and job aids. Job Aid 5-1 will aid in selecting an intervention.

JOB AID 5-1: INTERVENTION SELECTOR

Based on the cause analysis and performance gap analysis, select interventions that would improve the situation. Place a check next to each intervention to be considered. Prioritize the possibilities and circle three interventions to begin the performance improvement effort.

Performance Support

- Instructional
- ❏ Learning Organization
- ❏ Action Learning
- ❏ Self-directed Learning
- ❏ Training
- ❏ Knowledge Capture and Management
- ❏ Education
- ❏ Interactive Technologies
  - ❏ Distance Learning
  - ❏ Telecommunications
  - ❏ Satellite Technology
- Noninstructional
- ❏ Job Aids
- ❏ Electronic Performance Support Systems
- ❏ Documentation (Job Specification) and Standards

Job Analysis/Work Design

- ❏ Job Specifications
- ❏ Job Rotation
- ❏ Job Enlargement
- ❏ Work Methods
- ❏ Quality (Control, Management, and Assurance)
- ❏ Continuous Improvement
- ❏ Value Engineering
- ❏ Interface Design
- ❏ Ergonomics
- ❏ Preventive Maintenance
- ❏ Safety Engineering

Personal Development

- ❏ Mentoring and Coaching
- ❏ Career Development
- ❏ Career Assessment
- ❏ Feedback

Human Resource Development

- ❏ Selection and Staffing
- ❏ Compensation and Benefits
- ❏ Literacy
- ❏ Retirement Planning
- ❏ Health and Wellness
- ❏ Motivation (Incentives and Rewards)
- ❏ Performance Appraisals
- ❏ Assessment Centers and Competency Testing
- ❏ Succession Planning and Career Pathing
- ❏ Leadership and Executive Development
- ❏ Management and Supervisory Development

Organizational Communication

- ❏ Networking and Collaboration
- ❏ Information Systems
- ❏ Suggestion and Grievance Systems
- ❏ Conflict Resolution

Organizational Design and Development

- ❏ Strategic Planning and Management
- ❏ Environmental Scanning
- ❏ Globalization
- ❏ Benchmarking
- ❏ Reengineering, Realignment, Restructuring
- ❏ Teambuilding Strategies
- ❏ Problem Solving and Decision Making
- ❏ Culture and Diversity
- ❏ Ethics
- ❏ Spirituality in the Workplace

Financial Systems

- ❏ Financial Forecasting
- ❏ Capital Investment and Spending
- ❏ Cash Flow Analysis
- ❏ Mergers, Acquisitions, and Joint Ventures

Other Interventions

Developed by Darlene Van Tiem, James Moseley, and Joan Dessinger.
Sources: Gayeski, Hutchinson and Stein, Stolovitch and Keeps, Hale, and Whiteside and Langdon.

CLASSIFICATION OF INTERVENTIONS

There are several classifications of interventions. A performance improvement specialist's diagnostic skills and creative energies can help determine broad classifications and listings. It can be said, however, that all interventions are classified into instructional and noninstructional intervention systems. The Conifer Consulting Group identified 20 strategies and tactics for performance improvement systems: instructional, communication, career, career development, feedback, information, human development, quality improvement, resource, reward/recognition, etc. For example, organizational design and development is represented by the concepts of change management, conflict management, management structure design, team-building, and values clarification, among others.[1]

Another classification system focuses on 12 interventions that are the fruit of the Hierarchy model.[2] Here we see interventions aligned with need. The families of interventions include: define and clarify, standardize and systematize, create structure, redesign, document, motivate, etc. Other examples of motivating interventions are recognizing employees in a public forum for a job well done or paying them for effective team performance. Examples of an informing intervention are to communicate goals and expectations and to keep people informed through announcements and releases, progress reports, interim and preliminary reports, concluding reports, and internal reports. Sitting down with an employee to determine performance goals and giving constructive and frequent feedback are other examples.[3]

Another classification system ranks interventions by level of invasiveness.[4] Six interventions are listed here from least to most invasive:
1. Interventions designed to increase competence
2. Interventions designed to develop or clarify goals and standards or to establish feedback systems
3. Interventions that try to improve performance by changing work processes
4. Interventions that broaden the scope of a job by changing the things that employees are allowed or expected to do
5. Interventions that change the incentive system
6. Interventions that attack the total performance system

Examples of interventions designed to increase competence are job aids, reference manuals, methods designed to store information for easy and efficient retrieval, varieties of training experiences, and a host of developmental

programs. Carr said that interventions that attack the total performance system are deeply ingrained, most invasive, and show the greatest need.[5] They require considerable time to implement—months, even years—and they require attention, support, and follow-up by a champion in a top management position.

K.S. Whiteside distributed a Performance Technology Interventions Checklist that included 14 categories of interventions.[6] The classification of ergonomics interventions, for example, includes such subcategories as handicapped access/EEO, facilities design, person/machine interfaces, interior design and decoration, safety planning, and access systems.

Marc J. Rosenberg, a human performance guru, categorized four major areas of interventions: human resource development (performance of individuals); organizational development (performance of groups and teams); human resource management (managing, coaching, recruiting, staffing); and environmental engineering (tools, resources, and facilities that support workplace performance).[7]

Another author looks at performance by considering interventions external to the performer and internal to the performer. External interventions are divided into environmental interventions (intangibles), such as organizational systems and incentives, and resources interventions (tangibles), such as cognitive support, tools, and physical environment. Internal interventions are skills/knowledge and inherent ability.[8]

Another useful intervention classification system is the organizational scan. It is a systems-approach matrix (input, conditions, process, output, consequences, feedback) looking at four organizational levels: individuals, processes, workgroups, and business unit. Six categories of interventions are listed for each organizational level. For example, at the individual level, work methods interventions (process system) focus on work tools, job aids, work flow, skill update and enhancements, documentation, and skill maintenance and development. At the business unit level, business results interventions (consequences system) focus on measures of success, satisfaction of stockholders, satisfaction of customers, and market share.[9]

Revisiting their earlier contribution to interventions, Hutchison and Stein reordered and reconceptualized their 20 systems and categories.[10] Cultural anthropology becomes organizational anthropology, and each of the intervention systems is updated and streamlined to reflect current human resource development practice and examples.

Still another classification set identifies six major categories: instruction, work design, performance support, incentive systems, organizational communication, and organizational design and development. Examples of the latter include team-building, reporting and management structure, strategic planning, and vision development.[11]

Spitzer views performance improvement interventions with a systems approach that follows the steps of analysis, design, development, implementation, and evaluation. He suggests a six-step outline for the intervention design process:
Step 1: Organizing the effort
Step 2: Clarifying expectations
Step 3: Identifying intervention requirements
Step 4: Identifying intervention components
Step 5: Determining intervention specifications
Step 6: Documenting and approving the design[12]

He also suggests a five-step intervention development process involving team effort, prototype testing, revision, and production.[13]

A useful glossary of 48 interventions and their corresponding definitions is offered by the DLS Group from Denver. Some entries have examples and advantages listed.[14] Performance International defined over 121 performance technology interventions.[15] This list is unique in that intervention classification codes appear after each definition.

Another helpful listing of 50 performance improvement tools was edited by Langdon, Whiteside, and McKenna.[16] Each intervention follows a standard design format with the following components: performance change/level grid classification of interventions, alternative names, definition, description, when and when not to use, case study, resources and references, intervention and case study author(s). It is by far the most detailed listing of interventions published to date. The introductory sections, which include place and use of interventions in performance technology, selecting interventions, and implementing interventions, are particularly helpful.

A final intervention listing is the one suggested with the HPT Model in this book. It consists of eight categories of interventions: performance support, job analysis, personal development, human resource development, organizational communication, organizational design and development, work design, and financial systems. Those interventions selected for this section have been refined or restructured to reflect more current human resource development practices.

All of the intervention listings have their origins in the works of such "pathfinders" as Thomas Gilbert, Robert Mager, Joe Harless, Clay Carr, Geary Rummler, Donald Tosti, Warren Bennis, Peter Drucker, George Odiorne, and others. A more comprehensive and detailed discussion of interventions may be found in *Performance Improvement Interventions*, the companion book to this publication.

PERFORMANCE SUPPORT INTERVENTIONS: INSTRUCTIONAL

Once a performance problem, opportunity, or challenge is identified and the causes are determined, the PT practitioner must determine which interventions are most appropriate, timely, and cost-effective. Performance support interventions affect the workplace, the work, and the worker through planned change efforts in job performance and knowledge transfer (see Table 5-2). Performance support is "the label we give to the various techniques used to apply a systematic approach to analyzing, improving, and managing performance in the workplace through the use of appropriate and varied interventions."[1] Performance support is "a doohickey that tells you just what you need to know, just when you need to know it."[2] Performance support interventions can be either instructional or non-instructional. Instructional performance support interventions are selected when the problem is a lack of knowledge or skill. Noninstructional per-

formance support interventions are selected to improve individual, group, or team performance; to improve processes, products, and services; and to guide business plans, deliverables, results, and success measures.

Typical instructional categories of performance support interventions include (but are not limited to) learning organization, action learning, self-directed learning, training, knowledge capture and management, education, and the interactive technologies of distance learning, telecommunications, and satellite technology.

Learning Organization

The concept of the *learning organization* is a relatively new phenomenon. Its origins stem from organizational development, industrial relations, and public administration.

TABLE 5-2

PERFORMANCE SUPPORT INTERVENTIONS COMPONENT OF THE HPT MODEL

- **Instructional**

  Learning Organization
  Action Learning
  Self-directed Learning
  Training
  Knowledge Capture and Management
  Education
  Interactive Technologies
     Distance Learning
     Telecommunications
     Satellite Technology

- **Noninstructional**

  Job Aids
  Electronic Performance Support Systems
  Documentation (Job Specification) and Standards

TABLE 5-3

LEARNING LEVELS AND CHARACTERISTICS

Levels of Learning	Characteristics
Individual Learning	• Learn continuously • Rewards for learning • Knowledge, skills, and competencies focus
Team Learning	• Learn through dialogue • Build new mental maps • Actively transfer new learning • Civilized disagreement • Clear purpose with open communication
Organizational Learning	• Create market opportunities • Continuously adjusting • Infrastructure to deliver new capabilities[4]

It is based on the belief that an organization's competitive advantage can be enhanced through the use of knowledge as a competitive strategy. A learning organization continuously improves its processes, facilitates the education of all its members, and expands its capacity to produce.[3] Represented in the following Table 5-3 are three levels of learning.

In learning organizations everyone is a learner. People capitalize on both formal and informal opportunities to learn from one another. In this environment, education or training is an investment in human capital, not an unnecessary expense.

Action Learning

Another performance support intervention that has received much favorable attention is action learning. It builds opportunities for learning around real problems brought to the workplace by people. The mission and goals of the work and the workplace gain credibility because workers are focused on tasks and problems that are critical to success.

Action learning combines the experiences of direct work with learning. Through training and education, an individual's skill advancement is enhanced, which in turn strengthens the operational effectiveness of the organization.[5] The following Table 5-4 provides guidelines for the action learning process.

Self-directed Learning

Self-directed learning is training designed to allow the employee to master material independently, at the employee's own pace. Reading the safety features of a new machine, practicing a multimedia program or visiting a local public library to trace family history are examples of self-directed learning. From a corporate standpoint, it is useful in situations where there are diverse training needs, when training staff is limited, or when there is great need for individual development.[6] The following Table 5-5 highlights major advantages and disadvantages of self-directed learning.

Training

When people lack the necessary skills, knowledge, or appropriate attitudes to accomplish a task, they may need training. *Training* refers to instructional experiences provided by employers for employees. These experiences are expected to be applied on the job immediately or soon after the training episode. Training deals with what employees need to know and/or what they need to do to perform the job with a high degree of competency. It addresses attitudes as well as behaviors. It can be conducted internally by the training or human resource development departments or it can be conducted externally. Trainees can choose from a broad range of training events: symposia, seminars, workshops, courses, conferences, lectures, case studies, role plays, and others.[7] The performance system used should be carefully analyzed to determine if it is an appropriate intervention. Performance improvement most likely occurs via well-researched, cost-efficient training opportunities. Training must be endorsed by the organization's support system, and management must be involved every step of the way if it is to succeed.

Training solves a performance problem 20 percent of the

TABLE 5-4

ACTION LEARNING GUIDELINES

Components	How the Process Works
• Groups of 6–30 employees	• Representatives from different businesses or from different functional areas
• Reflection on lessons learned from previous experiences	• Apply knowledge to create more effective future performance
• Take action on issues or problems brought to group	• Group wrestles with problem; finds alternative with help of group process expert
• Selection of appropriate problems	• Lasts weeks, months, years depending on projects selected and needs of members
• Action learning vehicle: common problems and tasks	• Action learning focus: learning and development of group members
• Highly charged environment	• Collaborative efforts with keen listening skills[8]

TABLE 5-5

SELF-DIRECTED LEARNING GUIDELINES

Advantages			Disadvantages		
Trainee	Trainer Developer	Corporation	Trainee	Trainer Developer	Corporation
• Based on trainee readiness • Material individually selected • Learner sets pace	• Fewer repeated classes • Increase in development time • Time to serve as coach or mentor of resources	• Allows multiple site training • Allows continuous learning process to begin • Foundational to learning organization and teaching organization	• Learner unable to function in a self-directed capacity • Uncomfortable relying on objectives • Uncomfortable with self-evaluation	• Difficult to develop • Context in which self-directed learning is used must be carefully analyzed • Study habits of target population must be fully known	• Cost factor is high (production, reproduction, distribution, revision)[9]

time, whereas nontraining solutions are effective 80 percent of the time.

Knowledge Capture and Management

Knowledge capture and management, another of the instructional performance support interventions, is the process of acquiring, storing, and managing access to bodies of knowledge that assist people in performing their jobs with focus and precision. Knowledge capture and management can result in knowledge databases of an organization's best practices, critical job characteristics and corresponding outcome measures, and performance standards for dissemination across the organization. Organizations need to collect the scattered knowledge within their infrastructure and channel it into knowledge databases that can be easily retrieved by current and new employees so that work, worker, and workplace can quickly add to the value chain. Knowledge capture is unsuccessful without management's support and commitment. Management must actively demonstrate its support by systematically assessing content that is needed by employees throughout the organization and by identifying best practices of exemplary performers. Management needs to also support funding of corporate intranets to guarantee access to all employees.[10]

Education

The use of education is widespread and refers to human resources development activities that are designed to improve the performance of employees in a focused direction beyond their current job. The emphasis is on broad knowledge, understanding, comprehension, analysis, synthesis, and evaluation, and on transferring knowledge to future objectives as well as immediate, job-related applications. Measurable and precise objectives are stressed in an educational environment.

The Greek philosopher Maimonides offered advice to people seeking a broader, more global educational perspective when he said, "May there never develop in me the notion that my education is complete but give me the strength and leisure and zeal continually to enlarge my knowledge." Learning is a lifelong privilege. Education is not a task to be completed, but a process to be continued.

Interactive Technologies

There are three common instructional performance support interventions highlighted here that focus on interactive technologies: distance learning, telecommunications, and satellite technology.

The fundamental concept of distance learning is easy to understand: Learners and instructors are separated by distance (and sometimes by time). As a result, it's necessary to introduce an artificial communication medium that delivers information and provides a channel for interaction between the instructor and the learner.

Telecommunications refers to videoconferencing and computer conferencing. In a teleconferencing course, the instruction is quite normal except that part of the class is in another location. Teleconferencing also refers to live, interactive meetings of various kinds. In computer conferencing, the learner connects by modem to the conferencing system's software, which enables the instructor and the student to engage directly.

Satellite conferencing is the most widely recognized distance learning format. Using well-planned and -designed instructional materials, satellite instructors, subject matter experts, and on-site facilitators reach learners at multiple sites over wide geographic locations.[11]

To be effective, each of these technologies requires a thorough understanding of the target population; a curriculum that is needs-driven and meticulously designed; special instructional techniques; practice and feedback mechanisms; an evaluation plan; and special organizational and administrative arrangements.

Other interactive technologies to consider include multimedia, virtual reality, networking opportunities, and authoring tools for learning technologies. Another focal area is the technology for managing knowledge, especially networks like the Internet, intranet, Web, local area networks (LANs), and wide-area networks (WANs). In an increasingly wired world, businesses are moving ever closer to accepting a paperless workplace.

PERFORMANCE SUPPORT INTERVENTIONS: NONINSTRUCTIONAL

Typical noninstructional categories of performance support interventions include, but are not limited to, job aids, electronic performance support systems, documentation (job specifications), and standards. The use of these interventions is determined by their appropriateness to specific conditions.

Job Performance Aids

Job performance aids (also known as job aids) are used during a task to facilitate job performance and efficiency (see Table 5-6). Job performance aids are useful when employees need immediate assistance to help them get the job done. Tasks that are performed infrequently and are not part of a person's regular job are ideal situations for job performance aids. On the other hand, job aids that are quickly outdated, that convey complex information, or that compromise performance are inappropriate.[1] Job performance aids can be checklists or worksheets, matrix/decision tables, flowcharts, mixed varieties, and virtual reality. Those that guide job performance, reduce the length of time recall is necessary, signal when to take some action, and give directions on actions, are successful job performance aids. Table 5-6 is an explanation of a job performance aid.[2]

Electronic Performance Support Systems

A performance support system is "an integrated electronic environment which is available to and easily accessed by each employee and is structured to provide immediate, individualized on-line access to the full range of information, software, guidance, advice and assistance, data, images, tools, and assessment and monitoring systems to permit the employee to perform the job with a minimum of support and intervention by others."[3] In short, an electronic performance support system is a highly sophisticated technological job aid, with the following advantages:
- Access to large databases of information
- Designed to coach the user through questioning, assessing answers, evaluating responses and to offer recommendations
- User-friendly[4]

Documentation (Job Specifications) and Standards

There are a variety of ways to code information, to preserve it, and to make it accessible in the workplace. Written descriptions, policies, procedures, guidelines, reference manuals, quality assurance documents, bylaws, articles of incorporation, partnership agreements, contracts, and letters of intent are most frequently used to codify.[5] When we codify job specifications, we are providing written descriptions of the knowledge, skills, abilities, and other characteristics (interests, personality, training, etc.) that are necessary to be successful on the job. Documented job specifications can be used for employee selection, performance appraisal, and training.

TABLE 5-6

JOB AID VIEWPOINTS

	Traditional View	**Expanded View**
What Job Aids Do	• Provide information • Support procedures	• Provide information • Support procedures • Influence perspective and decision making
When Job Aids Are Useful	• During performance	• Prior to performance • During performance • After performance

Performance standards are concise statements that serve as a gauge for measuring accomplishment. The organization sets the standards around which performance is judged and the criteria that guide the performer.

Case Study: J.C. Penney Company

J.C. Penney is a mecca for value-conscious shoppers in the U.S. and abroad. It is a comprehensive department store rich in the traditional values of integrity, initiative, and work ethics. Traditionally, it was noted for good products and services at reasonable prices and a clean and inviting atmosphere with friendly personnel. Employees are called "associates" and enjoy a partnership with the company. Penney's decided to launch an ambitious expansion plan aimed at making it a major player in the international market.

Situation

J.C. Penney was one of the largest retailing chains in the U.S., operating more than 1,000 stores and a major retail catalog business. Keeping track of inventory and product changes was a major corporate challenge. To keep up, the company has become one of the top users of information services in the retail industry, with a host of mainframe computers supporting over 45,000 terminals.

J.C. Penney's training and documentation needs generated over eight million pages of paper documentation in one recent year. Each store has more than 100 reference manuals that need constant updating.

A performance analysis found updating to be a massive problem in the stores. As systems were expanded and modified, the need for timely training in so many locations posed significant logistical challenges.

Furthermore, employees required more and more time to access information, with no assurance that the reference materials were up-to-date. One new system, the Electronic Order File (EOF), part of J.C. Penney's purchase order management system, was so complicated that it required trainers to train people face-to-face, going through the entire system with them, a time-consuming and labor-intensive process.

Intervention

Applying performance technology to job redesign, Penney's developed a performance support system that resides with the EOF application. This system consists of features such as on-line documentation and training that is integrated with the application to help people successfully perform their jobs. When employees used an application system and had a question or needed information, they accessed the performance support system and gained "context-sensitive" information instantaneously. Users could search out additional information or training based on their needs.

The value of performance support was expressed by a company spokesperson: "We want to make people's jobs as easy and user friendly as possible ... if it takes our people an hour to figure out how to do 30 minutes of work, they're going to feel frustrated, and their productivity suffers."

Results

Although the integration of performance support systems into on-line applications was in its initial stages, results were gratifying. Instead of systems, documentation, and training being three separate units, they were integrated. "This will be very helpful," a user said. "Often I know I've read about something, but can't remember where. I think I will use it a lot, and I like it much better than a phone call to a help desk."

Lessons Learned

1. Plans were developed for more performance support systems. A J.C. Penney manager commented, "People costs are high and continue to go higher. Enhancing productivity is one way of addressing that controllable expense. Future applications will have performance support built right into the design; the hard copy documentation we know today will disappear."

2. Through a performance technology integration of documentation, training, and information systems, J.C. Penney enhanced worker competence, productivity, and job satisfaction.

Deterline, W.A. and Rosenberg, M.J. Eds., (1992). Workplace productivity: Performance technology success stories. Washington, D.C.: NSPI, pp. 15–16. Used with permission of the International Society for Performance Improvement.

JOB AID 5-2: PERFORMANCE SUPPORT TEMPLATE

Directions: Complete the chart to guide your choice about the performance support interventions. Two interventions are completed for you. Give a work-related example from your present employment.

Performance Support: Instructional	Definition	Unique Feature	Guidance Questions	Work-related Example or Advantages
Learning Organization	Organization's competitive advantage enhanced through knowledge	Individual Learning Team; Organizational Learning	• How is learning valued in your company? • How do people learn in your organization?	Employees capitalize on both formal and informal learning opportunities.
Action Learning				
Self-directed Learning				
Knowledge Capture and Management				
Education				
Interactive Technologies: Distance Learning				
Interactive Technologies: Telecommunications				
Interactive Technologies: Satellite Technology				

ISPI © 2000 Permission granted for unlimited duplication for noncommercial use.

JOB AID 5-2: PERFORMANCE SUPPORT TEMPLATE *continued*

Performance Support: Instructional	Definition	Unique Feature	Guidance Questions	Work-related Example or Advantages	
Job Performance Aids	A tool or technique for facilitating performance	Varieties of formats: Used prior to, during, after performance	• How does the job aid interact with user and system? • What constitutes an effective job aid?	If evaluation is this type:	The meaning is:
				Level 1	Reaction
				Level 2	Learning
Electronic Performance Support Systems					
Documentation and Standards					

ISPI © 2000 Permission granted for unlimited duplication for noncommercial use.

JOB AID 5-3: EVALUATING TRAINING

Directions: Training experiences. Use two (2) notecards to evaluate it.

<u>**On Notecards**</u>	<u>**Instructions**</u>

Front　　　　**Notecard 1**

Divide notecard in two by drawing a line down the center. On one half, say how you liked the training. On the other half, say how your training could be improved.

Things I like	Improvements

Back　　　　**Notecard 1**

List three (3) things that you learned in your training session.

1.

2.

3.

Notecard 2

List one (1) way that you will apply what you learned from the training session.
Review the card in two weeks.

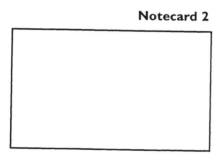

JOB AID 5-4: PERFORMANCE SUPPORT— INTERVENTION PLANNER

Directions: Answer the following with an organization of your choosing in mind.

Learning Organization	
How is learning valued in the organization?	
How do people learn?	
Are employees at every level expected to learn?	
Is there an evident spirit of flexibility and risk taking?	

Action Learning	
How does action learning differ from traditional, work-related learning?	
Which types of problems are appropriate for action learning?	
Which types of problems are inappropriate for action learning?	
Why is the focus of action learning on the learning and development of individual members?	
Action learning is neither product nor outcome. It is a process. Discuss the process-oriented nature of action learning.	

Self-directed Learning
Give an example of a self-directed learning project in which you were recently involved.
How is it decided that self-directed learning is either appropriate or inappropriate as an intervention?
Why would a place of employment value self-directed learning?

JOB AID 5-4: PERFORMANCE SUPPORT—
INTERVENTION PLANNER *continued*

Training
Why is training a vital component of any changes that occur within an organization?
What kinds of training are supported by organizations?
Why do perfectly good training programs fail to improve skills on the job?
How do companies link training to business needs?

Knowledge Capture and Management
Why are organizations beginning to pay attention to knowledge capture and management?
What are competitors doing to capture knowledge?
What unique roles does management offer in knowledge capture?
How can this intervention be effectively applied in the organization?

Education
How do education and training differ?
How do companies value education? Training?
How do education and training contribute to the value chain?

JOB AID 5-4: PERFORMANCE SUPPORT— INTERVENTION PLANNER *continued*

Interactive Technology (Distance Learning, Telecommunications, Satellite)

Which of the interactive technologies do companies use most often? Why?

What was the instruction like? How was it evaluated?

Job Performance Aids (Job Aids)

Job performance aids cannot be effective unless they are designed specifically for the conditions under which they are used. Why is this so?

How does the job performance aid interact with the user as well as with the system?

Why is buy in from supervisors and managers, as well as from users, critical to the use and, therefore, to the effectiveness of job performance aids?

Electronic Performance Support Systems

In what ways do job performance aids and electronic performance support systems represent similar paradigms?

Why is it that electronic performance support systems are not revolutionizing the workplace?

How does the absence of organizational infrastructure prohibit use?

Documentation (Job Specifications) and Standards

Which knowledge, skills, attitudes, and other characteristics are specified in job performance?

What standards guide performance?

How are job specifications and standards communicated to employees?

JOB ANALYSIS/WORK DESIGN INTERVENTIONS

Job analysis is the first step in the work design process. Job analysis lists and describes the tasks required to perform a job and the knowledge, skills, and attitudes that the worker needs to perform the tasks (see Table 5-7). Once the job is analyzed, work design interventions offer alternative work structures and create blueprints for organizing jobs in a way that will maximize performance in a given organizational or work environment.

TABLE 5-7

JOB ANALYSIS/WORK DESIGN INTERVENTIONS COMPONENT OF THE HPT MODEL

- **Job Descriptions and Specifications**
- **Job Specifications**
- **Job Rotation**
- **Job Enlargement**
- **Work Methods**
- **Quality (Control, Management, Assurance)**
- **Continuous Improvement**
- **Value Engineering**
- **Interface Design**
- **Ergonomics**
- **Preventive Maintenance**
- **Safety Engineering**

Job Analysis Interventions

Job analysis is often seen as the cornerstone of human resource development and management functions because the information collected contributes to hiring, training, recruitment, career development, counseling, and performance management activities. Job analysis is collecting information about the duties, tasks, responsibilities, etc. for specific jobs. Human resource personnel use these data to develop job descriptions and specifications. The ultimate purpose of a job analysis is to improve organizational communication, performance, productivity, and outcomes; it is an extension of the organization's overall mission and strategic planning efforts.

This discussion focuses on job analysis interventions, particularly job specifications and job descriptions.

Job Descriptions and Specifications

Job analysis data are used for writing job descriptions and stating job specifications. Whereas the job description describes duties, responsibilities, working conditions, and job activities, the job specifications describe the qualifications employees must have to do the job, namely, educational background, experience, knowledge, skills, abilities, etc.[1] The physical demands of a job—working, standing, reaching, bending, lifting, etc.—may be included in job specifications.[2]

Job specification is important because some jobs have qualifications that are set by law (medical doctor, dentist, teacher, etc.); others are required by professional judgment (a master's degree or doctorate for college-level teaching); still others are determined by the dictates of employers (typing at 110 words per minute). Job specifications must be linked to the relevancy of the job.[3]

Job Rotation

Job rotation involves moving employees from job to job within an organization for designated periods ranging from an hour or two to longer, depending on the goal. Organizations employ this strategy to familiarize employees with broad functional operations and processes and to reduce boredom. Assembly workers, for example, often rotate from one job to another on the assembly line to reduce boredom and the risk of injury. This cross-training procedure improves participants' job skills, increases job satisfaction, and provides networking opportunities. On the negative side, job rotations may increase the workload for employees due to frequent job change.[4]

Job Enlargement

Job enlargement expands the number and variety of different tasks performed by the employee so that the job is more interesting. A salesclerk's job, for example, may be enlarged by having the individual perform inventory control and merchandise returns. A reference librarian's job may be enlarged to encompass ordering books and indexing entries. This approach can improve job satisfaction and productivity. "Job engineering focuses on the tasks to be performed, methods to be used, work flow between employees, layout of the workplace, performance standards, and inter-dependencies between people and machines."[5] Job enrichment adds tasks to employees' jobs by making them accountable and responsible for planning and executing the job. Sometimes it involves changes in how the job is done, when or where one works, or with whom one works.[6]

Case Study: California-based Aerospace and Defense Corporation

Situation

In the mid-1980s through the mid-1990s, the large California-based aerospace and defense corporations were slowly losing market share. They began laying off large numbers of highly skilled employees. But the corporations were losing the capability to produce highly sophisticated products for a rapidly emerging and expanding competitive global market. As they continued to downsize, they lost highly skilled people in very specialized fields.

Intervention

The intervention chosen was to conduct a wide-range job and task analysis on existing jobs across the corporation's aerospace, aviation, electronics, and rock engine divisions to determine required skill sets. Then the PT practitioners analyzed and evaluated those skill sets to identify similarities. Once similarities were identified across common jobs, the jobs were combined (job enlargement) into larger work units. For example, the milling, lathe, and profiling machinists were combined to form a larger unit called machinists (network). This analysis work completed the first of two phases in the program.

The second phase entailed the development of a contextually designed assessment instrument that was a byproduct of the task analysis. The instrument consisted of a basic skills component and a technical component. Each person in the newly formed work unit was asked to complete the instrument in a classroom setting. The results of the assessment were used to determine the skill strengths and weaknesses of the employee population in each work unit and to identify where training would initially be concentrated.

To complete an analysis of this magnitude, a lead team was formed to (1) develop data collection tools that would maintain the quality and integrity of the analysis; (2) establish database systems to compare data across jobs, (3) develop training and logistical tools for analysts; (4) create common procedures to process the data after they were captured; (5) develop lines of organizational communication with regional, national, and local union members; and (6) develop interview schedules for each of the six rounds of analysis.

During the task analysis phase, each analyst documented a set number of jobs at each of the organization's facilities. The process was straightforward and consistent; observations and interviews were common. They documented physical demands, math and reading skills, equipment and tools, safety requirements, and environmental conditions. Managers reviewed the analysts' work to verify content accuracy.

Results

After combining the jobs, the analysts sorted tasks into a hierarchy based on complexity, frequency, and criticality. This enabled the organization to employ four strategies. First, it developed contextual assessment instruments to determine each individual's level of proficiency within the newly formed unit. Second, it designed training systems to build stronger and more efficient work units. Third, it established pay scales based on the hierarchy of skills for new employees. Fourth, it updated job descriptions throughout the organization (see Job Aid 5-5).

Lessons Learned

1. Programs of this magnitude are often difficult to manage from a strategic and tactical viewpoint because of the many variables that may conflict with organizational communication.
2. Communication among team members and supervisors at the different facilities needed to be encouraged. An understanding of organizational culture was important.
3. Job analysis improved organizational communication, performance, productivity, and outcomes.

The content for the California-based Aerospace and Defense Corporation case study was contributed by David A. Grant, M.Ed., Site Manager for Raytheon Systems Company. Used with permission.

JOB AID 5-5: TASK ANALYSIS CHECKLIST

Directions: List the job tasks for the job identified; then check (✔) the appropriate requirements.

Job Title: _____   **Date :** _____

Job Tasks	Quality Requirement	Safety Requirement	Math Skills	Reading Skills	Communication Skills	Physical Demands	Environment Demands
1.							
2.							
3.							
4.							
5.							
6.							
7.							
8.							

Job Tasks	Quality Requirement	Safety Requirement	Math Skills	Reading Skills	Communication Skills	Physical Demands	Environment Demands
1.							
2.							
3.							
4.							
5.							
6.							
7.							
8.							

Work Design Interventions

For purposes of this discussion, *work design* and *job design* are similar terms. How a job is designed has significant impact on the effectiveness of the organization and the quality of work life for employees. Work design should be tied directly to the strategy and goals of the organization. Job design is a blueprint of tasks required to accomplish a job successfully; its purpose is to structure the job to improve organization efficiency and employee satisfaction. Rothwell sees job design as a four-fold activity involving work duties, activities, responsibilities, and desired outcomes.[7] It determines "how the job is performed, who is to perform it, and where it is to be performed."[8] Sherman, Bohlander, and Snell see job design as a combination of four basic components, which are reflected in Figure 5-2.[9]

The job design interventions selected for review are ergonomics, preventive maintenance, work methods, value engineering, safety engineering, quality (control, management, and assurance), continuous improvement, and interface design (see Table 5-7). These interventions will increase knowledge about the psychology and service components of work.

Ergonomics

The word *ergonomics* comes from the Greek words *ergos* (work) and *nomos* (laws). Thus, the science of ergonomics is the study of how the laws of nature affect the worker and the work environment. It is the study of the relationship between people and their occupations, equipment, and environment. It is the science of making the work that is done, and the tools that are used, compatible with the physical abilities of the person doing the work. Ergonomic principles help guide the job design process.

Current market demands require workers to work smarter instead of harder. Implementing ergonomics in the workplace is one of the best ways to minimize on-the-job stress and strain. Poor ergonomic conditions can cause cumulative trauma disorders (injuries and illnesses that affect muscles, tendons, nerves, and blood vessels, such as carpal tunnel syndrome and chronic lower back pain). At times, the PT practitioner will be called on to improve performance by fixing the workplace, not the worker.

Job design principles that will assist PT or HRD specialists are suggested by Ostrom:[10]
1. Fit the task and the workplace to the individual.
2. Design the workplace for people who represent a range of body sizes.
3. Design the workplace for individuals at the extremes of the body size range.[11]
4. Design the workplace for individuals with different physical abilities (see Job Aids 5-6 and 5-7).

Preventive Maintenance (PM)

When a child is taken to the pediatrician for a well-baby checkup, when it's time for a six-month dental cleaning, when the car is prepped for the cold winter months, preventive maintenance is engaged. PM is a proactive approach to getting things done. In a work setting, a PM schedule involves such tactics as oiling and greasing gears and machinery; checking parts for flaws, cracks, chips, and replacing them; calibrating precision tools to make

FIGURE 5-2

COMPONENTS OF JOB DESIGN

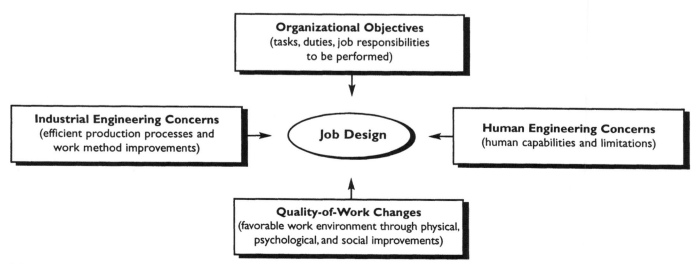

certain they are functioning within established specifications; aligning vehicles and their parts to make them stable; labeling parts and fixtures; cleaning tar and grease from workstation floors; and a host of similar tasks. PM and safety engineering are workplace cousins.

Work Methods

Work methods are techniques by which an organization defines what work needs to be done and how it will be accomplished. The goal is two-fold: (1) effective use of the organization's resources consistent with its mission to maintain a competitive position and market share in a global economy and (2) effective use of people's competencies to create and deliver efficient products and services. Topics of job design and redesign, reengineering, job specialization, task simplification, repetition factors, job autonomy issues, automation, job instructions, work flow design and/or redesign processes, etc., are elements of work methods.

Value Engineering

Value engineering is determining the amount of value added to the organization by each job and unit. The nature of the work, the worker, and the workplace play significant roles in maintaining a value-engineering thrust. People in industry see it as a fancy term for cost reduction. Engineering and manufacturing personnel brainstorm ways to redesign the parts, products, processes, services, etc. Design and production engineers work together to accomplish designated goals. Value engineering is driven by customer needs and requirements.

Safety Engineering

Safety engineering is an area undergoing continual evaluation. Materials that in the past were not thought to be hazardous are now known to be dangerous, thanks to studies of their long-term effects. Some ailments are now known to be caused by acts performed or equipment used on the job. In 1970 the Occupational Safety and Health Act was passed by Congress. This act was designed to ensure every working person a safe and healthy working environment. The Occupational Safety and Health Administration (OSHA) was created to act as the administrative agency for the Occupational Safety and Health Act. Under this legislation, employers must furnish and maintain a healthful work environment, keep records of occupational injuries and illness, and comply with OSHA standards. OSHA conducts workplace inspections periodically to enforce its standards. For example, safety engineering programs focus

TABLE 5-8

JAPANESE SAFETY APPROACHES

Approach	Challenge
Continuous Improvement	Formal training to help managers and employees think about production processes that improve safety and health.
Morning Exercise and Safety Check	Stretching exercises and safety check (two employees check each other for safety or health problems, e.g., jewelry that might get caught in machinery).
Articulation of Hazards and Contingencies	Identify hazards involved in workstations; develop contingency plan should hazard occur.
Hazard Prediction Cards	Cards listing potential hazards are given to workers to carry.

on accidents in the workplace, asbestos, blood-borne pathogens, boiler safety, confined space entry, hearing conservation, ladder safety, rigging, hazardous materials and waste, chemicals, fires, indoor air pollution, smoking, stress, tuberculosis, violence, and other concerns such as AIDS, drug testing and rehabilitation, and fetal protection. The Japanese have an exemplary approach to improving workplace safety as reflected in Table 5-8.[12]

Quality (Control, Management, and Assurance)

Of all the interventions in this chapter, the one that has received the most attention in recent years is quality. It is a popular, yet elusive concept that is an issue and concern for virtually every organization. Management defines it as a system of values, concepts, and methods for maximizing value. It is a degree of excellence. Quality is also defined by customers. To them, quality is meeting their needs to their satisfaction. Quality control is another name for total quality management. It brings together customers, employers, suppliers, and owners. It involves evaluating quality performance, comparing actual performance to quality goals, and acting on the differences.

Quality management is the process employed to facilitate communication of quality improvement functions among leaders, managers, staff, customers, and suppliers of an organization. It is guiding, collaborating, networking, risk-taking, sharing information, and team-building that lead to effectiveness. Core concepts that are part of the total quality management process are customer focus, work-as-process, continuous improvement, prevention versus correction, partnering and team effectiveness, employee empowerment, and fact-based decision making. Quality assurance is the process of setting standards and employing methodologies that work units must meet for the quality standards requirements of the organization.

Continuous Improvement

Continuous improvement is doing the job right the first time. It is an ongoing, organizationwide framework in which stakeholders are committed to and involved in monitoring and evaluating all aspects of a company's activities (inputs, processes, and outputs) to continuously improve them.

No discussion of continuous improvement is complete without mention of three leaders in the quality movement: W. Edwards Deming, Joseph M. Juran, and Philip B. Crosby. Deming's 14 points for quality have two major steps: (1) establish and perpetuate an environment in which quality improvement is integral to the work of all employees and (2) statistical analysis is used to support

efforts to improve quality. Juran's Quality Trilogy explains quality planning, quality control, and quality improvement. Crosby, who coined the terms *zero defects* and *do it right the first time*, outlines 14 steps to quality improvement that focus on prevention and zero defects.[13]

Virtually any organization practicing continuous improvement will use some or all of the following quality tools: checksheet (data collection/analysis form), mathematical tools (scattergrams, histograms, run charts, and control charts), cause-and-effect diagrams (fishbone), and the Pareto chart.[14]

Interface Design

When workers, machinery, and processes interact for smooth and easy, user friendly functioning, we see the results of interface design. For example, a jet plane has a complex set of electronic instructional panels, which pilots must master. The color-coded switches, knobs, and buttons that guide a pilot's choice of functions constitute interface design. The instruction manual for newly purchased stereo equipment should have solid interface design principles to ease the set-up process. Interface is also the link between two pieces of equipment and how they function, including consideration of such factors as position for ease of operation, displays, illumination, and interrelationships that minimize errors and maximize performance.

Case Study: The Michael James Clinic

The Michael James Clinic, located in Wichita, Kansas, is a large group practice of 45 physicians. The clinic employs about 160 employees and serves a regional population of about 180,000. The clinic offers medical and surgical specialities and operates its own lab, x-ray room, and outpatient surgical center.

Situation

For some time, the clinic had been receiving complaints from its patients that appointment times were not being kept, resulting in long waits. Clinic personnel felt that delays were unavoidable because physicians needed adequate time to examine patients. This problem was further complicated by the need to accommodate emergency patients.

Intervention

A quality improvement team was charged with evaluating the process. Team members questioned some of the basic assumptions about unavoidable delays and who should be scheduling appointments. A Pareto chart was used to evaluate factors such as emergencies, central appointments, examinations times, and overbooking. A cause-and-effect diagram (fishbone graphic) was constructed to study the problem in even more detail.

Results

The quality improvement team recognized that the central appointment desk's personnel needed data on and training in how long appointments should be. Nurses needed to take a more active role in routine scheduling. Furthermore, clinic managers' and physicians' attitudes about patient service needed to change.

Lessons Learned

* Everyone has a stake in the quality improvement process.
* Pareto charts, cause-and-effect diagrams, checklists, and mathematical tools are staples in the toolkit of a practitioner.
* Behavior is changed from a competitive to a collaborative approach to business.

This case study was written by James L. Moseley, Ed.D., Wayne State University. Used with permission.

JOB AID 5-6: STUDYING A WORKSTATION

Directions: Check (✔) yes or no to the following questions. Then discuss the four workstation components with friends at their workstations.

Assessment Questions	Yes	No
Posture		
• Are worker ears, shoulders, and hips aligned, maintaining the back's natural curves?		
• Are the shoulders relaxed?		
• Are forearms parallel to the floor?		
• Are wrists straight?		
• Are knees even with or slightly lower than hips?		
Chair		
• Is chair height adjusted so the forearms and thighs are parallel to the floor?		
• Is lower back fully supported?		
• Are feet resting comfortably on the floor or on a footrest?		
Work Area		
• Is screen about arm's length from the eyes?		
• Is a wrist rest used for support?		
• Are objects used frequently within easy reach?		
Lighting		
• Is the light from outside windows blocked to prevent glare?		
• Is screen free of smudges and dust?		
• Are contrast and brightness adjusted for maximum brightness without blurring?		

JOB AID 5-7: HAND AND WRIST PROTECTION FROM CUMULATIVE TRAUMA DISORDERS

Directions: After you read each statement, check (✔) the appropriate box. Discuss your results with a coworker.

Guidance Checklist	Yes	No	Don't Know
• Neutral positions place least amounts of stress on hands and wrists.			
• Reach the most commonly used items without bending wrists.			
• Place frequently used items closer; less frequently used items farther away.			
• Sit or stand so that hands and wrists can move straight out from body toward the desired item of reach.			
• Better positioning reduces pressure on muscles and tendons.			
• Cumulative trauma disorders take months or even years to develop.			

ISPI © 2000 Permission granted for unlimited duplication for noncommercial use.

PERSONAL DEVELOPMENT INTERVENTIONS

Responsibility for personal professional development in the workplace is the duty of the individual (see Table 5-9). The demand for new knowledge, new skills, tolerant attitudes, and new ways of doing things is constant. Moving beyond short-term fixes and solutions to long-term goals helps position people for future success. (Short-term fixes are sometimes appropriate.)

One way to approach personal development interventions is to help the employee develop an action plan.

Reasonable long- and short-term goals are set, guideposts for achieving them are determined, and measures of success are noted. An action plan should focus on:
1. Where am I going? (Long-term career plans)
2. Where am I now? (Current position)
3. How am I going to get there? (Effective strategies and tactics to achieve goal)
4. How will I know when I have arrived? (Personal assessment and satisfaction)

TABLE 5-9

PERSONAL DEVELOPMENT INTERVENTIONS COMPONENT OF THE HPT MODEL

- **Mentoring and Coaching**
- **Career Development**
- **Career Assessment**
- **Feedback**

Four personal development interventions are suggested here: mentoring and coaching, career development, career assessment, and feedback. These are considered personal interventions because individuals assume ownership. Each intervention is determined by how it fits into the employee's personal action plan.

Mentoring and Coaching

There is a difference between mentoring and coaching. In Homer's *Odyssey* a character named Mentor is a friend of the hero Odysseus who undertakes the education of the hero's son, Telemachus. Today mentoring is offering emotional support and guidance by an experienced person to a less experienced one. Mentors offer a wealth of experience to their students. It's a relationship of mutual trust and respect between two people with a common goal of professional development and learning. Mentors know their organization, have exemplary managerial and leadership skills, can give and share credit, have good common sense, and, above all, are generally patient people.

Coaching is the help that managers give to employees by examining and guiding on-the-job performance. It's teaching the "ropes" of the organization by providing relevant positive and negative feedback to improve both performance and potential. The coach is usually a manager of a unit or a team leader. Coaching allows for rehearsing and practicing. In job performance, coaches help people set goals, provide support, analyze barriers, and plan for the future. They are people who set good examples, inspire loyalty, celebrate successes, and empower by saying "we" instead of "I."

Organizations that support mentoring and coaching programs allow employees to grow. Both the organization and the employees win.[1]

Career Development

Career development concerns the match of a person's abilities, interests, etc., to the person's position and career plan with the focus on professional growth and enhancement of the work role. The process is continuous. The individual and the organization share an interest in an individual's career, and both parties to influence that career. As technology and rapid change drive continuous skill development and lifelong learning and job market skills continue to change, people are increasingly taking responsibility for their own career development. The workplace is becoming more globally oriented and far more diverse than ever before.

Organizations also need to manage the career development process by analyzing what will increase the value of the individual and his or her position. The knowledge, skills, attitudes, aptitudes, interests, and values of individuals must be periodically assessed to ensure a fit with the mission, goals, and business of the organization. Through career development, both parties contribute to the value-added chain.

Career Assessment

Career assessment can be considered an employee selection tool and an opportunity for advancement. In both cases employees are engaged in simulations, role playing, group discussions, and various self-assessment inventories. These are assessment and processes during which feedback is provided to the employee for increased self-awareness. This information helps the employee develop career goals, strategies, instructional support modalities, and a personal evaluation plan. The process of career assessment will help align individual career goals with institutional goals. And because most people will hold numerous jobs during their careers, continuous assessment for development may make them more marketable.

Three popular career assessment instruments are frequently used by companies to assist individuals along their career journey: self-directed search, career ability placement survey, and the Myers-Briggs Type Indicator. Table 5-10 below examines each.

Feedback

Everyone appreciates constructive feedback whether it is positive or negative. A cook wants to know how the white sauce tastes. At the end of a semester a teacher asks for impressions of the course. The facilitator during a week's training frequently solicits thoughts and builds them into the training sessions. Similarly, people look for feedback in a work setting. Feedback about on-the-job performance strengthens learning and transfer. It also increases self-efficacy, and people with high self-efficacy tend to be more motivated and, in the long run, achieve more.[3] Feedback performs three functions: (1) It tells employees whether or not their responses are correct, allowing for adjustments in behavior; (2) it makes an activity more interesting, encouraging people to continue; and (3) it can lead to specific goals for maintaining or improving performance.[4]

Frequent feedback opportunities should be part of any work-related function. With new or inexperienced employees, reinforcing feedback should immediately follow successful performance to remove ambiguity or uncertainty about work acceptability.[5]

TABLE 5-10

TYPICAL CAREER ASSESSMENT INSTRUMENTS

Career Assessment Instruments[2]		
Self-directed Search (SDS)	**Career Ability Placement Survey (CAPS)**	**Myers-Briggs Type Indicator (MBTI)**
• Based on Holland's personality theory • Focuses on long-term career planning • Examines choosing a career, changing careers, or selecting a course of study • 40–45 minute inventory • Self-scored and interpreted	• Multidimensional battery of tests • Efficiently measures abilities keyed to job entry requirements • Consists of eight five-minute tests • Investigates individual interests, values, and abilities	• Based on Carl Jung's theory of psychological types • Distinguishes between taking in information and organizing that information • Helps to identify strengths and unique gifts

Case Study: The Simonini Company

The Simonini Company, located in the metropolitan area of greater Pittsburgh, Pennsylvania, produced baskets of all sizes, shapes, and colors, for all occasions and functions. Baskets produced for special holidays and at seasonal times were big sellers for this small company of 1,275 employees. The people were proud of their jobs and prouder of their exemplary work record and stellar job performance. Rewards and incentives were not uncommon to these folks. A banner in their workplace read: "If we cannot find you a basket, we'll make one for you." The training manager was studying protocol and applications for International Standards Organization (ISO) certification later in the year.

Situation

Basket sales were declining over the previous year's receipts. All indications pointed to a 35 percent decrease in sales. There were increasing complaints from customers that the product was not what it used to be. The baskets were looking cheap and lopsided, not sturdy; in general, they represented poor craftsmanship. Concurrent with the product concern was an employee concern. Workers were asking to transfer out of the work unit to other units of the organization. The former manager, a benevolent, firm-but-fair fatherly figure, had recently retired. A new, freshly scrubbed college graduate was hired to replace him. She was clothed in creative genius but lacked experience. In fact, she had no previous work experience. Where the previous manager had offered feedback, she complained. Where the previous manager's feedback had been frequent and performance-related, hers was infrequent, neither timely nor helpful, personal and, sometimes, unfair. Enter Beth Zoloft, a trusted, seasoned employee who had worked in various capacities in the company for the past 11 years. Zoloft was asked by the company's president to devote three months' time to examining the unit's work performance and account for employee turnover and product quality concerns.

Intervention

Beth Zoloft took the bull by the horns. She first observed people in the unit; then she interviewed each of them. She went out to the stores that carried her product in the greater Pittsburgh area to discover their concerns about the product's quality. All in all, she spent more time with employees and clients than anyone else had spent. People inside the plant perceived her as one of them. Those outside the plant saw her as customer-driven and devoted to total quality.

Results

Zoloft began to coach the newly hired manager. She gave the young woman job and people-handling advice. Zoloft helped the manager set goals, analyze barriers, and plan future activities for the unit. She taught her how to give feedback that was timely, constructive, and work-related. It wasn't long before workers began to feel appreciated and took a more active interest in the quality of their work. Complaints began to decrease and people began to smile again. Customer service and product quality were once again becoming familiar themes at Simonini's. At the manager's request, Zoloft helped the young woman with career development and career assessment concerns. As this effort drew to a close, the young manager was preparing to leave the company to use her psychology degree in a recruiting capacity for the Joseph Horne Company.

Lessons Learned

1. Feedback, if properly given, is a valuable intervention to increase performance.
2. Coaching (and mentoring) are based on relationships of trust.
3. Coaches provide relevant positive and negative feedback to improve performance and potential.
4. Quality and customer service are PT issues and everybody's concerns.

The Simonini Company case study was contributed by Ms. Elizabeth A. McQuiston, B.S., R.N., Nurse Specialist for Administrative Network, Inc. Used with permission.

JOB AID 5-8: FEEDBACK CHECKLIST

Directions: For each statement, check (✔) the appropriate response to describe how consistently you use the described behavior in the workplace.

	Rarely	Sometimes	Often
1. I provide frequent opportunities for feedback.			
2. I promote feedback when I work with teams.			
3. I provide constructive feedback that is both positive and negative.			
4. I time my feedback appropriately.			
5. I encourage feedback that indicates an employee can master a task.			
6. I listen before I provide feedback.			
7. I like to provide reinforcing feedback.			
8. I encourage formative feedback (modifying or changing performance from unacceptable to acceptable).			
9. I use language that is appropriate and understandable in providing constructive feedback.			
10. I tailor my feedback to fit the needs of the performer and the performance.			
11. I refrain from using punitive feedback.			
12. I help people understand that some kinds of performance depend on a continuous flow of feedback.			
13. I use a nonjudgmental attitude in providing feedback.			
14. I often provide feedback that deals with correctable items over which the employee has some control.			
15. In giving feedback, I provide clear and concrete data.			
16. I refrain from delivering feedback that is delivered inconsiderately or that is vague.			
17. When new employees come aboard, I orient them to the feedback improvement effort.			
18. I use nonverbal cues (smiles, nods, etc.) to give feedback.			
19. I consistently try to improve my feedback efforts.			

JOB AID 5-9: PLANNER FOR SELECTING A MENTOR

Directions: Answer the following questions.

What criteria should be used by the employee when choosing a mentor for guidance through the organizational channels?

For what reasons is an employee likely to choose a same-sex mentor or one of the opposite sex?

How does an employee ask a person for mentorship?

Why is mentorship a valuable intervention?

How does an organization track and evaluate the results of a mentoring process?

ISPI © 2000 Permission granted for unlimited duplication for noncommercial use.

HUMAN RESOURCE DEVELOPMENT INTERVENTIONS

Human resource development (HRD) is an essential function within a human resources management department (see Table 5-11). The nature of the function and its scope are shaped by the organization's mission and its ability to maintain market share. McLagan defines it as "the integrated use of training and development, organization development, and career development to improve individual, group, and organizational effectiveness."[1] Many studies have identified roles, outputs, and competencies for HRD professionals.[2]

The purpose of this section is to identify frequently used HRD interventions such as those in Table 5-11.

Employee Selection

Employee selection is choosing the right person for the job. The process begins with a precise description of the skills and/or knowledge, experiences, and personal characteristics needed to accomplish the job tasks. Valuable sources for identification are knowledgeable people and personal observations of competent performers. The selection process differs in complexity among organizations. Some fill positions quickly and inexpensively by perusing resumes and application forms. Other organizations select potential employees by elaborate, and sometimes costly, selection systems involving job-related tests, a series of interviews, and background checks[3]. Decisions regarding selection are crucial for effective organizational performance.

Compensation and Benefits

Compensation programs are monetary and in-kind payments used by organizations. Goals of compensation policies include rewarding employees' past performances, remaining competitive in the labor market, maintaining salary equity among employees, motivating employees' future performances, maintaining the budget, attracting new employees, and reducing unnecessary turnover.[4] Compensation typically includes pay for work and performance, disability income, deferred income, health, accident, and liability protection, loss-of-job-income, and continuation of spousal income when there is a loss due to a employee's relocation.

Benefits are the non-cash portion of the compensation program that are intended to improve the quality of work life for an organization's employees. Benefits include the employer's share of legally required payments (e.g., FICA, unemployment compensation, retirement and savings plan payments, 401k, profit sharing, stock bonuses, medical benefit payments, etc.)[5] Benefits were once viewed as gifts from the employer; they are now considered entitlements.

Motivation (Incentives and Rewards)

Incentives link pay with a standard of performance. They are future-oriented with the objective of inducing desired behavior. They can be short or long term, and they can be tied to individual and/or group performance. There are variations in incentives. Monetary incentives include salary, differential pay, allowances, time off with pay, deferred income, loss-of-job coverage, and other perquisites (product samples, an expense account, tax service, legal service, a company apartment, club membership, free housing, parking privileges, stock bonus, etc.). Nonmonetary incentives include desirable working conditions, training, and adequate equipment and materials. Examples of management incentives are participatory goal setting and decision making, and career opportunities.[6]

TABLE 5-11

HUMAN RESOURCE DEVELOPMENT INTERVENTIONS COMPONENT OF THE HPT MODEL

- **Compensation and Benefits**
- **Motivation (Incentives and Rewards)**
- **Performance Appraisals**
- **Assessment Centers and Competency Training**
- **Succession Planning and Career Pathing**
- **Leadership and Executive Development**
- **Management and Supervisory Development**
- **Literacy**
- **Retirement Planning**
- **Health and Wellness**

Rewards can change and reinforce behavior. Skinner's research showed that rewarded behaviors are more likely to be repeated. Rewards need to be timely, specific, and matched to the preferences of the person and the achievement of goals.[7] Rewards can be formal, such as public recognition, gift certificates, etc., or informal such as field trips. Nelson has catalogued more than 1,000 ways to reward employees.[8] Wilson suggests that rewards should be SMART: specific, meaningful, achievable, reliable, and timely.[9]

Performance Appraisals

Performance appraisals help individuals manage their performance by providing them with feedback. Organizations also have performance appraisal programs that provide criteria for salary decisions, promotion, and improving job performance. Gohrman discusses the many potential benefits of regular performance appraisal: increase in employee self-esteem and motivation to perform effectively, job clarification, communication between employee and rater, clearer organizational goals, and better human resource planning.[10] Morissey suggests that some positive advantages of performance appraisals are increased probability of promotion for good performance, decreased likelihood of receiving undesirable assignments, clear understanding of supervisor's expectations, and greater personal reward and recognition for meeting those expectations.[11] He also sees benefits for the organization in reduced turnover, reduced liability for potential legal action, improved overall productivity, improved organizational results, and greater attractiveness to potential new hires. Research suggests that the performance review should be approximately 60 minutes long and conducted as a mutual discussion.[12]

Examples of performance appraisal methods used by organizations include checklists, weighted checklists, graphic rating scales, mixed scales, forced-choice scales, and critical incidents (written descriptions of a highly effective or highly ineffective performance), and behaviorally anchored rating scales (BARS).[13] The HRD literature is filled with positive techniques for conducting effective performance reviews. It also reports stories of anxiety, frustration, uncertainty, and ambiguity when performance appraisals are handled improperly.

Assessment Centers and Competency Testing

An assessment center is "a place where standardized selection procedures are applied, usually to separate management from non-management candidates and executive candidates from middle managers."[14] Candidates are evaluated and selected by testing mechanisms to determine if they are capable of performing predetermined skills. Others see it as a process where trained professional evaluators observe, record, and evaluate how a candidate performs in simulated job situations.[15] In-basket techniques, leaderless group discussions, role playing, and speech making are common practices for testing job candidates.

It is important for an organization to study its jobs to identify and assign weights to the knowledge and skills each one requires. Testing people for current job skills, or for attributes or skills needed for future performance, helps the organization fulfill its strategic goals for human resources. Interviews, psychological profiles, intelligence testing, etc., are sometimes used in competency testing.

Succession Planning and Career "Pathing"

Succession planning is a systematic identification of employees for senior management positions. It involves long-term planning and is often developmentally oriented. Succession planning is likely to involve input from several managers and recommendations for experiential assignments to ensure the ability of the candidates to fill positions as they open.[16]

A career path is a sequence of jobs, usually involving related tasks and experiences, that employees move through over time.[17] For example, a career path in a school setting may include the positions of teacher, counselor, department head, principal, central office administrator, and superintendent. Career paths are generally vertical lines of progression; however, they can include horizontal assignments as well. This is increasingly the case as management positions disappear.

Leadership and Executive Development

Leadership development is necessary at all levels of an organization. High-potential employees receive special training and experience that translate into personal and professional growth. Leadership development includes coping with changes that occur during the life cycle of an organization, from growth to decline. It is about changes in the external environment, specifically about rearranging priorities and overturning assumptions about how the business operates and the role of leadership.[18]

Executive development deals with the organization's vision, values, and business strategies, and the goal is to develop leaders who can ensure the strategic development of the organization.[19] Leadership and executive development are successful when the process is embedded in the organization's HRD efforts.

Management and Supervisory Development

Management development is "the education, training, knowledge transfer, and, ultimately, skills demonstration of those individuals who are defined as managers by their respective organizations."[20] It is about coping with complexity. Effective management development supports the organization's mission, strategy, goals, objectives, and market position. Supervisory development is designed for front-line managers who work with and through non-management employees to meet the objectives of the company and the needs of its employees.[21] It is broader than management and executive development. Bittel and Newstrom state the unique roles the HRD and PT personnel play in supervisory development as follows:

1. Recognition of the innate qualifications, limitations, and aspirations of supervisors
2. Genuine knowledge of specific competencies required to complete work assignments
3. Sensitivity to the roles and relationships imposed on the supervisors by the company
4. Realization of the continuing evolution of the supervisor's role[22]

Literacy

Literacy is a person's knowledge, especially one's reading and writing abilities, which enables the person to function in society. Literacy programs are efforts by businesses to improve workplace communication, job understanding, and job skill development.

Literacy rates are often directly connected to quality of work and job performance. Raising the literacy skills of workers is likely to increase productivity and lower production costs.

Retirement Planning

To have positive experiences in retirement, people must plan ahead. No longer is retirement looked at as withdrawal, retreat, and solitude. Current gerontological thinking suggests new words for retirement: reorientation, recommitment, reinvention, reinvolvement, regeneration, renewal, renovation, redirection, reinvestigation, replenishment, reexploration, and more. Retirement planning is usually part of a benefits package. People want to know about finding part-time employment (should they want it), legal issues, housing arrangements, health and wellness, etc.[23]

Health and Wellness

Health and wellness programs are commonly offered by organizations and can serve to enhance employee morale and productivity and to reduce absentee rates and health care costs. According to the National Centers for Disease Control, more than 60 percent of all disease is caused by lifestyle risks. The most powerful lifestyle risks are smoking, inattention to diet, lack of exercise, substance abuse, back problems, mental distress, failure to use safety belts, and excessive stress. Employees who participate in workplace wellness programs tend to have better attitudes and behavior, exhibiting more loyalty, enthusiasm, motivation, and energy.[24]

Case Study: Aetna Life and Casualty Co.

Aetna Life and Casualty is one of the world's leading providers of insurance and financial services to corporations, public and private institutions, and individuals. Aetna ranks as the nation's largest stockholder-owned insurance and financial services organization. The company employs about 47,000 people in the U.S.

Situation

The environment for insurance and financial services was becoming increasingly competitive and, some would say, even hostile. For that reason, it was especially important that Aetna retain superior managers, with even stronger skills in areas such as problem solving and decisionmaking, leadership, and building teams.

For the top 10 positions of the company, the longest tenure of any executive had been six and a half years. This turnover rate had resulted in a diminished talent pool at lower levels. The company realized that many positions could not be easily filled from inside because of a lack of internal breadth or depth of skill. As competition in the industry grew, strong managerial skills became more critical.

"Additional experience in the current job" was sometimes the extent of a manager's developmental plan. Job descriptions did not always focus on the specific skills, knowledge, and behaviors required for success in a position. Development plans did not always focus on clear measurement criteria as required to determine progress or success.

Without the identification of specific competencies and measurable development plans required for a job, Aetna realized filling management positions would continue to be a problem. Additionally, the company realized that even those managers with good skills were not necessarily adequately prepared for the future. Aetna also knew that it needed to ensure that people were participating in training to develop their skills and to decrease performance gaps.

Intervention

Because Aetna already had a planning and direction-setting tool called the Aetna Management Process (AMP), it was applied to the development planning process. AMP is a systematic, seven-stage planning and assessment process that clarifies the organization's critical success factors, scans and describes the environment, recognizes gaps between current and desirable performance, sets objectives, develops and implements action steps, and monitors performance.

Aetna executives decided to use performance technology to develop a comprehensive human resource response plan based on identified competencies that would be needed in the future. Included in this systematic response were:
*   Identification of management competencies.
*   Development of processes to identify performance and competency gaps.
*   Creation of development plans and identification of education programs.
*   Design and publication of a development planning guide that would tie the process together for the entire organization.

This comprehensive program was also integrated into Aetna's interviewing and selection process, succession planning, and the rewards systems. The resulting program enabled employees and management to identify work elements critical to success and to define the required competencies. After determining the gap between current practices and desired proficiency, specific development and training plans were designed, implemented, and monitored. Companywide implementation of this process is now under way.

Results

This initiative was first introduced only a few years ago, but preliminary results indicated that:
*   There were more focused and specific development plans for employees.
*   There was increased understanding by employees and their managers of how to implement and monitor these development plans.
*   More people were selecting training and education programs based on identified skill or knowledge gaps relative to specific competencies.
*   Corporatewide bench strength was improving and performance gaps were more clearly understood and actively worked on.
*   Focus on a person's competencies and development was now treated as serious business throughout Aetna. Additionally, the company began a complete reorganization process. The new processes enabled the company to successfully redesign all of its jobs and redeploy people to those jobs in less than one year.

Lessons Learned

1. Performance technology is used to develop a comprehensive human resource response.
2. A common language is now in use companywide.
3. The focus is clearly on the mastery of competencies and development planning.
4. All employees of an organization need to be trained, including those in leadership, managerial supervisory, and executive positions.

Deterline, W.A. and Rosenberg, M.J. Eds., (1992). Workplace productivity: Performance technology success stories. Washington, D.C.: NSPI, pp. 5–6. Used with permission of the International Society for Performance Improvement.

JOB AID 5-10: HUMAN RESOURSE DEVELOPEMENT—SKILLS SET

Directions: Assess and fill in the present and future skills-set necessary for an organization's personnel to maintain competitive strength.

Leadership Development Skill Set	
Present*	Future†

Executive Development Skill Set	
Present	Future

Management Development Skill Set	
Present	Future

Supervisory Development Skill Set	
Present	Future

Answer These Questions:

• What would be included in a program for leadership development?

• What would be included in a program for executive development?

• What would be included in a program for management development?

• What would be included in a program for supervisory development?

*Present: The immediate present   †Future: Three to five years hence

JOB AID 5-11: RETIREMENT PLANNING—DETERMINING NET WORTH

Directions: Complete the following worksheet. Discuss the results with a financial advisor.

DETERMINING NET WORTH

As of _____

Date

ASSETS	LIABILITIES

ASSETS

Cash

Checking Account(s) _____

Savings Account(s) _____

Investments
(Current market value)

Stock, Mutual Funds _____

Bonds _____

Tax Shelter Annuities _____

IRA _____

U.S. Savings Bond(s) _____

Other _____

Life Insurance
(Cash value) _____

Real Estate
(Market value)

Home _____

Other _____

(Vacation property?)

Personal Property
(Market value)

Appliances/Furniture _____

Jewelry _____

Stereo, Piano, Organ _____

Automobile _____

Other Assets _____

Total Assets _____

LIABILITIES

Mortgage Balance
(or annual rent) _____

Installment Debt(s)

Auto Loan(s) _____

Appliance/Furniture _____

Other _____

Personal Loans

Credit Union _____

Bank _____

Loan Company _____

Life Insurance _____

Current Bills

Credit cards _____

Medical expenses _____

Association fees _____

Others _____

Other Liabilities _____

Total Liabilities _____

NET WORTH

Total Assets _____

Minus Total Liabilities _____

Equals Net Worth (- or +) = _____

ISPI © 2000 Permission granted for unlimited duplication for noncommercial use.

JOB AID 5-12: RETIREMENT PLANNING—MONTHLY INCOME/EXPENSES

Directions: Complete the following worksheet. Discuss the results with a financial advisor.

Expenses	Now	At Retirement
Mortgage or rent	$ _____	$ _____
Utilities (phone, electric, gas, water)	_____	_____
Food (meals at home and out)	_____	_____
Clothing	_____	_____
Transportation (gas, parking, bus fare)	_____	_____
Medical/Dental Care	_____	_____
Insurance Premiums		
Life	_____	_____
Health	_____	_____
Homeowners	_____	_____
Automobile	_____	_____
Taxes		
Income	_____	_____
Property	_____	_____
Entertainment/Recreation	_____	_____
Charities	_____	_____
Furnishings and Equipment for Home	_____	_____
Personal/Miscellaneous		
Credit Cards	_____	_____
Auto Loan	_____	_____
Other Loans	_____	_____
Total Expenses	$ _____	$ _____

Income	Now	At Retirement
Salary (less taxes)		
Your own	$ _____	$ _____
Your spouses	_____	_____
Commissions	_____	_____
Bonuses	_____	_____
Interest		
Savings account	_____	_____
Other	_____	_____
Dividends	_____	_____
Rental Property	_____	_____
Social Security	_____	_____
Pension Benefit	_____	_____
Annuities	_____	_____
Life Insurance	_____	_____
Others	_____	_____
Total Income	$ _____	$ _____
Total Expenses	- _____	- _____
Difference	$ _____	$ _____

ORGANIZATIONAL DESIGN AND DEVELOPMENT INTERVENTIONS

The onset of the Information Age has forced industry to continuously seek new and innovative business practices to remain competitive. This has compelled companies to examine the way they do business and to restructure their organizations. Organizational design and development is a process that examines the operation and management of an organization in an effort to ensure efficiency and competitiveness (see Table 5-12).

Organizational operations are affected by both internal and external factors. Political environments, the economy, technology, and social norms all have an impact on how an organization does business. Successful company leaders incorporate a variety of interventions to address these factors and to maintain an edge in their respective markets. The interventions frequently used to affect organizational design and development are shown in Figure 5-13.

TABLE 5-12

ORGANIZATIONAL DESIGN AND DEVELOPMENT INTERVENTIONS COMPONENT OF THE HPT MODEL

- **Strategic Planning and Management (Vision, Mission)**
- **Environmental Scanning**
- **Globalization**
- **Benchmarking**
- **Reengineering, Realignment, Restructuring**
- **Team-building Strategies**
- **Problem Solving and Decision Making**
- **Culture and Diversity**
- **Ethics**
- **Spirituality in the Workplace**

Strategic Planning and Management

Strategic planning and management are the core interventions of organizational design and development. Successful strategic planning and management operations are at the heart of an organization and reflect the essence of what the company does. When organizations change, strategic planning and management provide direction to employees and serve as a guide to organizational purpose. This is expressed in terms of the mission, or the purpose of the organization, and the vision, or how the organization will appear when it achieves success.

Strategic planning is the process by which an organization envisions its future and develops the necessary goals and procedures to achieve that vision. To garner support and achieve success, a strategic plan must be easily communicated and must apply to the entire organization.

Strategic management supports the organizational vision through the day-to-day implementation of the strategic plan. Successful organizational change occurs when daily operations and innovations are directly connected to the strategic plan. The results are shared common goals and a sense of ownership by employees and other stakeholders.[1]

Environmental Scanning

Environmental scanning is a strategic planning technique for monitoring the trends in the external environment of an organization. This includes any political, economic, technical, social, national, or international factors that affect the operation of an organization. For example, political unrest in a foreign country may determine the price of a resource essential to the operation of a company, thus having an impact on the cost of doing business.

Environmental scanning provides management with much of the information needed to develop and implement its strategic plan. The process focuses decision making on trends and issues that may have an effect on the organization's future. It can also help determine the education and training needs of current or future employees and assist in developing plans to meet those needs. Environmental scanning also supports other organizational development interventions such as globalization, benchmarking, and reengineering.[2]

FIGURE 5-3

INTERVENTIONS FOR ORGANIZATIONAL DESIGN AND DEVELOPMENT

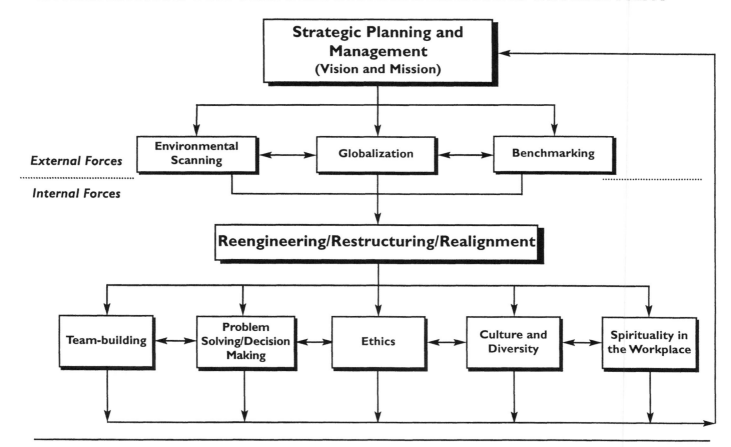

Globalization

Globalization is a means of achieving higher productivity and efficiency by identifying and focusing an organization's efforts and resources in key world markets. The fundamental ideals behind globalization are free flow of commerce, capital, and labor, and the belief that individuals can significantly influence large social and economic systems. Globalization is accomplished in several ways. Outsourcing noncore activities, combining purchasing volumes, and centralizing key support activities are examples of globalization techniques. Production and distribution activities are often consolidated to create more efficient operations. Success is based on the ability to quickly adjust to the needs of the customer. For this reason, globalization is often more successful in smaller organizations. Globalization often includes acquisitions, joint ventures, and coproduction. It affects employees, customers, and suppliers. Globalization encourages people to attain a new awareness of both their company and the world in which they live. Through this realization comes new opportunities for personal and professional advancement and satisfaction.[3]

Benchmarking

Through benchmarking, organizations compare themselves to the best industry practices in their field. Understanding best practices helps company leadership identify what must be changed within an organization to achieve its vision. Benchmarking helps define customer requirements, establish effective goals and objectives, develop true measures of productivity, and identify education and training needs for current and future employees. Effective use of benchmarking requires an understanding of the total environment, including:

- What others have done
- What standards and practices have been implemented
- The organization's past performance
- Changes that affect current and future organizational performance[4]

Reengineering, Realignment, and Restructuring

Reengineering, realignment, and restructuring mean bringing about change in the culture of a business by moving toward team-based management and individual ownership. Many organizations realize that profit, quality output, efficiency, and employee satisfaction are attained only when people share more responsibility in the organization and for its product. This can happen with a radical restructuring of the basic values held among leadership, management, employees, and stakeholders. Total Quality Management (TQM), stewardship, and learning organizations are examples of this type of change. Some of the outcomes resulting from successful reengineering are:

- The establishment of common and consistent goals
- Organizational commitment from all stakeholders
- Team leadership
- Role clarity among team members
- Mutual accountability within teams
- Complementary knowledge and skills
- Power, both real and perceived
- Shared rewards[5]

Teambuilding

A key intervention associated with restructuring and reengineering is teambuilding. Teambuilding subscribes to the philosophy that people work better and more creatively in groups than they do alone. Teams may consist of representatives from various groups within an organization. Teambuilding interventions focus on trust, collaboration, openness, and other interpersonal factors. Successful use of this intervention requires commitment and acceptance through organizational readiness, leadership support, and the support and consideration of workers.

Teambuilding strategies are often used to strengthen an organization's culture. Quality circles, organizational matrices, and participative management are examples of teambuilding interventions. Teambuilding encourages people to create common guidelines for conducting business and for promoting ownership of ideas and tasks. The practice encourages confidence, unity, and a sense of belonging and satisfaction in employees and customers.[6]

Problemsolving and Decisionmaking

Problemsolving and decisionmaking are empowerment tools that allow employees and teams to deal directly with problems. Such empowered employees learn how to analyze problems and to select the right solutions using their own experiences and resources. The process provides a structure for organizing work, setting priorities, identifying and diagnosing problems, evaluating alternative solutions, and creating and implementing plans to solve problems. The results of these interventions are often reflected by:

- Fewer repeat problems
- An increased ability to anticipate problems, reducing the time spent solving them

- Fewer conflicts between teams and individuals
- Increased self-confidence, commitment, and satisfaction among employees
- More efficient implementation of action plans.[7]

Culture

Culture is a shared system of values, beliefs, and behaviors that characterize a group or an organization. In business, it is demonstrated in the way that things are done. Culture often originates from an organization's mission and vision. It consists of the key values of the organization and the practices that support those values. Culture change is the alteration or modification of an organization's values, beliefs, or behavior system. Culture interventions redefine, clarify, emphasize, or create desired practices within a group. The goal is to influence both employee behavior and production output.

Success is likely when it is clear to employees that strategic goals are consistent with organizational and strategic visions. An example of inconsistent values and goals is when an organization attempts to instill "quality" as a strategic value, but continues to base its operations on production "quantity."[8] In performance-enhancing cultures, managers share values and methods of doing business. The culture is strategically appropriate for the marketplace and it is adaptable. Risk-taking, proactivity, and trust are supported.[9]

Diversity

Diversity is an element of organizational culture. Diversity means differences; differences in employees' ethnic, cultural, and religious backgrounds; education; values; attitudes; and gender. A diverse workforce enhances creative output because people are able to contribute from their varied experiences. A diversity commitment is especially important when dealing with international markets because it prepares an organization to better understand and serve its customers' needs.[10]

Ethics

Ethics define good and bad standards of conduct. Standards are cultural. They vary among countries, companies, incidents, and situations. Ethical standards provide a basis for exercising judgment in day-to-day business operations. They support and help define the culture of an organization. Successful implementation of ethical standards requires that they be applied to every person within a group or organization, as well as outside individuals or groups that do business with the organization.[11]

Spirituality in the Workplace

Work can be not only a place where we go to do a specific job, but also a place where we can experience and express our soul and spirit. Spirituality in the workplace encourages organizations to recognize people's needs and to promote their involvement. Many companies are finally beginning to realize that their employees come to work with a full range of needs and desires, all of which affect the quality of employee efforts and therefore organizational success. Federal Express and Southwest Airlines are two companies integrating workplace spirituality as a performance intervention. "Soul Committees," where employees meet regularly to share experiences and provide mutual support, and "Spirit Awards," which honor employees who practice and encourage creativity, are forms of spirituality practiced in the workplace.[12] The benefits are many: improved communications, increased creativity, enhanced partnerships, greater self-respect, deepened respect for others, and higher morale all emanate from spirituality in the workplace.[13]

In today's marketplace, organizations that wish to remain competitive must reexamine and restructure their operations and implement the changes necessary to ensure continued efficiency and effectiveness. Employee satisfaction, contribution, and ownership are key ingredients to the success of any organization. When consideration for people and the individual pursuit of excellence becomes the standard, organizational excellence blossoms.

The content for the Organizational Design and Development Interventions section, including the job aid, was contributed by Kristin Olin-Sullivan, M.Ed., Henry Ford Community College, and by G. Kevin Sullivan, M.Ed., Freelance Video Producer/Editor. Used with permission.

Case Study: Morrison-Knudsen Corporation

Morrison-Knudsen Corporation (MK) is a world-leading construction, design, service, and engineering company. The projects it has completed include the Alaska pipeline, EPCOT Center, the Hoover Dam, mining and environmental remediation, and building locomotives. It has a backlog of new work that exceeds $4 billion.

Situation

MK's business is highly competitive. Its marketing efforts are typified by the writing of competitive proposals for multimillion dollar construction, design, and engineering jobs. The cost of writing a proposal can range from a few hundred dollars to more than $200,000. Writing proposals and presenting oral support are labor intensive and time-consuming. The marketing arm of MK wanted to improve the presentation performance of its speakers, who are usually engineers with no public speaking training or experience. Improved oral presentations would increase the company's chances of winning millions of dollars of new work.

Intervention

A PT practitioner conducted an extensive needs analysis, which consisted of watching "live" presentations, videotaping and reviewing practice presentations, and interviewing prospective clients post-presentation. The PT practitioner became involved in the analysis of typical groups as they prepared and practiced their presentations. As a result, some needs that became apparent were (1) to change from an information-only orientation to a sales presentation style; (2) to produce, in a short period, a team presentation; (3) to demonstrate a team responsiveness to technical content and client concerns; (4) to show leadership on the part of the proposed project manager; (5) to strongly communicate specific technical knowledge and team and individual experience; and (6) to demonstrate effective organizational ability to do the proposed work.

The solution to meeting these needs is usually a training intervention; lack of presentation skills would seem to warrant establishing new skills via training. However, certain constraints (e.g., limited time to develop a presentation) precluded intervention training to meet the short-term needs. Training could be used for a more long-term supporting role. The combination of interventions that was utilized included a form of team-building, job aids, coaching, feedback, and modeling.

Team-building was needed so that the presentation would model the team effort that would be used to execute the project. Job aids (e.g., checklists) were needed to guide the sequential development of the presentation. Coaching by an expert presenter, feedback (e.g., videotaping review), and modeling (e.g., samples of well-structured presentation booklets) were also considered useful interventions.

Team-building was accomplished by having the presenters, as opposed to the marketing department, develop the presentation, which helped establish ownership in the presentation. A series of job aids guided the process. An experienced person skilled in developing and enhancing presentations provided coaching. Feedback took many forms, including the coach's comments, the participants' review of their videotaped sessions, evaluation forms, and comparisons to examples of exemplary presentations. Modeling was achieved by showing the presenters examples of winning presentation documents and videotapes. The interventions were well-integrated and did not conflict with one another.

Results

A series of 10 presentations using the above model were compared with presentations developed by various marketing departments. The conventional approaches they used usually included evaluative feedback designed to enhance overall group and individual presenter skills. Although the conventional presentations did win contracts, after the new model was put to use, there was an increase of about 250 percent in contracts.

Moreover, clients indicated that the presentations were "some of the best they had ever seen," and this was sometimes expressed even when the project was not awarded to MK for other reasons (economic, experience, etc.). The general reaction of participants who experienced the multiple intervention approach was that it was more systematic and focused on results.

Lessons Learned

1. One intervention is often insufficient to solve a company's problems. Multiple interventions work best.
2. By using alternative solutions to overcome constraints, the company won new work.
3. A thorough needs assessment is critical to selecting appropriate interventions.

Deterline, W.A. and Rosenberg, M.J. Eds., (1992). Workplace productivity: Performance technology success stories. Washington, D.C.: NSPI, pp. 17–18. Used with permission of the International Society for Performance Improvement.

JOB AID 5-13: EVALUATING TEAM ATTITUDES

Directions: Use this survey to acquire information about how team members feel about their team and the job they are doing. Areas with lower scores indicate potential areas for team-building intervention. Use the following scale to respond to each statement below as it applies: **3 - AGREE   2 - DON'T KNOW   1 – DISAGREE**

	Agree	Don't Know	Disagree
1. SELF-PERCEPTIONS	3	2	1
a. I communicate with members of my team regularly.			
b. I contribute to team discussions.			
c. I participate in team activities.			
d. I work well with the other members of my team.			
e. I respect the members of my team.			
f. The members of my team respect me.			
g. I value the contributions of other team members.			
h. The other team members value my ideas.			
2. PERCEPTION OF TEAM MEMBERS	3	2	1
a. Everyone on my team contributes to its success.			
b. Everyone on my team contributes to problemsolving.			
c. My team works well together.			
d. Everyone on my team is shown respect.			
e. Everyone on my team participates in team discussions.			
f. The members of my team communicate regularly.			
3. IDEAS	3	2	1
a. My team has good ideas.			
b. All ideas have potential.			
c. All ideas presented are considered and discussed.			
d. There are no bad ideas.			
e. All ideas presented to my team are shown respect.			

JOB AID 5-13: EVALUATING TEAM ATTITUDES *continued*

Directions: Use this survey to acquire information about how team members feel about their team and the job they are doing. Areas with lower scores indicate potential areas for team-building intervention. Use the following scale to respond to each statement below as it applies:

3 - AGREE   2 - DON'T KNOW   1 – DISAGREE

	Agree	Don't Know	Disagree
4. TEAM WORK	3	2	1
a. Everyone on my team listens with an open mind.			
b. Opinions are expressed freely among team members.			
c. Everyone on my team is encouraged to participate.			
d. No one monopolizes the team discussions.			
e. Team members work together to solve problems.			
5. GROUP DYNAMICS	3	2	1
a. My team is diverse in age.			
b. My team is diverse in gender.			
c. My team is diverse in ethnicity.			
d. My team is diverse in knowledge.			
e. My team is diverse in experience.			
f. The diversity of my team makes it easier to solve problems.			
g. The diversity of my team is a valuable asset.			
6. PROGRESS	3	2	1
a. My team works efficiently most of the time.			
b. Work in my team is completed on time.			
c. Recommendations from my team have been implemented in the organization.			
d. My team consistently achieves success.			
e. My team does not always succeed in reaching our goals.			
f. My team solves problems well.			
g. We have achieved more as a group than we would have working individually.			
h. Management has denied some of our recommendations.			

JOB AID 5-13: EVALUATING TEAM ATTITUDES *continued*

Directions: Use this survey to acquire information about how team members feel about their team and the job they are doing. Areas with lower scores indicate potential areas for team-building intervention. Use the following scale to respond to each statement below as it applies: **3 - AGREE   2 - DON'T KNOW   1 – DISAGREE**

7. SATISFACTION	Agree 3	Don't Know 2	Disagree 1
a. Working with my team has been a positive experience.			
b. It is easier to solve problems when working as a group.			
c. I have learned from group solutions that did not work out.			
d. I enjoy working as part of a group.			
e. Group work promotes creativity.			
f. Working as part of a group has helped me personally.			
g. I look forward to working with my team.			

ISPI © 2000 Permission granted for unlimited duplication for noncommercial use.

ORGANIZATIONAL COMMUNICATION INTERVENTIONS

Although the word *communication* has many meanings, it is defined here as the transfer of meaning between sender and receiver. The sender has an idea that is put into a letter, memo, or conversation so that it can be sent. The transmitted idea is then received, whereupon the receiver interprets the message. The receiver then provides feedback. More broadly, communication is a process through which people, acting together, create, sustain, and manage meanings through the use of verbal and nonverbal signs and symbols within a particular context.

> ## TABLE 5-13
>
> ## ORGANIZATIONAL COMMUNICATION INTERVENTIONS COMPONENT OF THE HPT MODEL
>
> - **Networking and Collaboration**
> - **Information Systems**
> - **Suggestion and Grievance Systems**
> - **Conflict Resolution**

An organization's success depends on the effectiveness of its people working together, supporting common goals and understanding critical issues, all of which is dependent on effective communication. Gibson and Hodgetts define organizational communication as "the transfer of information and knowledge among organizational members for the purpose of achieving organizational efficiency and effectiveness."[1]

This section examines the impact of four organizational communication interventions on employee behavior: networking and collaboration, information systems, suggestion and grievance systems, and conflict resolution (see Table 5-13).

Networking and Collaboration

Networks are patterns of communication interactions. They are defined channels within an organization that expedite the timely transmission of messages to their intended receivers. Defined network channels add predictability to an organization by directing the access of information. Communication networks facilitate the dissemination and collection of information, the coordination of work effort, and the achievement of goals. Many smaller networks exist within the larger organizational networking system. For example, there are personnel and individual networks, and there are departmental networks.[2] Researchers have studied network structures, formal and informal networks, communication roles of networks, descriptive properties, and network analysis.

Collaboration is cooperating in the communication process by working together for an improved quality of work life. The organizational culture has a dramatic impact on how people communicate. Communication patterns should be matched to the organizational culture because each reinforces the other. Positive organizational communication exists in a collaborative setting; a competitive setting often fosters negative organizational communication.

Information Systems

Information systems refer to the various manual or automated communication mechanisms within an organization that store, process, disseminate, and sometimes even analyze information for those who need it. Computer hardware, networks, and software are most commonly associated with this communication mechanism. Their increased use over the past decade is due to the fact that, if used correctly, information systems offer many advantages over other organizational communication devices. Table 5-14 illustrates these advantages.

The introduction of information systems as an organizational communication mechanism carries with it many implementation considerations.
- **Security.** Sensitive information made available by and transmitted through information systems must be protected with passwords, encryption, firewalls, and virus protection.
- **Integration.** Information systems should ideally be integrated. However, when this is not possible, consideration should be given to making the various systems, as much as possible, compatible with other departments as well as with suppliers and customers.
- **Consistency.** An important consideration, especially in nonintegrated systems, is maintaining consistency to avoid the use of inaccurate or out-of-date information.
- **Policies.** Consideration must be given to ensure that information systems are used in a manner compliant with company policies, code of ethics, and governmental regulations.

TABLE 5-14

ADVANTAGES OF INFORMATION SYSTEMS

Mode	Advantage
E-mail	Immediate dissemination of information to employees, suppliers, customers, and any other constituents
E-mail, listservs, audio/video conferencing	Synchronous or asynchronous text, audio and video communication unobstructed by geographic separation
Corporate databases made available through corporate local area networks (LANs) or the World Wide Web (Web)	Dissemination of the most up-to-date information
Networked Computer-based Training (CBT), computer training labs, Web-based Training (WBT) accessible through a corporate intranet	Training-on-demand
Databases, data warehouses, online analytical processing (OLAP) tools, executive information systems, statistical software	Integration of departmental data and information for executive decision making
Groupware with synchronous communication features such as whiteboards and real-time file sharing	Facilitation of collaborative teamwork unobstructed by geographic separation
Varied software that supports text, images, audio, video, and interactivity	Multimedia communication
Enterprise resource planning (ERP)— integration of organizations with supplier and customers	Automated business transaction with supplier and customers, such as inventory reordering

- **Ease-of-use and training.** Information systems bring with them new and sometime more complicated methods of use and thus require development of user-friendly interfaces and, when necessary, the appropriate training on their use.
- **Dehumanization.** Finally, information systems should only be used as an organizational communication instrument when face-to-face communication is not possible or necessary. Examples where information

systems, in isolation, are not advisable include employee terminations, diversity or safety training, and labor relations.

Suggestion and Grievance Systems

Communication is at the heart of all employee involvement efforts. Companies that support employee involvement strategies allow workers more responsibility and

TABLE 5-15

CONFLICT RESOLUTION DO'S AND DON'TS

Do	Don't
Ask for feedback and reflect on what you think the other person is saying	Use "You should/shouldn't" statements
Give nonverbal supportive messages	Use overly long statements
Make sure the problem is clear, concise, and specific	Use putdowns and sarcasm
Express problems as soon as you are aware of them	Interrupt others in mid-sentence
Admit when you are in the wrong	React defensively
Argue only one point at a time and resist temptations to get off the subject	Fight about an issue as a way to avoid a more serious issue
Keep discussions private when appropriate	Ignore the statements of others
Create neutral atmospheres when mutual agreements are more likely to be reached	Act in a commanding or threatening manner
Express facts and feelings regarding the problem ensuring everyone has an equal chance to speak	Respond to an unfair comment with an equally unfair remark
Back up from solutions to needs	Use double messages
Depersonalize the argument	Hold resentments
List possible solutions, being as creative as possible and considering all solutions	Express more anger than you really feel just to intimidate the person
Develop specific actions that have a good chance of being successful and that are developed from shared input	Give up before the issue is resolved just to keep peace
Try to keep a sense of humor	Make unfair comparisons

accountability for preparing products or offering services. A suggestion system is one of the employee involvement strategies. Others are empowerment efforts, ownership in the firm, and total quality management. With a suggestion box format, people are encouraged to participate. Identity is anonymous until a suggestion is implemented and an award is presented. The Consolidated Edison Company of New York, for example, requested that employees who work directly with customers suggest ways to improve service. Ideas earned $50 and a write-up in the company newsletter. This public recognition for a winning entry can boost self-esteem.[3]

Grievance systems, on the other hand, provide a mechanism for the employee or union to dispute a decision that is believed to be in violation of the contract. Grievances have several causes, with the primary being a misunderstanding or misinterpretation. Whatever the cause, grievances are organizational communication issues.

Conflict Resolution

Conflict is generally defined as disagreement between two or more people who share differing views. Conflict may be caused by either miscommunication or a lack of communication. However, the conflict can only be resolved through open, honest, direct communication channels.[4] The U.S. Postal Service has established a variety of conflict resolution programs to address violence-prone employees. Other organizations are similarly engaging their employees in a variety of conflict resolution programs.

Because the goal of conflict resolution should be to resolve, rather than win, communication should be neither hostile nor negative. It should be clear, direct, and as open as possible. Table 5-15 highlights some of the useful tools, as well as pitfalls, in conflict resolution.

In the end, be sure to evaluate the solution by asking if everyone is satisfied with the outcome. If the problem remains unsolved, decide on the reason. Perhaps the wrong problem was discussed. If so, reconsider possible solutions. Perhaps the solution was inadequately implemented. If so, rethink the plan to carry out the solution. And finally, if conflict cannot be avoided, minimize the negative effects of hurt feelings, anger, resentment, grudges, and blame.[5]

Some content for this section was contributed by David Maier, M.S., A.B.D., Web Developer, Karmanos Cancer Institute. Used with permission.

Case Study: Bugaj, Incorporated

Bugaj, Inc., is a large, Detroit-based conglomerate. It was founded in 1956 and reached the billion dollar mark in 1996. The firm's growth has in part been a result of acquisitions and mergers. During the last nine years, the conglomerate has purchased 11 firms in unrelated industries.

Situation

One of the small companies that Bugaj acquired is Grombala Brothers, a moderately successful retail chain in the southern part of the U.S. Grombala was founded in the early 1950s and soon became one of the dominant retail houses in its geographic region. The chain's greatest growth years were during the 1960s and 1970s. During the 1980s Grombala's sales began to slow and the company was surpassed by three major competitors. When Bugaj considered Grombala operations, the conglomerate management was convinced that there were great opportunities for profit. The chief executive officer reported, "Grombala has not been run properly for at least one and one-half decades. Transfer of information and knowledge among organizational members is neither efficient nor effective. The organizational culture sends mixed messages. The managerial philosophy is old-thinking. If we purchase this chain and put in our own management, we can turn the company around." The final arrangements for the sale were completed in September 1998. Within nine months, the conglomerate had installed its own employees in the upper ranks of Grombala.

Intervention

The new management communicated openness and trust. Delegation of authority was essential and staff assumed greater responsibility for company decisionmaking. In an attempt to address organizational communication needs, Grombala supported formal suggestion systems, progress reports, management audits, and a host of training opportunities for employees. The company paid for outside education and training. A wellness center was established, followed by child care and adult day care centers. Although employees were generally accepting of these changes, people were neither happy nor did they experience high morale. The company decided to contract Pitts' Consulting, an agency that specializes in organizational communication and change, to observe workplace dynamics and offer recommendations.

Results

Pitts' spent a considerable amount of time on-site to determine the communication problems. The consultants talked to employees to understand the Grombala control mentality. They heard about managers being passed over for promotions and the hectic pace of business in the new company. They networked and collaborated with similar businesses and with competitors. Their report was submitted to Bugaj, Inc.

Lessons Learned

1. Mergers and acquisitions take a toll on employees. Companies need to address the people issues that accompany major change efforts.

2. Grombala Brothers represented old thinking patterns and outdated management approaches. Bugaj, Inc. represents the new. The organizational culture—norms, attitudes, values, beliefs, and philosophies—of both companies needed to be compatible.

3. People represent the heart of organizational communication. Management needed to talk to the employees and listen to their concerns.

4. The Bugaj, Inc., group had the foresight to contract with Pitts' Consulting. Bugaj had to be prepared to follow the suggestions in the consulting report and to remember that change efforts take time.

This case study was written by James Moseley, Ed.D., Wayne State University. Used with permission.

JOB AID 5-14: COMMUNICATION NETWORKS PLANNER

Directions: Networks are patterns of communication interactions. Analyze your company's level of networking.

Levels of Networking	Examples from Your Company
• Entire organizational communication system	Describe your organization's communication system network. _____ _____ _____ _____ Which formal and/or informal systems are predominant? _____ _____ _____
• Individual or personal networks that people use in getting things done.	Describe your organization's grapevine network. _____ _____ _____ Discuss the positive and negative influences of your organization's grapevine. _____ _____ _____ _____
• Group networks, e.g., departments, similar occupations, etc.	Describe the departmental group networks in your organization. _____ _____ _____ How do group networks remain healthy? _____ _____ _____

FINANCIAL SYSTEMS INTERVENTIONS

To benefit from a healthy economy, an efficient and effective financial system is needed. Economic activity affects small and large businesses, interest and mortgage rates, the stock market, and the global marketplace. In a sense, it affects the nation's entire purchasing power. The financial system's primary role is to move savings from one business or individual into investments for another business or individual. It is extremely important to have general familiarization with basic financial concepts to communicate with the finance division, or the accountant, or the marketing specialist, or with anyone in the organization concerned about money and its true cost. There may be a time in the future of a company when a PT practitioner will intervene in financial forecasting or suggest protocol and criteria for capital investment and spending. There may even be involvement in cash flow analysis. Knowledge in these areas will serve well. As non-instructional interventions, financial systems deal with economics and decisions tied to the financial aspects of business (see Table 5-16). The financial systems interventions considered here are financial forecasting, capital investment and spending, and cash-flow analysis. Mergers, acquisitions, and joint ventures, three multiorganizational arrangements, are included as financial systems interventions because of their bottom-line results.

TABLE 5-16

FINANCIAL SYSTEMS INTERVENTIONS COMPONENT OF THE HPT MODEL

- **Financial Forecasting**
- **Capital Investment and Spending**
- **Cash-flow Analysis**
- **Mergers, Acquisitions, and Joint Ventures**

Financial Forecasting

Financial forecasting is anticipating the future cash needs for a particular business. Financial managers use forecasts to determine whether or not their plans are consistent with the goals and objectives of their businesses. Financial forecasts play a major role in the planning of business strategies, monitoring the firm's financial affairs, and controlling and investing cash. Forecasts help management

anticipate problems so that appropriate actions can be taken to minimize financial problems. These activities help to increase profits and reduce risk and are, therefore, vital components in the continuing effort to make businesses successful.

Financial forecasting methods are scientific in nature, meaning that two people applying the same methods and using the same data should be able to arrive at the same conclusion. Although this may be true, theoretically, statistical manipulations do not guarantee accurate financial forecasts. Successful financial forecasting also relies on solid judgment combined with an objective analysis of the data available. All variables, domestic and foreign, must be reviewed to come up with a financial forecast that is accurate and reliable. Information for financial forecasts may come from various locations, such as the balance sheet, the income statement (or cash-flow forecasts), or trend forecasts.

Financial forecasting affects all employees. Companies invest excess cash in stocks, bonds, and securities of other companies to generate extra revenue. All of this affects the bottom line of current and future business. Employees need to learn about their company's financial goals and objectives so that they can become better consumers. A review of company financial statements may help people understand the connection between their efforts and the bottom line of the company.[1]

Capital Investment and Spending

Capital investments yield returns during future periods and may include property, buildings, equipment, and securities of other companies. Property may include the land on which the firm's facilities are located. Equipment may include furniture, tools, computers, and machinery that the company uses to produce the goods that it sells to customers. Capital investments are made in the anticipation of returns in the future and usually involve large sums of money. Resources and cash often are committed for long periods, so it may be difficult to reverse the effects of a bad decision. Uncertainty about return on investments is a risk factor.

To decide whether an investment or strategy should be pursued, the analyst must decide whether it has the potential of value for the firm's stakeholders. To create value, the investment or strategy's returns must exceed its costs. Determining which costs and benefits are relevant to the particular investment or strategy must also be determined. Capital invested in new products has a cost. To use capital, the company has to pay for its use. Money invested in new products, equipment, or facilities could be diverted to other uses, such as paying off debt, making a pay-out to stockholders, or investing in stocks or bonds. These all result in economic benefits to the company.

Once management has decided to make an investment in property, plant, equipment, or working capital, a decision must then be made to fund the project. Funds that are invested in these types of endeavors may come from stockholders and/or bondholders. The capital budgeting problem is essentially balancing the benefits from these new capital expenditures with the costs needed to finance them. The cost of this capital, adjusted to a minimum acceptable rate of return, plays an essential role in ranking the relative effectiveness of different types of capital projects and in establishing acceptable guidelines for project acceptance. A sound capital expenditure program will recognize the need to search for investment opportunities, to conduct long-term planning, to estimate future benefits from projects, to appraise the state of the economy, to establish guidelines for return on investment, and to review all completed projects.

Many companies experience uneven cash flows during the year. An example is department stores, which generate a large portion of their revenues during the months of November and December, resulting in a large cash inflow during the holiday season. In many instances, these large amounts of cash are not immediately needed to fund the operations of the company. Many of these companies may elect to put some of their excess cash into short-term investments until the cash is needed for operations. These investments usually produce higher earnings than those available from bank accounts, enabling companies to increase their earnings.

The time value of money is a key concept in investment analysis. The time value of money refers to the fact that a dollar received today is more valuable than a dollar received one year from now. The dollar received today can be invested at some interest rate so that it will be worth more than the dollar received one year from now, which cannot be invested until that time.[2]

Most workers do not understand the strategies involved in deciding whether money should be invested in capital equipment, land, facility expansion, or securities. To many, machinery is bought to build products, products are sold to make money, and money pays the bills and gives the person a paycheck. But these investments must create value, which means that they must be able to produce a product that, when sold, will produce revenues

that exceed the cost of the production of that product. These decisions are important, especially when one bad decision can bankrupt a company or stress it enough financially that it can never fully recover.

Cash-flow Analysis

Cash-flow analysis provides information about the inflows and outflows of cash during a specific period. The ability of a business to generate cash is important because it affects the ability of the business to pay its debt obligations. Cash also enables the business to replace old equipment, to expand product lines, and to provide dividends to shareholders. Cash flow is the difference between revenues—the amount of money taken in from the sale of a product or service—and the cost of the product or service that was sold. These costs could include materials, labor, equipment, and overhead, among others.

It must be remembered that not all healthy businesses have a large, positive cash flow. Businesses that are experiencing extensive growth often use their excess cash to expand their production facilities, acquiring new equipment and labor and thus reducing the amount of cash on hand.

Financial statements provide financial managers and others with historical data about cash. Sufficient cash must be available on an ongoing basis so that the firm can meet its commitments. The information contained in the financial statement will enable the financial manager to make proactive decisions about the company's financial situation, not reactive decisions. The management of cash begins with projecting the amounts and timing of future cash flows. If positive cash flows are forecasted, management must identify some profitable uses of the excess cash. If negative cash flows are forecasted, then alternative sources of cash must be found so that obligations can be met. Possible sources include short- and long-term debt, an infusion of cash by the owners of the company, or the liquidation of assets. Other possible strategies include trying to hasten up collections from customers and delay payments to suppliers.[3]

The extent of many employees' knowledge of cash-flow analysis is that they want the company to have enough money in its bank account so that their weekly paycheck is covered on payday. But cash flow plays a very important role in the everyday running of a company. Being able to pay its obligations in a timely manner is just one part of doing business. It also needs to produce profitable products, to replace old or defective equipment, expand productive and profitable product lines, and provide dividends to shareholders to keep them happy. These are the other steps that need to be taken to make a company successful. Employees need to know how cash flow in their business operates. They may be in a business that has cycles, as in department stores, which get most of their revenues during the holiday season. If workers know how cash flow operates, they may be able to suggest areas where money could be saved when excess cash is at a minimum.

Mergers, Acquisitions, and Joint Ventures

A merger is when two separate companies combine operations and become one company. An example of this is if Company A and Company B merge, resulting in a new or surviving company called Company A (or it could be called Company B, or it could be called something new). Mergers are usually negotiated by the management of the two merging companies. The surviving company acquires either the stock or the assets and liabilities of the nonsurviving company, and the nonsurviving company no longer exists as a separate company.

The advantage of a merger is that it can lower the costs of product development, management, financing, research, and marketing. The most common economies are from the reduction of duplicate fixed costs for production and management, since fewer production facilities may be needed post-merger, and fewer managers will be needed to run the facilities. A reduction in the accounting and personnel departments, as well as in upper management, may be accomplished because of duplicated job functions. Research economies may also be achieved by eliminating duplicate research efforts and personnel. Marketing economies may be produced through savings in advertising and from the advantages of offering a more complete product line.

An acquisition is when one firm acquires more than 50 percent of the voting stock of another firm, thereby controlling that firm. The buyer firm is referred to as the parent company, while the acquired firm continues to exist and operate as a subsidiary of the parent company. This type of arrangement offers several advantages when compared with mergers. The parent company may obtain effective control without having to acquire 100 percent of the acquired company, substantially reducing the amount of capital needed for the transaction. Because the subsidiary continues to exist as a legally separate company, the parent company has only a limited liability for the debts of the subsidiary. If the parent company should ever decide to increase or decrease its investment in the subsidiary, it is very easy to either sell or purchase shares. Other advantages of an acquisition include complete control over operations, new technology, immediate access to new markets, and instant credibility and gains realized by owning an already established company.

Acquisitions may take place under two different circumstances: in the form of a tender offer or via a hostile takeover. In a tender offer, one corporation will ask the shareholders of another corporation to sell to them their shares in the targeted corporation, at a specific price. This is typically done after approval from the targeted corporation's board of directors. In a hostile takeover, a corporation sends the board of directors of another corporation a letter announcing the acquisition proposal, requiring the board of directors to make a quick decision on the proposal. If the board of directors rejects the proposal, the corporation may appeal directly to the targeted corporation's shareholders by way of a tender offer for their shares.

A joint venture is undertaken by competitors for a specific purpose. This may include acquiring new technology, entering new markets, generating new products, or meeting customer demands quickly. It may also include accessing new distribution systems or new capital or personnel resources. Joint ventures can be more involved when a domestic firm enters into a partnership with a foreign firm. There is the possibility of disagreements regarding objectives, such as how much profit is desired and how fast it should be paid out to stakeholders.[4]

Often during mergers and acquisitions employee morale drops because of concerns about an uncertain future, the stress of change, and job losses. However, if people know the ramifications of a merger, acquisition, or joint venture beforehand, they may be able to better position themselves in the new organization by acquiring additional training to reduce their risk of job loss.

Case Study: Muller-Roberts

Situation

Roberts Manufacturing, a New Jersey producer of apparel fasteners, announced a merger with Muller Manufacturing, a German producer of various small machinery replacement parts and apparel fasteners. The merger with Muller Manufacturing significantly increased Roberts Manufacturing's ability to compete with their major competitors in China. With the merger, the new company became the largest single manufacturer of apparel fasteners, with four production sites in the U.S. and two in Germany. Muller-Roberts, as the new company was called, expected to reap the benefits of economies of scale. The stated objective of the merger was to integrate Roberts Manufacturing's technological superiority and higher profit margins with Muller Manufacturing's distribution system and expanded markets. Muller Manufacturing sells its products in 20 countries, whereas Roberts Manufacturing sells 97 percent of its products in North America.

Although both companies produce similar products, there are many differences between the two companies. Roberts Manufacturing employed union production employees in all four production facilities in the U.S., where six-day workweeks were the norm. Muller's employees were not union and worked a standard 40-hour workweek. Differences in language, wages, health benefits, work environment, safety programs, employee training programs, currency, and culture were also strongly evident when comparing the two companies.

Once the merger announcement was made, Roberts Manufacturing noticed a decrease in worker morale as well as a 12 percent decrease in production and a 16 percent decrease in the quality of their products. Employees' anxiety levels seemed to increase because of their sense of insecurity and uncertainty as to how the merger would affect them. Although the new, combined management announced that there were no planned layoffs or reductions in the workforce, most believed that layoffs and workforce reductions were imminent. Many Roberts Manufacturing employees felt that the merger was not really a merger of equals, but that Roberts had actually been bought out by Muller. Upper management of the new company seemed to be split between the management personnel of both companies, with Muller's CEO taking his position at the top of the new company. Key positions in the new company were filled by management from Muller.

The challenge was to get production and quality levels back to premerger levels as soon as possible, since these two major problems were costing the company millions of dollars. To accomplish this, the employee morale, culture, and quality differences of the two companies would have to be reviewed. Feelings of insecurity and uncertainty among the people would have to be dealt with to combat the problems.

Intervention

Several interventions were used to deal with the merger issues. Clear goals and objectives were written and conveyed to employees by the upper management of the new company. The hope was for all employees to accept the new direction that the company was going to follow. Training sessions were held to discuss production and quality problems as well as new production procedures that were to be implemented as a result of the merger. These training sessions were followed by team-building sessions so that each production group could work on problems in their specific areas. Upper management made decisions regarding wages, the elimination of overtime work, and health benefits. Many employees felt that these decisions were solely based on what was good for the company, not taking into account what was good for the employees as well. These decisions were conveyed to the employees in town hall-type meetings presented by upper management.

Results

Many longtime employees felt betrayed by the whole merger process and believed that nothing management ever could do would change their feelings. Some of the employees decided to retire instead of adjust to the new company environment. Others, after attending training sessions, team-building sessions, and the town hall meetings, had a better attitude toward what had taken place and what was planned for the future. Upper management decisions seemed to make more sense to the employees when they understood the rationale behind the decisions. The insecurity and uncertainty levels exhibited by employees right after the merger announcement decreased, while morale increased. Production and quality levels soon returned to pre-merger levels before surpassing those levels as new production processes were implemented.

Lessons Learned

When dealing with mergers, employees' feelings of insecurity and uncertainty are probably unavoidable no matter how prepared a company is ahead of time to combat those feelings. It is common for employees to feel that way when change occurs. But it is still management's job to calm those fears.

The content for this section and the Muller-Roberts case study were contributed by Leonard M. Constantine, Jr., M.S., M.B.A., Daimler-Chrysler. Used with permission.

JOB AID 5-15: MULTIORGANIZATIONAL ARRANGEMENTS ANALYSIS

Directions: Identify the problems and benefits associated with the three multiorganizational arrangements. Discuss your findings with your group. How would you explain their differences to an HPT or an HRD colleague?

Mergers	Potential Problems		Potential Benefits	
	Worker	Workplace	Worker	Workplace

Acquisitions	Potential Problems		Potential Benefits	
	Worker	Workplace	Worker	Workplace

Joint Ventures	Potential Problems		Potential Benefits	
	Worker	Workplace	Worker	Workplace

JOB AID 5-16: BASIC FINANCIAL STATEMENTS

Directions: One way to distinguish between basic financial statements is to consider the following points. Check (✔) the appropriate category (categories).

What We Need to Know	Balance Sheet	Income Sheet	Statement of Cash Flows
• Itemization of all the firm's assets and claims against the firm at a point in time, at least yearly.			
• Summarizes the operations of the firm.			
• Format and content prescribed by the Financial Accounting Standards Board (FASB).			
• Shows amounts owed to the corporation from its customer.			
• Assets listed in order of liquidity, cash being the most liquid, followed by marketable securities, and accounts receivable.			
• Shows accounts payable—goods the company has received on credit from its suppliers.			
• Assets, liabilities, and owner's equity.			
• Shows more clearly the source of all funds the firm acquired in a given period and how the firm used them.			

JOB AID 5-17: TEMPLATES OF BASIC FINANCIAL STATEMENTS

Directions: Review the elements included in each of the financial statements. Discuss the rationale for including them.

(TEMPLATE 1)   MULLER-ROBERTS COMPANY, BALANCE SHEET
(as of December 31; 000s of dollars)

Assets
Cash
Marketable Securities
Accounts Receivable, Net
Inventory
    _____

      Current Assets

Gross Fixed Assets
Less: Accum. Depreciation
    _____

      Net Fixed Assets
      TOTAL ASSETS

Liabilities and Owners' Equity
Accounts Payable
Notes Payable, Short-term
Accurals
Taxes Payable
Current Maturities of Long-term
  Debt and Capital Leases
    _____

      Current Liabilities
      Long-term Liabilities
      Total Liabilities

Common Stock
Paid-in-Excess of Par
Retained Earnings
    _____

      Total Equity
      TOTAL LIABILITIES AND
        OWNERS' EQUITY
    _____

JOB AID 5-17: TEMPLATES OF BASIC FINANCIAL STATEMENTS *continued*

(TEMPLATE 2)   MULLER-ROBERTS COMPANY, INCOME STATEMENT
(Year ended December 31; 000s of dollars, except per share)

Net Sales Revenue
Cost of Goods Sold   _____

Gross Profit

Operating Expenses:
       Depreciation
       Selling, General, and Administration   _____

Earnings before Interest and Taxes
Interest   _____

Earnings before Taxes
Provision Taxes   _____

Net Income   _____

Less: Dividends Paid   _____

Addition to Retained Earnings   _____

JOB AID 5-17: TEMPLATES OF BASIC FINANCIAL STATEMENTS *continued*

(TEMPLATE 3)   MULLER-ROBERTS COMPANY, STATEMENT OF CASH FLOWS
(Year ended December 31, Year ___)

Opening Activities:
      Net Income

Adjustments to Reconcile Net
      Income to Cash Provided by
      Operating Activities:

Depreciation
Decrease (increase) in accounts receivable
Decrease (increase) in inventories
Increase (decrease) in accounts payable,
  accrued liabilities
Increase (decrease) in short-term notes payable
Increase (decrease) in taxes payable,
  deferred taxes   _____

Net cash provided by operating activities

Investing Activities:
  Decrease (increase) in gross-fixed assets   _____

Net cash from (used) investing activities

Financing Activities:
      Insurance of (payments) on long-term debt
      Dividend paid   _____

      Net cash from (used) financing activities

Increase (decrease) in cash and short-term investments

Cash and short-term investments, beginning of year

Cash and short-term investments, end of year

CHAPTER

6

INTERVENTION IMPLEMENTATION AND CHANGE

FAXING EMPLOYEES IS A POPULAR WAY FOR SOME
BUSINESS TO REDUCE TRAVEL EXPENSES.

INTRODUCTION TO INTERVENTION IMPLEMENTATION AND CHANGE

At this point in the HPT Model, PT practitioners have already determined the organizational and individual performance gaps, defined the measures of success, identified various causes for the gap, and determined appropriate interventions.

Definition and Scope

Although analysis and intervention planning are critical to the success of any performance improvement effort, actual changes in performance result from intervention implementation and change (see Figure 6-1). As car-loving Detroiters say, "That's when the rubber hits the road." The stage of intervention implementation and change is critical because as interventions are implemented, changes begin to affect individuals, groups, and organizations. Some change is desired and anticipated; but much of the change that actually occurs is the result of human adaptation to the planned change (intervention). Although this resulting adaptive change can be expected, its exact nature cannot

FIGURE 6-1

HPT MODEL: INTERVENTION IMPLEMENTATION AND CHANGE PHASE

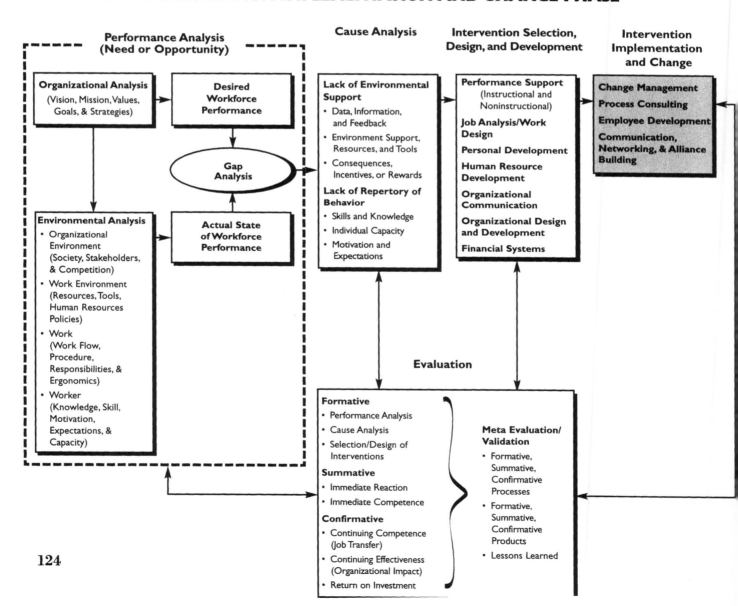

be predicted. A PT practitioner "ensures that interventions are implemented in ways consistent with desired results and that they help individuals and groups achieve results."[1]

Implementation Methods

Intervention implementation and change are as important as the previous stages of the HPT Model. Rothwell points out that, "A good solution that's poorly implemented becomes a poor solution."[2] There are four typical methods for implementation and change:

1. The quickest and most basic method is developing support through effective communicating, networking, and alliance building. Communication is critical for creating and maintaining a clear understanding of the organization's direction and change efforts. Networking and alliance building allow individuals and organizations to team up with others who already perform the desired behavior.
2. Employee development includes learning activities, such as training, job rotation, on-the-job training, mentoring, and job aids. Employee development enhances workforce capabilities in an organized manner to maintain competitive advantage or to prepare the organization for anticipated knowledge and skills requirements.
3. Change management refers to gradual improvement through structured problem solving.

4. Process consulting results in revising processes and often involves reengineering or restructuring an entire organization.

Novice PT practitioners may find it helpful to use methods that are familiar, have proven value, are consistent with desired results, and are supportive to individuals and groups. The PT practitioner's first step is to ensure adequate commitment from stakeholders, such as senior management, line management, and workforce representatives. There must be sufficient ownership, resources, time, and energy. All stakeholders must agree on clear roles, objectives, strategies, and procedures. Resistance to change can be a powerful inhibitor. Strong support from management and workers is critical.

Intervention implementation and change need to include plans for (1) introducing the initiative, (2) consolidating and supporting the change effort, and (3) minimizing resistance. Measurement throughout intervention activities will help monitor the change progress and clarify decisions for corrective actions. Establishing tracking systems that are designed to compare actual with ideal progress help people realize their change efforts are having results. Financial and nonfinancial metrics allow determination of the value of the change activities and enable PT practitioners to calculate their return on investment.

CHANGE MANAGEMENT

Problems have a way of cropping up. Even if an organization is almost perfect, forces outside the organization change constantly. Every organization must be willing and able to adapt to pressures. Healthy organizations recognize changing conditions and adjust. Unhealthy organizations hang on to "the usual way of doing things" long after they should change. The old saying "If it ain't broke, don't fix it" is misguided advice for today. Instead, it is important to recognize trends, to identify causes of the trends, and to search for ways to keep up with or ahead of trends.

Basically, there are two common methods for adapting to changing conditions: empowering employees as problem solvers (such as quality teams) or assigning process consultants to develop solutions. Many organizations combine methods using problemsolving teams to implement ideas developed by an internal or external process consultant. Employees as problem solvers means that the people closest to the problem identify causes and solutions. Problem solving usually focuses on a single issue, department, or

process. This usually results in many small projects involving several departments, but seldom a single, major impact.

Process consulting, on the other hand, is usually coordinated by a centrally assigned person or team. Typically, process consulting involves major divisions of the organization, or the entire organization, in a coordinated effort.

Definition and Scope

Change management requires sensitivity to workers' and to managers' feelings and capabilities. PT practitioners, acting as change agents, need to be honest about the issues. Ideas need to be framed in positive ways to defuse resistance. PT practitioners consider the organization's culture, organizational structure, and external conditions. Key groups from all levels need to be involved. Successful change teams need to carefully select the right intervention strategies. Workers need to prepare for the change.[1]

Role

The role of the change manager has evolved from controlling to facilitating the change process. In the past, changes were decreed by executives. Today, change efforts require worker involvement to maximize each person's contribution. Change managers were once responsible for planning, commanding, and coordinating the effort. Today, change managers (e.g., PT practitioners) consult, communicate, collaborate, and mediate to minimize resistance or fear.[2] They need to be effective negotiators and equitable resource allocators to maintain confidence. In addition they need to be effective communicators to alleviate foot-dragging.

Ownership

Fostering ownership among employees is necessary for change to be sustained.[3] Employees need to identify the new processes and procedures as their own, rather than regarding them as imposed. Too many managers naively believe resistance will evaporate in the natural process of change. PT practitioners need to ensure employee support by:

- Delegating teams and empowering employees to make change happen.
- Building incentives for using the new policies, practices, and processes.
- Unleashing the power in the group and utilizing worker's talents and skills in every phase of the implementation.
- Fostering involvement of everyone to promote a feeling of ownership.

To achieve support, effective PT practitioners often use indirect methods to get people to recognize and articulate the need for change. By dropping hints, stimulating ideas, and encouraging reflection, change managers foster ownership by allowing people to solve problems for themselves. At first, it may be necessary to use direct suggestions. However, this direct approach should not continue because without ownership resentment will build.[4]

Empathy is the first key to successful change because it enables the PT practitioner to realistically anticipate probable employee reaction.[5] Empathy is not an innate personality characteristic. It is a skill developed by listening, questioning, and welcoming comments and feedback. Empathy enables change managers to appreciate the other person's point of view and to predict whether people will accept, resist, or reject a change idea.

Resistance

When people feel threatened or do not believe change is in their best interest, they will resist, which can under-

mine success.[6] Employees worry that their feelings are not being taken into consideration. Longer-term employees often believe that the good aspects of the previous processes are not adequately preserved. When feeling threatened, employees can dwell on seemingly trivial details instead of visualizing the bigger picture. It is important for PT practitioners to acknowledge the employee's concern and to explain the reasons behind the changes. In some cases, it may be necessary to agree to disagree in order to move ahead. The key is to acknowledge and respect each individual's reactions.

Employee's concerns tend to occur according to the following stages: information, personal, implementation, impact, collaboration, and refinement.[7] In the beginning, people want to be informed about the positive and negative details of the change effort. They are worried about the impact change has on each individual, including the benefits, losses, and new skills needed. It is important to talk about the details of the implementation process, including timeframes and what happens if the change doesn't work out. Impact concerns revolve around results relative to employees and the organization. Collaboration questions focus on how people will cooperate and work together. Finally, employees will often have ideas for making the original changes better and will want to work toward continuous improvement. As employees work through the change process stages, they will come to appreciate the value of the changes.

Continuous Performance Improvement

Because markets and customer expectations change, it is necessary for organizations to continuously improve. The basic steps are:

- Determine customer requirements.
- Analyze processes to determine gaps between current performance and customer expectations.
- Gather starting-point data and set targets to eliminate gaps.
- Implement process improvements on a trial run to assess impact.
- Standardize good processes to sustain the improvement process.
- Measure and monitor ongoing improvements.

System Components

For successful continuous improvement, the following components should be present.[8]

- Leadership commitment by all levels of management
- Planning that links customer requirements with business priorities
- Policies and practices that emphasize customer focus

- Process management that involves the entire supplier-producer-customer relationship
- Education and training in measurement, problem solving, team-building, and continuous improvement
- Involvement of all individuals in the entire organization
- Measurement through continuous feedback from customers
- Benchmarking by comparing key processes with similar processes
- Performance accountability by establishing specific performance indicators linked with customer expectations
- Rewards and recognition systems to communicate success and motivate people

Problemsolving

As global profitability requirements change, processes that work perfectly well today are not necessarily adequate for tomorrow. There is a need to detect performance gaps and to discover new solutions for closing them. PT practitioners need to have methods for documenting and explaining causes through use of brainstorming, histograms, trend charts, cause-and-effect diagrams, or force-field analysis. Problem-solving activities need to lead employees and managers to address problems holistically.[9]

Quality Methods

Quality methods have a long history of effectiveness. Quality methods can start a chain reaction, leading to increased productivity, lower costs, and increased market share.[10] These methods begin by:
- Correctly identifying the customer.
- Understanding the customer's needs and expectations.
- Providing measurement against customer needs.
- Developing controls to create products and services that customers value.[11]

There are two types of customers: internal and external. Internal customers are the employees in departments affected by the work. The departments are known as "downstream" or "upstream" depending on whether they come before or after the problem. Determining the expectations of upstream and downstream departments is part of determining internal customer needs. In contrast, external customers are the purchasing consumers of the goods or services.

Quality Tools

Problem solving uses quality tools to collect, analyze, and interpret data to acquire sufficient understanding of the problem to accurately select and implement an appropriate intervention. For example, brainstorming encourages team members to share ideas without the ideas being judged by the group. Ideas are then prioritized by discussing their merits and voting for the best suggestions.

The first step in data analysis is to determine what data should be collected and documented. Data is frequently charted using the method that best illustrates the problem.[12] Common data charting techniques include:
- Histograms that indicate quantities on a grid using dots with lines to connect the dots, thus illustrating trends.
- Cause-and-effect diagrams are known as "fishbone" diagrams because of their data-reporting shape. Typically, information is organized according to materials, methods, equipment, and measurement.
- Force-field analysis that creates a T-shaped chart to capture the factors that encourage (positively influence) and those that impede (negatively influence) the situation.

Project Management

All too frequently, interventions are carried out ineffectively because project management methods were not used.

Definition

Project management combines common sense with practical, universal tools to accomplish targets in a systematic manner.[13] The intent of project management is to accomplish the goal on time and within budget.[14] Project management uses a systematic approach.

Deliverables

As project managers, PT practitioners begin by describing deliverables, which are the tangible outcomes (e.g., gap analysis or cause analysis summaries, intervention steps, improved products or services, or evaluation reports).

Gantt Chart

The next step is for the project team to identify the tasks and subtasks needed to produce each tangible deliverable. The duration of tasks or subtasks is estimated. A Gantt chart (see Figure 6-2) is created to represent the tasks and deliverables. Completed deliverables (products) are indicated as milestones using a triangle or similar mark.

Schedule

At this point, the problem-solving team and management jointly determine the acceptable finish date. The schedule is created based on deliverable milestones, task and subtask durations, and finish dates.

Constraints

It is critical for project teams to realize that no project is without glitches; the team should attempt to anticipate setbacks. Suspected problems are known as *constraints*.[15] Good project managers realize that projects do not go perfectly smoothly and build in slack time to compensate for anticipated constraints.

Project Meetings

Project team meetings should occur with sufficient frequency to ensure that all problem-solving team members are informed and able to contribute any needed information.[16] When projects are completed, close-out meetings focus on lessons learned (positive and negative project results) and ways to improve processes for the next project.

Benchmarking

Once the decision has been made to conduct a problem-solving effort, it is important to understand the competitive environment and to understand how to serve customers more effectively.

Definition

Benchmarking enables problem-solving teams to use a "systematic process for evaluating the products, services, and work processes of organizations that are recognized as representing best practices."[17]

Benefits

Benchmarking helps organizations set realistic goals designed to meet customer requirements, improve produc-

---

FIGURE 6-2

EXAMPLE OF PROJECT MANAGEMENT GANTT CHART

D	Task Name	Duration	Start	Finish	January — Jan	February — Feb	March — Mar	April — Apr	May — May	June — Jun	July — Jul
1	**Company Profile**	6d	1/13/99	1/20/99	◢						
2	Group Resumes	6d	1/13/99	1/20/99	■						
3	Individual Matrices	6d	1/13/99	1/20/99	■						
4	**Situational Analysis**	6d	1/20/99	1/27/99	■						
5	**Justification**	11d	1/27/99	2/10/99	■						
6	**Proposal**	6d	2/10/99	2/17/99		■					
7	**Design Document**	6d	2/17/99	2/24/99		■					
8	**Prerequisite /Testing**	16d	2/24/99	3/17/99			◢◣				
9	Prerequisite Skills Assessment	16d	2/24/99	3/17/99			■				
10	Pretest and Post-test	16d	2/24/99	3/17/99			■				
11	**Prototypes**	6d	3/17/99	3/24/99			◢				
12	Manual	6d	3/17/99	3/24/99			■				
13	Job Aid	6d	3/17/99	3/24/99			■				
14	**Handouts**	6d	3/24/99	3/31/99			◢				
15	Self-study Materials	6d	3/24/99	3/31/99			■				
16	Walk-through Materials	6d	3/24/99	3/31/99			■				
17	**Evaluation Forms**	11d	3/31/99	4/14/99				■			
18	**Final Presentations**	11d	3/31/99	4/14/99				■			

Project: Date: 4/14/99	Task ▬▬▬ Progress ▬▬▬ Milestone ◆	Summary ◥▬▬◤ Rolled Up Task ◥▬▬◤ Rolled Up Milestone ◇	Rolled Up Progress ▬▬

tivity, and become more competitive by adopting industry best practices. According to Cheney, benchmarking requires:
- Wholehearted management commitment
- Resources, including time and money
- Planning to identify the best-in-class for comparison
- Solid understanding of your own company's operations
- Analysis to determine performance gaps
- Openness to change and new ideas
- Willingness to share information with partners
- Integration to set new goals and standards
- Dedication to continuous benchmarking efforts[18]

Benchmarking Process

Cheney identifies 10 benchmarking steps.
1. Determine what to benchmark in order to focus on nettlesome practices that affect customer values, company performance, and competitive status.
2. Identify the best-practice organizations to benchmark by searching public records, databases, and publications. Communicate and network with industry gurus, talk with customers and suppliers.
3. Collect data to analyze, such as cost, quality, and timeliness. Decide what kinds of information will provide insight.
4. Determine current performance gaps by comparing common factors between organizations.
5. Anticipate future performance levels of your benchmarking partner for three to five years. Determine if it is possible to use these benchmarked performance levels as targets.
6. Communicate benchmarking findings to win support for the desired change.
7. Establish functional goals.
8. Develop action plans with input from line management and workers.
9. Implement actions and monitor progress.
10. Recalibrate benchmarks based on changing market forces and competitive business practices.[19]

Caution

Benchmarking usually involves site visits to best-practice organizations. There is a particular protocol that is usually adhered to by benchmarking partners.[20] American Productivity and Quality Center (APQC) (at www.apqc.org or 1-800-776-9676) can assist with protocol and site visit expectations. The key is reciprocity, confidentiality, and respect. Each benchmarking partner plans to share its findings and to provide comparable information equally. It is important that findings remain within the partnership and not be shared outside the partnership without permission.

Although most people realize that change is a necessary and normal part of life on an intellectual level, employees are accustomed to certain ways of doing things. When planning and implementing change, it is best to base any efforts on the understanding that "People are the most important part of any organization. People work best in an atmosphere of trust, sharing, and mutual contribution. Investing in them is well-rewarded." [21]

Case Study: Epilepsy Foundation of Michigan

Situation

Prior to the 1940s, little research or medical treatment was available for people with epilepsy in Michigan. The Epilepsy Foundation of Michigan was founded in 1948. Its primary purpose was to promote diagnosis and medical treatment for people with epilepsy. These early centers were academically oriented and staffed by medical experts in neurological and psychosocial issues. In the late 1970s, the federal government began to finance studies and medical care through nonprofit, specialized programs. The Epilepsy Foundation of Michigan did not win one of these contracts.

By the 1990s, medical treatment became available through the mainstream health care delivery system because of advances in technology and research. Major hospitals and clinics offered excellent medical treatment for epilepsy and were beginning to create comprehensive epilepsy programs.

The Epilepsy Foundation of Michigan realized that it could not duplicate what was now available in large health care clinics. For example, it was not possible to purchase adequate new equipment, which was readily available in major hospitals, or to attract the specialized physicians necessary to provide advanced services. In addition, the foundation faced cuts in state funding as the philosophy regarding delivery of public services changed. It also faced cuts from other traditional funding sources.

However, there was also a need for psychosocial assistance for people with epilepsy and their families. Community and school-oriented education and advocacy were emerging needs. Clearly, client needs and funding priorities had changed, creating a performance gap between the old (1940s–1980s) nonprofit research and medical service delivery model and the emerging education/advocacy/psychosocial needs.

Intervention

The multiyear change process began by redefining the vision for services to people with epilepsy. Arlene Gorelick, president of The Epilepsy Foundation of Michigan, worked closely with the foundation board of directors to define a new service delivery model. The next step was to talk with mainstream medical facilities about creating a partnership to provide the medical care. This medical service migration was a lengthy process of negotiating with several health care providers to determine best fit and then creating a patient education program to facilitate the transition. Arlene communicated honestly with the foundation staff and kept them apprised of the plans and the negotiations. As expected, there was resistance to change. However, with consistent support from the foundation board and empathetic discussions between Henry Ford Health System (HFHS) and the foundation's medical staff, the migration of services was completed.

Arlene also had to manage the change of the foundation's service delivery process after the medical/academic services were replaced. Again with consistent support and direction from the foundation board, she discussed changes with primary funding sources to ensure that they would support the changes.

Currently, The Epilepsy Foundation of Michigan offers:
- Information and referral relative to first aid, treatments, school issues, pregnancy, health insurance, employment discrimination, transportation and driving issues, and financial assistance programs
- Seizure management
- Individual and family counseling and support
- Public policy and case or individual advocacy when a person's civil rights have been violated
- Employment support
- Public and professional education
- Disease management program (in planning), which is targeted for sale to managed care companies

Results

Service delivery for people with epilepsy improved by transferring medical care to a mainstream medical facility. The Epilepsy Foundation of Michigan could no longer afford to purchase modern equipment to provide up-to-date diagnosis and treatment. But Henry Ford Health System owned the necessary

equipment and also accepts most personal health insurance plans, facilitating the payment for medical care. In addition, there are HFHS staff doctors with expertise in treating epilepsy.

The foundation now provides psychosocial and community services rather than research and medical services. Modern seizure management procedures enable many people with epilepsy to lead almost normal lives. However, myths and misunderstanding about the disease remain. The foundation helps alleviate the misconceptions and assist persons with epilepsy as they deal with the stresses and challenges of managing daily life.

Lessons Learned

1. Honest communication and clear vision build trust and a sense of fairness.
   Although change management is complex, honest communication and clear vision help the process move forward with fairness. In the early 1990s, foundation employees were nervous and depressed because they recognized the problems with the old medical/academic model. However, they were unable to determine a new direction and make the transition. Arlene, as change manager, benefited from the confidence and support of the foundation board.

2. Unwavering resolve and early successes engender pride and confidence.
   Although people worried and rumors existed, the organizational climate improved as change progressed and new services were developed. Commitment to the new opportunities was essential. Early successes produced pride and confidence. Steady, unwavering movement toward new goals required determination and the ability to inspire a willingness to persevere and iron out any problems with the new approaches.

Epilepsy Foundation of Michigan case study based on interview with Arlene Gorelick, Foundation President, on December 9, 1998. Case study written by Darlene Van Tiem, Ph.D. Used with permission.

JOB AID 6-1: CHANGE MANAGEMENT PLANNER

Directions: Answer the following questions.

What changes in products or services are needed to meet customer expectations?
What performance gaps exist in meeting those expectations?
How will customer satisfaction be determined?
How will employees know when customer expectations are met?

JOB AID 6-2: CHANGE MANAGEMENT EVALUATOR

Directions: Answer the following questions.

Has the change expectation been thoroughly defined?
How will this change disrupt the current organization?
Does the organization have a history of implementation problems? If so, describe.
Are the sponsors sufficiently committed to the project? If not, would education or replacing sponsors help?
Does synergy exist between sponsors, employees, and change targets? If not, what can be done to improve relationships?
What resistance is anticipated?
Is planned change consistent with organizational culture?
Are employees sufficiently ready for change effort? Would training help?
Are the right people, right communication plan, and right measurements in place?

PROCESS CONSULTING

Process consulting involves major redesign of processes and jobs leading to significant organizational reengineering.

In this competitive, rapidly changing global marketplace, the need for flexibility and the willingness to adapt are necessary for survival. In many cases, it is possible for departments or work groups to observe a need, analyze the situation to understand it better, brainstorm alternative solutions, and implement the most favorable idea with minimal discomfort. In those situations, change is welcomed because it alleviates outmoded practices.

Sometimes business practices and processes become entrenched because they involve many departments or include processes that have served well in the past. Often, the need to change is not obvious to all employees and, as a result, change may be resisted.

Ambiguous situations, multidepartmental concerns, or problems with little agreement are often best suited for process consulting. As a result, process consulting can lead, at times, to significant reengineering.

Definition and Scope

Organizations change continually in subtle ways, and solutions to correct minor issues are implemented daily. However, there are times when a centralized approach, known as process consulting, is needed to ensure that change is coordinated and sustained. Process consulting is usually spearheaded by one leader (or team), such as a PT practitioner, who works closely with a sponsor and a project team. The process consultant may be either external or internal to the organization.

For smaller problems, work groups can accomplish change using traditional continuous improvement techniques. Process consultants, on the other hand, work in a mutual, collegial relationship on the bigger organizational issues. It is important that consulting recommendations are beneficial to employees.[1]

Process consultants use specialized skills to observe and interpret group dynamics, to bring insight to work process concerns, and to manage the stress and ambiguity of change relationships. PT practitioners, as process consultants, need to carefully observe interactions among and between various constituent groups, such as executives, managers, and workers and, perhaps, customers or suppliers. They create process flowcharts and analyze policies, procedures, and work standards to identify or confirm work problems. PT practitioners help clients anticipate the stress of change and the ambiguity of new situations. In addition, they prepare for resistance and the frustration of people who do not welcome the change effort.

Determining Performance Relative to Business Needs

Frequently people fear process consulting efforts because they believe that chaos and anxiety usually come with major change. Workers fear that they, or others, will lose power or their jobs. Employees become defensive because change efforts seem to imply that everything in the past was wrong.

Actually, process consulting is usually triggered by changes in shareholder expectations, increased competition, or a need to increase productivity and maximize the possibilities available through computers and automation. Typically, the results of process consulting are increased productivity, consolidated functions, or the elimination of unnecessary work.

Employees can benefit from:
- "Increased employee interest in and appreciation of the enterprise, its leadership, its products or services, and its customers.
- "Improved internal cooperation, communication, teamwork, and understanding of needs.
- "Increased employee knowledge of the organization's direction, its role in the marketplace, its competitors, and its identity.
- "Improved matching of employee skills and empowerment to responsibilities and processes.
- "New individual- and group-performance measures that are more closely aligned with the marketplace, the value of the work performed, and the contribution made."[2]

Consulting Phases

When PT practitioners serve as process consultants they usually follow a structured approach. According to Lippitt and Lippitt,[3] widely respected experts in consulting, ideally there are 6 phases and 14 work focuses in consulting.

Phase One: Contact and Entry

Making First Contact
Consulting services may be requested due to a problem or a desire to improve competitiveness, increase productivity,

ity, or enhance satisfaction, effectiveness, or organizational image. Typically, organizations search for potential consultants by considering internal talent, checking external referrals, and through professional associations. Internal consultants tend to know more about the existing problem or need for improvement. External consultants bring a "fresh pair of eyes" and neutrality.

Clarify the Need to Change
Internal or external consultants begin by seeking information via surveys, interviews, and official memos, reports, and other documents. Outsiders need to gain context and learn the history of the organization, whereas insiders may face defensiveness due to a perceived "in-the-family" status.

Exploring Readiness for Change
While the consultant is acquiring information, the client organization is determining the consultant's credibility, trustworthiness, sensitivity, and capability. At the same time, the consultant tests the readiness of the client to collaborate before mutual commitment to the change effort.

Potential for Working Together
The client and consultant need to feel comfortable working together, and they need to believe the change effort is worthwhile. The consultant needs to ensure that there is sufficient motivation within the client organization to implement interventions.

Phase Two: Formulating a Contract and Establishing a Helping Relationship

What Outcomes Are Desired?
The consultant and client need to agree about the problem and the likely outcomes of the change effort. Outsiders have a fresh outlook regarding the problem and tend to come up with a wider variety of potential solutions. Insiders more easily understand the organization's concerns and the feasibility of any planned change effort.

Who Should Do What?
At this point, the client wants an estimate of the time and energy needed for this project. The client also requires a commitment that the consultant has sufficient availability, skill, and knowledge to reach success. The consultant expects a pledge of support from top management and the necessary financial and time resources.

Accountability
There needs to be consensus about measures of success. Evaluation measures and strategies for documenting a baseline status also need to be established.

Phase Three: Problem Identification and Analysis

Force-field Diagnosis
Clarification activities should focus on forces that may impede progress and those that support reaching change goals. For example, the client organization is likely to encounter resistance to data collection and to change intervention. Force-field diagrams help illustrate driving forces and restraining forces that will have an impact on the change effort. It is the consultant's responsibility to interpret the causes of the problems and the implications for change. An internal consultant has greater awareness of available documents and needed data. The external consultant may need more data but is less likely to face resistance.

Phase Four: Goal Setting and Planning

Projecting Goals
At this stage, the consultant talks to strategic planners, the organization's futurists, and top management. It is helpful also to talk to designated representatives of all employee levels. Change activities need to be aligned with organizational goals and in tune with the internal and external environments.

Planning for Action and Involvement
Planning for implementation involves documenting and sequencing the steps in the change process. Criteria, or evidence of change, need to be established and agreed on. It is vital to conduct trial runs to predict pitfalls and to determine the best path to success.

Phase Five: Taking Action and Cycling Feedback

Successful Action
The consultant must marshal resources and inspire motivation within the organization before initiating change activities. At this point, the outsider probably has greater leverage for introducing interventions and initiating change. However, the internal consultant probably does a better job of assessing implementation requirements.

Evaluation and Feedback
Using a variety of procedures, the consultant periodically seeks feedback about the progress of the change initiative. The internal consultant may more easily get feedback because of his or her familiarity with the organization, although employees may try to hide information and opinions from internal colleagues. In contrast, the external consultant, who may find getting feedback more of a challenge, may more readily introduce new procedures and methodologies.

Revising Action and Mobilizing Additional Resources
"Feedback is only helpful if it is utilized rapidly to reexamine goals, to revise action strategies, and, perhaps, to activate decisions concerning the mobilization of additional resources and changes of assignments and roles."[4] The internal consultant knows how to get access to resources. The external consultant may find it easier to confront issues and suggest alternatives.

Phase Six: Contracting Completion: Continuity, Support, and Termination

Designing for Continuity
Process changes are hard to sustain. For example, employees may try new ideas and procedures and find them awkward. Days are spent deliberately thinking about processes that were previously automatic. Old methods were faster because new methods still have "bugs" in them. There can be intense pressure against change in the hope that management will revert to the old methods. This fragile situation should be anticipated and countermeasures established. Follow-up support for change initiatives should be consistent and strong.

Termination Plans
The consultant needs to prepare the organization to assume new responsibilities for continuing the changes. A termination timeline needs to be established that covers the following:

- An insider needs to be assigned responsibility for maintaining the change effort.
- The intervention budget may be decreased as maintenance activities are put in place.
- A termination celebration should be produced, such as a publication of results.
- A periodic maintenance plan, such as annual reviews, needs to be established to support continuation of the changed environment and to acknowledge accomplishments.

Although no intervention project adheres rigidly to each phase, using a similar overall plan promotes successful interventions. PT practitioners, as process consultants, listen and watch diligently, empathize with the entire workforce, and partner with the organization to achieve excellence and to institute exemplary processes and practices.[5]

Case Study: Roegan Enterprises

Situation

Each year, K-12 school leadership teams convene work sessions to prepare and/or update their school improvement plans (SIP). Typically, membership includes school administrators, representatives from each grade level and subject, and parents. Team responsibilities include collecting and analyzing student and staff performance data, researching best practices, and assessing the monitoring and evaluation processes utilized in the past year.

Intervention

Because SIP is a continuous strategic planning process, the role of a process consultant is to prepare the organization, obtain buy-in, and develop the organization's skills for transformation. Moreover, the process consultant uses her or his skills to diagnose bottlenecks in the school learning environment, to assess its performance outcomes, and to learn how to make these processes more efficient and cost-effective. Thus, the process consultant needs to utilize all three levels of facilitation skills—process, content, and intervention—to develop an effective transformation framework.

The SIP team can consist of 10–20 members. This larger group is generally divided into the following small planning groups:
- Values, mission statement, and goals
- Student and staff performance data
- Objectives and strategies
- Curriculum alignment
- Monitoring and evaluation

Objectives

The process consultant works with the SIP team to ensure they address barriers created by dysfunctional school cultures. Thus SIP teams:
- Define their organizational strengths, weaknesses, opportunities, and threats (SWOTs)
- Identify the subsequent top barriers to achieving growth over time
- Propose solutions
- Prepare their annual plan

Techniques

At the beginning of each session, the process consultant frames the issue, describing it in a couple of sentences using input from the SIP team. The consultant helps guide the team in determining objectives, listing sub-issues or underlying problems, and soliciting possible solutions. In addition, with the team's input, the process consultant determines the appropriate group to address the issue and the timelines for implementation.

Throughout the planning phase, the process consultant uses various techniques to help the SIP team obtain a deep understanding of the entire school and the district's overall direction and operations. Typically these will include round-robins, storyboarding, discussion, and consensus-building.

During the round-robin and storyboarding sessions, each member or team discusses and writes SWOTs on 3M Post-Its™ and attaches them to the appropriate charts. Members then discuss, clarify, consolidate, and use consensus to select top SWOTs, identify "killer" barriers, and propose solutions.

The process consultant provides summary and direction and ensures that any remaining issues are resolved, assigned to the planning groups for resolution, or carried over to the next meeting.

Results

The process consultant leads the team to its final outcome of the planning sessions, a SIP, that includes:

- A needs assessment based on student and staff performance, which includes specific recommendations for improvement.
- Improvements in the quantitative and qualitative monitoring and evaluation process.
- Performance-driven goals, objectives, strategies, action steps, and timelines.
- Professional development strategies that build strong, competent leaders and well-educated teachers.
- Effective teaching practices and highly engaging instructional methods.
- Strong school-family relationships.

Lessons Learned

1. The isolation that teachers face in the traditional K–12 classroom setting hampers transformation and contributes signifi-

cantly to the resistance to changing traditional practices. However, using the facilitation skills of a process consultant, a workable framework for change can be created. This collaboration between process consultant and SIP teams enables schools to use their SIP as a source for organizational renewal. This helps the school to solve its local problems, make changes, and gain focus for sustained improvement.

2. When school schedules do not provide adequate planning and discussion time or limit opportunities for internal and external cross-functional communication, curriculum and programming tend to narrow rather than grow far-reaching. Opportunities for developing external relationships decrease. If resistance occurs, the process consultant helps the team to unfreeze and remove the obstacles to its reform efforts. The process consultant helps the school develop better strategies for dealing with its problems, as everyone becomes comfortable with a process of assessment, goal setting, and implementation.

3. When teachers have job-embedded time to meet and have structured, collegial dialogue on student and staff performance, significant growth occurs. Thus, the process consultant can successfully help establish a school culture that values collaborative effort, sets high standards and expectations, and creates a challenging core curriculum.

4. When schools include parents, community organizations, and businesses in their planning and decision-making processes, staff perception and knowledge expands and becomes more global, student learning improves, and relationships among school, parents, and business improve. At this point, the process consultant has enabled stakeholders to focus the school's efforts on a shared vision and ensured that changes in the school respond to priority local problems rather than simply reflect on current "popular" problems. Thus, faculty, staff, administrators, and volunteers all attend to the same concerns.

Case study written by Joyce Beasley, President of Roegan Enterprises. Used with permission.

JOB AID 6-3: PROCESS CONSULTING PLANNER

Consulting Objective	Initial Observations and Issues
Describe situation and improvement opportunities.	
Why is the proposed process consulting project necessary?	
List project team members and document executive-level support.	
Sketch out consulting activities and sponsor's expectations.	

EMPLOYEE DEVELOPMENT

Most organizational initiatives require learning new skills and knowledge for implementation. Employee development is the organizational structure that supports learning. Employee development involves acquiring knowledge, skills, and attitudes through a number of learning opportunities including (1) traditional instruction; (2) newer technology-oriented formats; (3) informally by means of mentoring, coaching, and on-the-job training; or (4) team participation.

The knowledge era requires workers to continuously develop new skills due to advances in technology, improved processes to increase productivity, and to keep up with the competition.[1] Employee development is critical for succession planning and aligning leadership practices with business objectives. Organizations are becoming *learning organizations* that encourage, support, and celebrate personal mastery of knowledge. Motivation to learn can come as tuition reimbursement, structured on-the-job training, job aids, handy pocket guides, Franklin Planner inserts, or special assignments. In addition, formal instruction can be offered in traditional classroom settings or via newer CD-ROM multimedia with razzle-dazzle and videoconferencing that marries personal involvement with the convenience of learning at the worksite.

Knowledge Era and Human Capital

Clearly, the knowledge era rewards learning and education. The Organisation for Economic Co-operation and Development (OCED) reported that, globally, years of education positively affects literacy, earnings, and employability.[2] In addition, better-educated people tend to be healthier, with fewer sicknesses and disabilities and lower hospital utilization. "Knowledge, skills, and competencies constitute a vital asset in supporting economic growth and reducing social inequality… As we move into "knowledge-based" economies the importance of human capital becomes even more significant than ever."[3] "According to Strata, the rate at which individuals and organizations learn may become the only sustainable source of competitive advantage, especially in knowledge-intensive industries."[4] It is just good business practice to train and educate employees.

Learning Organization

Organizations recognize the need to maintain a competitive position or, especially for nonprofits and govern-

ments, to provide services desired by clients and citizens.[5] As a result, senior management realizes that employees must develop new skills and increase knowledge. U.S. Department of Labor Studies, OCED Literacy Studies, and American Society for Training and Development research indicate that effective employee development results in increased profits and improved economic well-being for the organization and the employee.[6] However, it is easy to argue that training is time-consuming and costly; training attendance diminishes time on the job, which affects productivity and attention to customers.

Although course participation is a significant part of the learning mix, learning can also take place on a day-to-day basis. Organizations are promoting learning as an integral part of worklife.[7] In fact, Shoshana Zuboff believes that learning and working should be fully integrated. "The behaviors that define learning and the behaviors that define being productive are one and the same. Learning is not something that requires time out from being engaged in productive activity; learning is the heart of productive activity. To put it simply, learning is the new form of labor."[8]

Many organizations promote continuous learning by crafting a learning organization. Peter Senge first described the following parameters of learning organizations in 1990 in his book, *The Fifth Discipline:*

- Systems thinking is the discipline of seeing wholes, visualizing and acting on the interrelationships of the organization. It is recognizing patterns that may span departments. Systems thinkers do not reason in narrow terms and resist straight-line analysis.
- Personal mastery refers to employee proficiency through continually clarifying and deepening their own personal vision, focusing their energy, developing patience, and seeing reality objectively.
- "Mental models are deeply engrained assumptions, generalizations, or even pictures or images that influence how we understand the world and how we take action."[9] Mental models of desired change are necessary before change implementation can be successful.
- Shared vision "binds people together around a common identity and sense of destiny. A genuine vision causes people to do things because they want to, not because they have to."[10]
- Team learning raises the collective intelligence and capacity of a group through dialogue, feedback, and problem-solving activities. Team learning is achieved

by overcoming defensiveness and the need for personal gain and attention.

According to Nancy Dixon, learning organizations support:

- Acquisition of information through external sources such as conferences, data collection, benchmarking, trend monitoring, collaborations, alliances, and consultants, and through internal sources such as organizational vision, job experience, feedback, and continuous improvement activities.
- Distribution and interpretation of information through messages in newsletters, e-mails, advertising, and press releases.
- Making meaning from shared unspoken but influential assumptions and through reflective, interpretative experiences such as action learning and special assignments.
- Organizational memory from the collection of information and experiences that can be found in records, processes, stories, and symbols.
- Retrieving information through databases and through informal stories and conversations among employees, even though they are limited by personal opinions, distorted perceptions, and aging memories.[11]

Learning organizations constantly strive to transform themselves. For example, learning organizations tend to encourage all employees to participate in decision making and view management decisions as "experiments," rather than edicts. Organizational information, formerly viewed as confidential, is used to inform and empower people. For example, accounting and control systems are opened up and designed to support employee inquiry. Employees are rewarded for ideas and actions that contribute to innovation and progress. Learning organizations link customers, suppliers, and the neighboring community with employees to increase communication and cooperation. Learning organizations produce a climate of self-development and inquiry.

Creating and sustaining learning organizations is challenging work. Peter Kline and Bernard Saunders have identified 10 steps for establishing learning organizations.[12]

1. Assess your learning culture.
2. Promote the positive.
3. Make the workplace safe for thinking.
4. Reward risk taking.
5. Help people become resources for each other.
6. Put learning power to work.
7. Map out the vision.
8. Bring vision to life.
9. Connect the systems.
10. Get the show on the road.

Sandra Younger compares learning organizations to basketball teams in this way:

"You do your job; you trust your teammates to do theirs.

If you can't make the shot, you pass the ball to someone who can. Forget showboating. It's one for all and all for one. Nobody slamdunks in a vacuum. … In essence, then, basketball is a game of collective intelligence, played best by organizations of players who are constantly learning as a team—in short, a learning organization."[13]

Corporate Universities

As organizations consider the best departmental structure for employee development, many are forming "corporate universities." They are created primarily to align training and employee development with business strategy, provide a highly visible curriculum, and to secure and maintain executive sanction and support.[14] For example, GM University was originally headed by the former president of the successful Saturn product line, who was promoted to Chief Learning Officer. GM University, a global learning network, includes the following colleges: quality, brand, sales and service, leadership, communications, purchasing, financial, legal, public policy, engineering, health and safety, human resources, lean operations, and manufacturing. GM's vision is to "be a learning organization with a bias for action. The GM University will be a network of learning opportunities to continuously improve our understanding and skills to conduct and grow the business of General Motors."[15]

Corporate universities are becoming vital to organizational strength. "Gradually, major companies are making human resource investments just as they would make capital investments—in essential education and training that will give employees skills, knowledge, and attitudes that will make them more productive and competitive."[16] In fact, "Corporate education and training has evolved from a fairly routine technically necessary but strategically insignificant activity to a potentially important source of competitive advantage."[17]

Definition and Scope

Four basic approaches are used for employee development: formal instruction, learning support, job experiences, and interpersonal relationships.[18]

1. Formal instruction can be traditional, classroom-based training, college classes attended through tuition assistance, distance learning events (such as Web-based programs), videoconferences, audioconferences, or self-study. Topics include:
   - Executive Retreats
   - Management and Supervision
   - Professional, Technical, and Skilled Trades
   - Clerical or Line Worker
   - Corporate Culture, Change Management, Problem-solving, Quality
   - Reengineering/New Product Launch

2. Learning support includes conference participation, assessment (e.g., performance appraisals, 360° feedback, and career inventories), performance support (e.g., embedded computer software help and telephone help desks), or corporate libraries.
3. Job experiences include on-the-job training, job aids and reference manuals, job rotation and special assignments, or team involvement.
4. Interpersonal relationships involve mentoring and coaching, informal suggestions "at the water cooler or mailroom," or advice received at lunch and breaks.

Both the employee and the organization are responsible for employee development.[19] In most cases, employees are responsible for learning and implementing changes in the workplace as a result of the learning opportunity. Employees are also responsible for enrolling themselves in the learning activity. Organizations have a responsibility to provide learning opportunities, to provide sufficient information about future jobs, and to honestly appraise current performance, thus allowing people to make wise and useful educational and learning selections.

Who Should Attend?

One of the challenges in employee development is determining who should have the opportunity. George Odiorne categorizes employees in four groups as follows:
"Employees with high job performance and high potential are stars; those with high job performance and low potential are workhorses; those with low performance and high potential are the problem children; and those with low performance and low potential are the deadwood."[20]

Odiorne recommended spending 10 percent of the training budget on stars, 10 percent on problem children, and 80 percent on the workhorses who are the bulk of the workforce. According to Odiorne, the deadwood should be confronted through performance appraisals, and their future should be based on their response to the confrontation.

Working With Requesting Departments/Managing Vendors and Consultants

Good relations between requesting departments and training and development providers is critical for success in employee development. Typically, a manager recognizes a problem and believes that lack of knowledge or skills is at the heart of the matter. The manager contacts the PT practitioner or the training department for assistance in resolving the situation.

Requesting Departments

PT practitioners need to investigate the reason for the request and determine if an intervention will alleviate the problem or enhance competence. Employee development can be provided by external vendors or consultants or in-house trainers. Cost-benefit analysis is used to calculate the costs of various options and to compare them. PT practitioners weigh the advantages and disadvantages to justify their decisions.

Vendor/Consultant Alternatives

Deciding to use external resources to provide employee development means choosing from existing options or designing customized approaches.[21] Vendors typically begin with existing materials and adapt their approach, as needed and as budget permits.

Tailoring involves using ready-made materials by supplementing with exercises, case studies, or simulations in auxiliary materials. Tailoring is effective for generic topics, such as computer software, interpersonal skills, benchmarking, or problem solving.

On the other hand, vendors use *customizing* to modify content and materials in more job-specific situations, such as new-hire orientation or technical training. Customizing is based on generic content that can be used with many other clients. Job-specific diagrams, directions, examples, and exercises are created and placed within the participant materials. For example, machine operation directions need to be clear and precise for safety reasons. If the training was based on generic directions, it would be confusing and could lead to accidents.

Consultants tend to create materials or courses that exactly match the requirements of the situation. Consultants are usually more expensive in the development phase, but can become more cost-efficient during delivery by requiring fewer participation days or by creating targeted learning events.

Selecting Vendors or Consultants

Getting the best vendor or consultant requires careful selection based on fairness. Networking and references are excellent starting points for identifying potential vendors or consultants. Client organizations usually like to create *bid lists* by prequalifying outside vendors and consultants. Vendors are usually selected by evaluating instructor guides, participant materials, auxiliary materials, and related media. In addition, vendors and consultants are evaluated on their relevant experience, financial stability (if appropriate), size and expertise, reputation and trustworthiness, and ability to fit into the client's organizational culture. The major question is, Will the vendor or consultant meet desired expectations on time and within budget?

Request for Proposals (RFP) and Proposals

Requests for employee development services begin by drafting specifications, including cost projections. Internal requesting departments, along with the PT practitioner, describe the current situation and problem, desired outcomes and deliverables, a timeframe, conditions (such as facilities or printing capabilities), and preferred experience of the bidder. PT practitioners send the requirements to pre-selected vendors or consultants as a *request for proposal (RFP)*. The RFP also includes proposal specifications such as bid date and location for deliverables, quality assurance expectations, and invoicing directions.

Proposals are written by vendors and consultants to convey to the requesting organization their willingness to deliver the desired employee development services. Proposals contain specific information to explain the vendor's recommended approach to resolving the situation, staffing resources, pricing, deliverables, and the conditions necessary to meet the bid requirements (such as access to someone knowledgeable about the situation). Proposals are reviewed using predetermined criteria. The chosen vendor or consultant is notified immediately, after which nonselected vendors are notified.

Confidentiality

Consultants, vendors, and requesting organizations have obligations to respect each other's confidentiality. It is expected that the requesting organizations will not disclose bid contents to other bidders nor will they use any ideas of bidders not selected. Consultants and vendors must keep problem situations, disclosed during the bid process, confidential.

Management and Employee Support

Employee development cannot be effective without the support of workers and management. Without trust, requesting departments are reluctant to share problems and ask for assistance. Participants resist applying what they have learned to the job. In addition, managers and employees might not attend sessions and there could be excessive cancellations.

McDermott recommends that PT practitioners inspire confidence and maintain appropriate communications by doing some of the following:

- Facilitate meetings, especially with senior executives, so they are viewed as helpful and capable of leadership.
- Provide results information by tracking budgets, attendance, post-course results, tuition assistance usage, mentoring successes, job assignments, job aids, etc.
- Chart employee development costs and create reports about the value of employee development.
- Advertise successes and encourage employees to take advantage of employee development opportunities.
- Treat employees and management as valued customers; create partnerships.
- Consult with management and employees about their needs. Focus on solving problems and making a difference in the workplace.
- Link employee development to the organization's objectives and plans.[22]

The previous list includes thought starters and represents the myriad of possible actions. The key is the flexibility, confidence, and enthusiasm of the PT practitioner.

Case Study: Managed Care College of Henry Ford Health System

Situation

The Managed Care College (MCC) is a professional health care educational development program designed to promote collaborative interdisciplinary practice and clinical improvement. Participants in the college study various approaches to continuous improvement within health care delivery. In addition, they are also introduced to the business side of health care and it how affects their daily work environment. Curriculum topics include Evidence-based Medicine, Continuous Quality Improvement (CQI), Outcomes Research, Population and Disease Management, Understanding Patient Needs, Benchmarking, Measurement and Statistical Tools, Team Development, and the Business of Health Care. The purpose of the MCC is to integrate concepts of managed care and CQI into the daily routines and practices of professional staff within the Henry Ford Health System (HFHS).

MCC began in 1993 as part of the Metro Medical Group, which was a professional practice group associated with HFHS. A need to educate physicians on managed care as a new and growing concept in the Detroit area became apparent. Shortly thereafter, this professional practice group was assimilated into the HFHS and, during the transition, the MCC was identified as a new type of applied learning. The concepts taught in the curriculum met a need within the HFHS for education pertaining to managed care principles and applied CQI.

Intervention

The MCC views managed health care as the deliberate integration of health care financing to:

- Provide comprehensive, continuous care to a defined population.
- Conserve human and material resources.
- Distribute resources effectively, rationally, and fairly.
- Enable the continuous improvement of the services being provided.

The MCC is open to all professionals within the HFHS including physicians, nurses, physician assistants, nurse specialists, administrators, and other disciplines. The program is designed to integrate managed care and continuous quality improvement by having participants identify a study population, evaluate risk factors, direct benchmarking efforts, collect and analyze data, plan and implement interventions, assess results, reevaluate, and redesign as necessary. This is accomplished through required classroom sessions of approximately 40 hours over a nine-month period including elective classes on various topics to support content. In addition, the participants complete an integrated work project (IWP) of their choice while participating in an interdisciplinary team. These projects are presented at the end of the curricular year by storyboard presentation and written assignment.

MCC faculty is drawn from medicine, nursing, research, administration, and a variety of other professional disciplines within HFHS. Many are nationally recognized in their field. The focus in the MCC on interdisciplinary teamwork is duplicated in the faculty composition.

Results

Evaluation of learning is both formative and summative. An ongoing formative evaluation of the learners' subjective responses to the material is completed after every class session. This information helps faculty meet participants' ongoing needs. To assist appropriate planning and finetune the following year's curriculum, a summative evaluation is conducted at the end of the curricular year, along with an analysis of events within the HFHS (i.e., impact of legislation on health care) that may need to be included. In addition, a review of each team's storyboard and presentation and the organizational needs of HFHS influ-

ence the suggested topics for the next year's interdisciplinary teamwork projects.

One-on-one interviews with various participants and identification of ongoing departmental/regional projects that began within MCC interdisciplinary teams provide further data for an analysis of MCC's effectiveness.

Lessons Learned

Lessons learned during the five years since MCC was established are:

1. Allowing teams to pick their own topics for integrated work projects produces a more enthusiastic team and a more sustainable project.
2. Adjusting class hours to meet the needs of the participants, relative to their job requirements, supports the needs of the system.
3. Soliciting topic suggestions from each session for the upcoming sessions allows for a less structured, learner-focused curriculum that better meets the needs of the learner.
4. Less didacticism and more dialogue promotes effective learning.
5. Ongoing, formative evaluation is critical to implementing effective change processes.
6. CQI is a proven process for improvement; however, conducting a formal cause analysis could help to identify other gaps in professional performance not readily fixed with training and education.
7. Organizational change affects the daily work practices of professional staff whether they are on an inpatient floor, in an outpatient clinic, in an administrative office, or another area of activity.

The MCC tries to instill an awareness of the interrelationship of these factors and how they all impact and improve patient care. Thus, MCC influences employees' daily professional actions and improves health care delivery.

MCC case study was written by Debra Demeester, M.A., R.N., Curriculum Manager, and John Wisniewski, M.D., M.H.S.A., Director, Managed Care College, Henry Ford Health System, Detroit, MI. Used with permission.

JOB AID 6-4: EMPLOYEE DEVELOPMENT STANDARDS

Questions	Yes	No
Objectives and Target Population		
Does the employee development event meet objectives through clear links to job performance?		
Will the employee development event benefit people and the organization?		
Will management and workers endorse the employee development event and apply the learnings?		
Does the employee development event match learner characteristics? (Are learners ready and prepared for employee development?)		
Does the employee development event include balanced learnings in cognitive (knowledge), affective (feelings), and psychomotor (manual skill) domains or procedures?		
Design Integrity		
Does the employee development event match findings of gap analysis and cause analysis?		
Is the employee development event based on action learning? (Action learning means working on projects related to actual job issues.)		
Is the employee development event interactive?		
Is the employee development event modular? (Modular learning allows flexibility for scheduling employee development.)		
Does the employee development event contain a variety of learning strategies? (Variety should enable employees with diverse learning styles and sensory needs to have opportunities to learn effectively.)		
Does the employee development event focus on "need to know" and minimize "nice to know"?		
Does the employee development event include accelerated learning features designed to simplify and enhance learning? (Accelerated learning features tap various parts of the brain to encourage learning.)		
Culture and Context		
Does the employee development event support current organizational initiatives?		
Does the employee development event accommodate quality, health, and safety standards?		
Does the employee development event include language and illustrations compatible with the organization's culture and ideals?		
Cost and Usability		
Is the employee development event available in-house? (In-house training is usually targeted to the organization and work environment, and supports the organization because it is designed to meet the organization's needs, be cost-effective, and minimize impact to cash flow.)		
Is the employee development event cost-effective? (Calculate costs: development, material purchase, instructor/facilitator delivery, facility [location, equipment, and food], and compare estimated total costs against estimated value to organization and employees. Some organizations also calculate participating employee wages and benefits as an expense. Other organizations consider employee development as a routine part of the job and not an additional expense.)		

JOB AID 6-4: EMPLOYEE DEVELOPMENT STANDARDS *continued*

Questions	Yes	No
Quality Assurance		
Was the employee development event designed by a team containing a performance technologist or an instructional technologist?		
Was the employee development event designed by a team containing a subject matter expert?		
Does the employee development event contain a variety of preassessments and postassessments that are job-related? (Evaluation tools should measure cognitive [knowledge], affective [feeling], and psychomotor [manual skill] outcomes.)		
Does the employee development event contain a reasonable quality standard? (A quality target of 90%/90% is recommended. That means 90% of the participants will score 90% or better on the post-assessments.)		
Other Standards Based on Organizational Requirements		
Conclusions and Comments		

COMMUNICATION, NETWORKING, AND ALLIANCE BUILDING

Communication can focus the organization on the positive value of intervention implementation and change. Networks and alliances increase the efficiency and effectiveness of people working together.

Communication is like an old-fashioned elixir. It is good for this and good for that. In fact, nothing works well without it. Communication is the glue that holds all of the pieces of a well-designed intervention together. Communication helps people understand what is happening and why it is happening. People have a chance to ask questions and grasp what they are supposed to do. Talking helps people work together instead of assuming what was meant.

Communication

Communication is the process of sharing thoughts and ideas to develop a common understanding. It is not necessary for people to agree with the idea. It is okay to disagree. However, communicators need to agree about what was actually said. Each communicator needs to be able to paraphrase, or repeat, the essence of what was said.

Frame of Reference

Communicating involves understanding other's frame of reference. People encode (put feelings and ideas into a verbal message) and decode (receive the message and internally translate the words into personal meaning). Each participant in the communication translates the messages differently based on his/her own frame of reference. People understand verbal messages based on their unique experience, educational background, race, sex, attitudes, personality, and values. For example, people are influenced by their ethnic and religious heritage, their environment (e.g., small town or big city), and their family (e.g., siblings, single-parent household). They are affected by vacations, hobbies, and their childhood community. Frame of reference influences everything. Effective communicators need to predict how the listener will receive a verbal statement. It is not sufficient to use perfectly accurate and clear descriptions. If the receiver has no way of grasping the ideas or visualizing the experience, then miscommunication will result. "*The message that counts is the one received* …Therefore, the burden of communication lies with you the sender."[1]

Code

Communication is more than words, it includes the entire body and the surrounding environment (context). Code is not the actual message but how the message is carried. There are three basic codes:
- Verbal—Spoken or written language
- Paralanguage—Voice elements such as tone, pitch, rate, volume, and emphasis
- Nonverbal—Voluntary and involuntary muscle movements, such as gestures, facial expressions, eye contact, appearance, posture, location of communication, arrival times, etc.[2]

R. L. Birdwhistell explained that "probably no more than 30–35 percent of the social meaning of a conversation or an interaction is carried in the words."[3] As a result, communicators should realize that 65–70 percent of the message comes from paralanguage and nonverbal means.

Interpersonal Relationships

PT practitioners need to establish trust and work closely with others. Without effective interpersonal communications, resistance ensues and confidence is not established. Effective communication depends on the ability to make

TABLE 6-1

GREGORC'S LEARNING STYLES

	Unrelated Ideas	Step-by-step/ Linear
Reflection	Abstract Random	Abstract Sequential
Take Action	Concrete Random	Concrete Sequential

personal expectations clear and to understand and respect the beliefs, values, and attitudes of others. This requires empathy and understanding of differences in people.

There are many ways to explain diversity among people. For example, people vary in their preference for thinking things through (reflection) or taking action. In addition, people differ in their thinking style. Some like to use a step-by-step approach and others like to think about ideas in a way that, at first, may seem random.[4]

Based on the Gregorc explanation of differences (Table 6-1), *abstract randoms* like to reflect on unrelated ideas and tend to be creative and artistic. *Concrete randoms,* committed to accomplishing targets, persevere and do not lose their commitment to action. *Concrete sequentials* have patience with details and are intent on doing things right. They provide checks and balances to others who tend to overlook small things. *Abstract sequentials* are inclined to think things through to be sure an idea is logical and sound. They research and test innovative ideas.

It is plain to see that each preference for thinking and doing has advantages in the workplace and that there is a need for people with all styles. It is imperative that PT practitioners acknowledge differences and plan to maximize the strengths of each person. In newsletters, memos, procedures, and other documents, it is important to accept the differences and accommodate for each type. For example, documents should have sufficient concrete detail, yet highlight important points for those who like to accomplish something quickly. There should be some illustrations and examples of various applications and an explanation of purpose for those grounded on logic.

Active Listening

Good listening requires the ability to accurately absorb what the speaker is saying with an understanding of the speaker's point of view. Effective listeners are able to paraphrase, or accurately restate, the speaker's ideas and feelings using similar words. Good paraphrasing requires listeners to minimize the influence of personal values, past experience, background, and educational level. Listening is an active process that focuses on the speaker's message. It requires the listener to test the accuracy of understanding by questioning the speaker.

Good listening involves a positive outlook towards the speaker's message. According to Hamilton, signs of poor listening include:

- Criticizing the speaker's topic by referring to it as uninteresting or boring.

- Criticizing the speaker's delivery.
- Interrupting to challenge or disagree with the speaker or silently build arguments.
- Listening only for facts.
- Making detailed outlines while listening.
- Pretending to listen to the speaker.
- Tolerating or creating distractions.
- Avoiding understanding difficult material.
- Reacting emotionally by tuning out the speaker.
- Daydreaming during long presentations.[5]

Feedback

Typically, employees want information about such things as progress towards a goal, quality of work, or an interpersonal situation. Feedback is an interpretation or judgment about a statement or a situation. Feedback can help employees know how they are doing, and it increases job satisfaction by realizing the need for appreciation. However, feedback can also make people feel under attack. It is time-consuming and difficult to convey because the person's response can be negative or positive.

It is possible to improve the quality and frequency of feedback by using the following, or similar, suggestions:[6]
- Tell people you want feedback.
- Identify the areas in which you want feedback.
- Set aside time for regularly scheduled feedback sessions.
- Use silence to encourage feedback.
- Watch for nonverbal responses.
- Ask questions.
- Paraphrase.
- Use statements that encourage feedback.
- Reward feedback.
- Follow up.

When giving feedback to others, it is best to:[7]
- Direct feedback toward behavior rather than toward the person.
- Use language that is descriptive instead of evaluative.
- Recognize that feedback involves sharing ideas, not giving advice.
- Include only as much information as the person can handle at one time.
- Remember that effective feedback is immediate and well-timed.

Meetings

Conducting effective meetings is an essential skill for PT practitioners. Meetings bring decision makers and supporters together, facilitating consensus and increasing support for interventions. Meetings allow direct, face-to-face communication and provide an opportunity to explain rationale and to discuss concerns and resistance.

Meetings strengthen groups and encourage collaboration. Meetings should be well-planned and include appropriate speakers and participants, necessary visual aids, and clear handouts. As soon as participants gather, the meeting leader should then welcome and open with introductions, objectives, and the agenda. The meeting proper includes informational presentations, group collaboration, decision making, and action planning. Closing includes summarizing decisions, making action assignments with deadlines, listing recommendations, and asking for feedback. Meeting leaders ensure that participants have sufficient information, full participation in discussions, and clear action plans for meeting follow-up.[8]

Presentations

PT practitioners frequently convey prepared remarks or speeches. These presentations are designed to influence management or employees to act or to convince them to provide support for an idea or change. The point of the presentation is to get listeners to agree with the speaker's way of thinking. It is also likely that listeners will be asked to change normal work activities and to adopt different methods, processes, or procedures.

Listeners, consciously or unconsciously, consider the evidence or logic of the message, the credibility of the speaker, the opinions of others, and their own needs and beliefs.[9] Well-organized speeches are clearer to follow and more effective. Begin by capturing listeners' attention with impressive facts, an example in a story format, a surprising comparison, or linking new ideas with old concepts as a form of transition. Convince listeners that their opinions and values are respected.

Listening has its limitations. Listeners are limited to what they can remember, but may be strongly influenced by a well-prepared speaker. It is necessary to convey transitions carefully and to prepare the listener so that new ideas can be accepted and remembered. The mind is like a file system that depends on a file folder to provide the structure to hold the ideas. The speaker should preview the talk's main points first to help the listener remember the details. Use specific information to convince or to explain main ideas and ensure that the body of the presentation matches the main ideas. Finally, wrap up the main ideas in the conclusion with a motivational message designed to engender action or confidence.

Speeches can result in a common commitment to change, keep employees informed of plans or progress, and explain reasons for organizational action. Presentations are an essential form of communication.

Networking

Networking, or forming informal relationships with people who have common interests or experiences, is an essential part of getting work done. Networks have no formal structure and no obvious authority. They can consist of vast numbers of people including outsiders, peers, bosses' bosses, and subordinates' subordinates.[10]

Individuals form their own personal networks based on integrity, trust, mutual benefit, and knowledge that can be shared. Networks are cooperative relationships with people who will respond to questions or requests for information or assistance.

PT practitioners need networks to affirm direction and ideas. They can provide examples or discuss similar experiences helping a PT practitioner anticipate change. Internal networks can explain actions and rally support. Networks depend on mutual advantage and must be nurtured and appreciated through reciprocation. Effective networking assumes political sensitivity and trust that shared information will be used discreetly.

Networks can be built and nurtured by joining professional associations, such as the International Society for Performance Improvement (ISPI) or the American Society for Training and Development (ASTD). In addition, graduate schools, study groups, and alumni organizations provide opportunities for frequent contact with people of similar interests.

Alliance Building

PT practitioners need to be able to create and sustain alliances. These agreements increase service delivery capabilities and encourage the sharing of resources. For example, noncompetitive organizations in close proximity can enroll each other's employees into unfilled training seats on an equity basis. Each organization will have more training sessions filled to capacity, and each organization can offer greater educational variety to meet individual needs.

Networks can be handy because they are readily accessed, informal, and personal. Alliances, on the other hand, are based on the mutual benefit of all parties. They are more formal, more organized, and often have protocol, rules, and restrictions. Typically, alliances are limited in scope.[11] Alliances are based on agreements relative to partnership participation and operations and work best if partners have similar strengths and influence, but non-conflicting organizations. Each partner keeps autonomy but needs flexibility to cooperate, as required. As the following case study will demonstrate, Michigan Virtual Automotive College, an alliance between government, academia, and business, effectively meets the needs of a particular industry.

Case Study: Michigan Virtual Automotive College

Situation

The need for the Michigan Virtual Automotive College (MVAC), part of Michigan Virtual University (MVU), was identified from a study conducted by the University of Michigan, Office for the Study of Automotive Transportation. This study was commissioned at the request of the Michigan Automotive Partnership, an industry-led roundtable established by the governor. The report, "Michigan: Driving America's Renaissance," predicts a retirement bubble that will create significant staff turnover among automotive firms from 1995 to 2003. The report included a recommendation to create an organization like the Michigan Virtual Automotive College that would facilitate delivery of higher education and provide a tool for meeting the rapidly changing educational and training needs of automotive manufacturers and suppliers.

The report predicts that Ford, General Motors, and Chrysler [DaimlerChrysler] will hire 250,000 new employees over that eight-year period. The quality of the workforce is expected to be a major factor in determining whether these jobs go to people in Michigan or other states. If the state maintains its current share of "Big Three" activity, an estimated 129,000 new hires could occur in Michigan.

The report outlined significant changes that would be needed in the state's educational system to help prepare new workers for automotive jobs, including the development of partnerships among government, education, and industry. The report recommended the creation of an entity like the Michigan Virtual Automotive College to facilitate delivery of knowledge and content from the educational community, to provide closer links to industry, and to take advantage of the benefits of distance learning technologies.

At the 1996 Society of Automotive Engineers Annual Conference, Governor John Engler stated his intention to act on the recommendation of the study by creating the Michigan Virtual Automotive College. This new virtual college would expand education and training opportunities available to employees of Michigan automotive plants; encourage companies to maintain industry headquarters in Michigan; and preserve economic advantages for the state and its residents. "We have a golden opportunity ahead of us to employ a new generation of Michiganians in the world's greatest industry. Michigan will meet this challenge," the Governor said.

In the spring of 1996, a work group began meeting to develop the concept for the Michigan Virtual Automotive College (MVAC). In the fall of 1996, the Michigan Virtual Automotive College task force began working with the consulting firm of Coopers and Lybrand (now PricewaterhouseCoopers) to conduct the market research needed to develop and implement a business plan for the college. Initial research efforts concluded in January 1997 with the development of a business and implementation plan. Table 6-2 indicates the current populations or employees in the various automotive job catagories. Initial staff

TABLE 6-2

POPULATIONS* IN AUTOMOTIVE JOB CATEGORIES

	Production	Skilled Trades	Manufacturing Engineering/ Technical	New Product Development Engineering/ Technical	Total
Michigan	109,400	26,500	7,900	47,200	190,900
U.S.	544,300	131,700	19,600	58,900	754,600
World	1,958,000	473,900	70,700	212,000	2,714,500

Population figures are based on data from the Department of Commerce, Automotive News, and the Autofacts Department of Coopers & Lybrand.

were engaged in February 1997, and the college began developing its programs and services throughout the spring and summer of 1997. Initial offerings began in the fall of 1997.

Intervention

Created specifically for the automotive industry, MVAC is a joint venture by 48 of Michigan's institutions of higher education; the state government; and the automotive industry and its employees. This private, nonprofit Michigan corporation is not a degree-granting institution. Instead, it acts as broker, coordinator, and facilitator of programs, courses, and services from colleges, universities, and other training providers. The target audience/consumers are original equipment manufacturers; automotive suppliers; labor organizations within the automotive industry; individuals interested in preparing themselves for employment in the auto industry; and others who have a need for or interest in the training and educational opportunities available through MVAC. It can even develop customized courses on specific subjects to meet customers' unique needs.

As MVAC continues to evolve, it will:
- Serve as a "one-stop shopping" clearinghouse for automotive education.
- Seek out and deliver the best education and training available, using customer feedback to continually improve programs and services.
- Develop a set of technology standards that will enable course providers, students, and corporate clients to work with common and consistent media interfaces.
- Offer a full array of student services for the adult working student.

- Develop a consistent method of assessing competency and reporting on how a learner has absorbed information and can demonstrate skills.
- Maintain a current base of knowledge about automotive industry training needs, industry skill sets, learning theory, and instructional technology from which all partners can benefit.

To make learning more convenient and cost efficient than ever before, MVAC lets students learn on and off the job, in company-sponsored training centers, or anywhere, anytime with the new distance-learning technologies (see Table 6-3). A comprehensive, searchable on-line catalog that lists courses ranging from Automotive Service Fundamentals to Computer Network Technology and from QS-9000/TE Supplement to Systems Engineering and Vehicle Design is available at http://www.mvac.org.

Results

The initial model for the development of MVAC was based on the training needs of individuals in the automotive industry. Although educational content was available from institutional partners, there was not a clear mechanism for directing potential automotive employees to a specific career path within the industry. This required the development of a career guidance model that incorporated a four-step process. This provides prospective clients on-line assistance at a variety of entry points, as illustrated in Figure 6-3.

MVAC has provided education and training to the automotive industry as shown in the Table 6-3, reprinted from *MVAC Training Report* (good through December 18, 1998).

TABLE 6-3

NUMBER OF STUDENTS BY TECHNOLOGY FORMAT*

Courses Offered By:	Internet/ Intranet	Satellite	Face-to-Face Classroom	Interactive Television	Total
MVAC/ College or University		308	148		456
MVAC/ Company	674		416	7	1,097
Totals	674	308	564	7	1,553

Based on MVAC Training Report, through December 18, 1998.

149

FIGURE 6-3

CAREER GUIDANCE MODEL

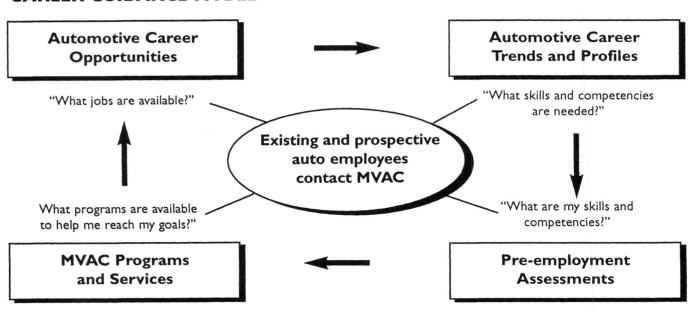

TABLE 6-4

NUMBER OF MVAC STUDENTS OVER TIME

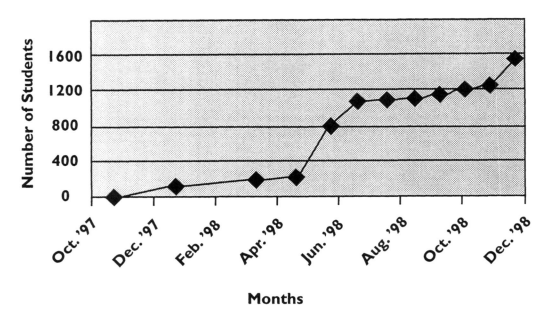

Student enrollment comprises those students who have completed training, are currently in training, or who have enrolled but not yet started training. All courses are noncredit (see Table 6-4).

Lessons Learned

Institutions are providing virtual (distance) content, more so than a year ago. Additionally, the community colleges have formed a virtual collaborative and are providing input to the newly formed MVU (http://www.mivu.org). MVU, formally established on October 1, 1998, has built on MVAC's existing relationships with community colleges and universities. MVU has served as an umbrella organization that hosts other industry-specific colleges including information technology, travel and tourism, plastics, aeronautics, furniture, and allied health.

1. Companies in the automotive industry want cost-effective media by which they can implement and achieve their training strategies. Although MVAC deals primarily with distance-learning technologies, some companies demand face-to-face instruction delivered at the plant site.

2. The desire for entry-level employees to have complete access to the Career Guidance System (Figure 6-3) became apparent. Initially, MVAC did not provide this service to clients. This system was rolled out in early 1999.

Success Stories

FANUC Robotics, one of North America's leading robot manufacturers, is using MVAC to address key training issues for its rapidly growing number of employees. In this collaborative arrangement, MVAC brings together FANUC Robotics executives with Eastern Michigan University faculty members. Together, they are establishing training programs that focus on reliability and maintainability, team problem solving, failure mode and effects analysis (FMEA), and value analysis and value engineering.

Ford Motor Company wanted to find an easier and more cost-effective means of disseminating training to thousands of engineers in every corner of North America. Today, Ford, MVAC, and MVAC's technology partner are mapping out a training program using Ford Motor Company's intranet site and MVAC's Web site. Two technical education modules are currently available: Global 8D (Decisionmaking) and FMEA. The current classroom-based 8D course requires three days of face-to-face training (about 24 hours). In the Ford/MVAC Web-based program, the same amount of information can be covered in just eight to sixteen hours.

Case study written by Rudy Morales, Director of Client Relations, Michigan Virtual Automotive College. Used with permission.

JOB AID 6-5: NETWORKING IS NECESSARY

Directions: Write **p** (*primary*) for the leading resource for getting a job. Write **s** (*support*) for any other resources that assisted in that effort.

	First Job	Most Recent Job	Next Job
People You Know			
Newspaper Ads			
College Placement Offices			
Executive Search Firms			
Outplacement Bureaus			

Directions: List the names of people in your network and their relationship to you (such as personal friend, former coworker, colleague, and professional association member) and list how you met the person. Have you talked to the persom recently? If not, when and where could you make contact?

Name	Relationship	How Met?	Recent Contact?	Future Contact?

Directions: List places where you are likely to meet people who would be helpful on a future job search.

_____

_____

_____

_____

_____

_____

_____

JOB AID 6-6: SKILLS DEVELOPMENT WORKSHEET

Directions: Based on your networking experience, identify skills that would benefit from improvement. Prioritize skills and select four that are most important. List skill in first box of each line. Jot down ways to develop or improve that skill. You may think of more than one way to improve your skills.

Needed Skill	Self-study	Experiential	Training

Needed Skill	Self-study	Experiential	Training

Needed Skill	Self-study	Experiential	Training

Needed Skill	Self-study	Experiential	Training

Evaluation

RAT MAZE

INTRODUCTION TO EVALUATION

Authors and practitioners alike seem to agree that to evaluate is to place a value on or judge the worth of a person, place, thing, or event. In the context of PT, evaluation is a way to "compare results with intentions and delve into the usefulness of methods and resources so that we may move toward the required results."[1]

The International Society for Performance Improvement (ISPI) has long supported "the integral role of evaluation in PT and in the ongoing functioning of any organiza-

tion."[2] According to ISPI's HPT Model shown below, evaluation is "one of the basic components of PT,"[3] along with performance analysis, cause analysis, intervention selection and design, implementation, and change management.

The authors of *Fundamentals of Performance Technology: A Guide to Improving People, Process, and Performance* have enhanced the HPT Model by adding the three types of evaluation—formative, summative, and confirmative—

FIGURE 7-1

HPT MODEL: EVALUATION PHASE

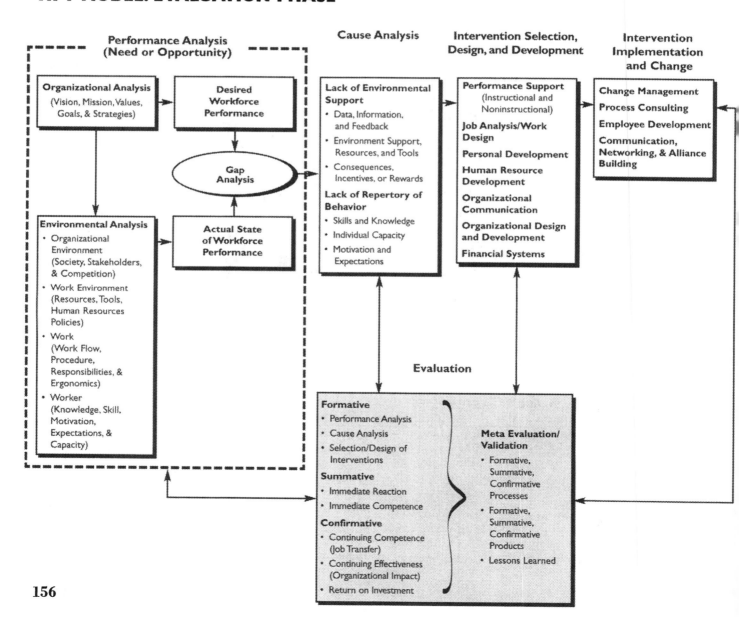

TABLE 7-1

THE FULL SCOPE OF EVALUATION

Formative

- Performance Analysis
- Cause Analysis
- Selection/Design of Interventions

Summative

- Immediate Reaction
- Immediate Competence

Confirmative

- Continuing Competence (Job Transfer)
- Continuing Effectiveness (Organizational Impact)
- Return on Investment

Meta Evaluation/ Validation

- Formative, Summative, Confirmative Processes
- Formative, Summative, Confirmative Products
- Lessons Learned

which literally evaluates the evaluation. Taken collectively, formative, summative, confirmative, and meta evaluation:

- Cover the life cycle of the performance intervention from analysis through implementation and evaluation.
- Guide the decision-making processes involved in why, what, when, and how to evaluate.

Table 7-1 illustrates the scope of evaluation within the HPT Model.

Formative Evaluation

Formative evaluation is diagnostic and is "used to shape or mold an ongoing process...to provide information for improvement...."[4] Formative evaluation is developmental and continuous; it begins during the analysis stage and continues through the selection and design of interventions and sometimes into early implementation.

Summative Evaluation

Summative evaluation focuses on the effectiveness of a performance intervention after it is implemented. Effectiveness is measured by immediate reaction and personal acquisition of knowledge and skills. Summative evaluation takes place during implementation and change management.

Confirmative Evaluation

Confirmative evaluation identifies and explains long-term or enduring effects.[5] It is "the process of collecting, examining and interpreting data and information in order

and the meta-evaluation process to the evaluation component. Enhancing the evaluation component (see Table 7-1) broadens the scope of the component and increases the value of the entire HPT Model.

Definition and Scope

There are three types of evaluation—formative, summative, and confirmative—plus a process called "meta evaluation,"

TABLE 7-2

OVERVIEW OF EVALUATION—TYPE, PURPOSE, TIMING

Type/Process of Evaluation	Why? (Purpose)	When? (Timing)
Formative	Improve performance intervention package	During performance analysis, cause analysis, and selection or design of interventions
Summative	Determine immediate competence of user and effectiveness of package	During implementation and change management
Confirmative	Determine continuing competence of user and effectiveness of package	6–12 months after implementation
Meta	Evaluate formative, summative, and confirmative processes to provide insight to evaluator	After confirmative evaluation

to determine the continuing competence of learners or the continuing effectiveness of instructional materials."[6] Confirmative evaluation builds on and goes beyond formative and summative to place a value on knowledge or skills transfer to the job, organizational impact, and return on investment.

Meta Evaluation

Meta evaluation is a process for "assuring and checking the quality of evaluations."[7] Through meta evaluation the PT practitioner or evaluator validates the formative, summative, and confirmative evaluations and acquires valuable insight into evaluation processes and products. The best way to distinguish among the three types of evaluation and the meta evaluation process is to look at why and when each type of evaluation and meta evaluation should occur during the life cycle of the HPT Model. Table 7-2 provides an overview.

Purpose

In broad terms, "the purpose of evaluation is to illuminate and improve the organization."[8] More specifically, the purpose of evaluation is to generate information that will accomplish two outcomes:
- Help the organization to value or judge the results of a performance
- Trigger or support a decision regarding the performance, the performer, or, ultimately, the organization itself.

Traditionally, quantitative and qualitative evaluation is used to prove or disprove the value of a performance intervention. When the HPT Model was first introduced in 1992, "Evaluation of Results" was the last step in the model. Marc Rosenberg, one of the authors of the HPT Model, summarized the evaluation component of the Model as follows: "After applying or implementing the PT solution, it's important to monitor it to determine its effect on performance improvement and on the organization."[9]

On the other hand, "Most evaluators would agree that the purpose of evaluation is to affect decision making."[10] Feedback from evaluation can determine whether to begin, maintain, change, or end the performance—or the performer. To provide feedback that will trigger or support decisionmaking, the PT practitioner or evaluator may focus the evaluation on one or more of the following goals:
- Confirm that a particular procedure or treatment is being carried out as prescribed.
- Indicate the effectiveness of some treatment or intervention in order to decide whether to continue, expand, or eliminate the treatment.
- Audit the current state of affairs.
- Determine whether the cost of an activity is justified by its effects.[11]

Earlier, this chapter indicated that the type of evaluation helps to determine the purpose of the evaluation. However, there is also a whole matrix of decisions (see Figure 7-2) that determines the purpose of evaluation, and the purpose of evaluation in turn determines when, what, and how to evaluate.[12]

When the purpose of the evaluation is explicit (clear, specific, and detailed), true (real and undistorted), and determined in advance, the resulting when, what, and how will unfold more smoothly.

When to Evaluate

PT practitioners should not think of evaluation as an afterthought or a one-time event. Ideally, "evaluation may occur at any time and with any frequency. It depends on the purpose of the evaluation."[13] Below are two supporting viewpoints from the literature.

- "During analysis one often carries out the activities earlier defined as evaluative: clarifying decisions to be made, collecting information, and feeding it into the decision process. A good part of the needs assessment—of front-end analysis in general—is evaluation."[14]

FIGURE 7-2

MATRIX OF EVALUATION DECISIONS

• "Establish a framework for accountability during the selection and implementation phases and ensure the personal involvement of key decision makers in choosing bottom-line measures to demonstrate the value of their efforts."[15]

Role of the PT Practitioner/Evaluator

Before completing this introduction to the evaluation component of the HPT Model, it is necessary to take a brief look at the role of the PT practitioner or evaluator. The PT practitioner or evaluator is responsible for performing or monitoring five major tasks,[16] whether the evaluation is formative, summative, confirmative, or meta. The tasks include:

• Setting the boundaries (or focus) by establishing the purpose, goals, objectives, and scope of the evaluation.

• Selecting the appropriate method(s) based on the purpose and the context (political environment, available resources, time, and cost).

• Collecting all the information that is feasible, available, and relevant.

• Analyzing the data using sound qualitative or quantitative methods.

• Reporting the findings after first determining who needs to know, what they need to know, how best to inform them, and how often to keep them informed.

The remaining sections in this chapter will help the PT practitioner or evaluator to plan and conduct a formative, summative, confirmative, and meta evaluation within the framework of the HPT Model.

JOB AID 7-1: TYPES OF EVALUATION: ADDRESSING THE ISSUES

Directions: The columns are labeled with the four types of evaluation; the rows are labeled to describe issues that must be addressed when planning an effective evaluation. Fill in each cell before the evaluation begins and revise as the evaluation progresses.

	Formative	Summative	Confirmative	Meta
Primary Audience				
Primary Emphasis in Data Collection				
Primary Role of PT Practitioner				
Primary Role of Evaluator				
Typical Methodology				
Frequency of Data Collection				
Primary Reporting Mechanisms				
Reporting Frequency				
Emphasis in Reporting				
Requirements for Credibility				

EVALUATION MODELS SHOW THE WAY

Models provide blueprints for conducting evaluation by illustrating when, what, or how to evaluate. Below are some models that are useful guides for the PT practitioner or evaluator.

Geis and Smith Model

Geis and Smith use the basic Instructional System Design (ISD) Model ADDIE (Analyze, Design, Develop, Implement, Evaluate) to illustrate when to evaluate PT interventions.[1]

Geis and Smith's model (Figure 7-3) emphasizes a proactive, continuous improvement approach to evaluating performance intervention processes and products.

Dessinger-Moseley 360° Evaluation Model

The Dessinger-Moseley 360° Evaluation Model[2] (Figure 7-4) uses spiralling concentric circles to represent "the proactive and iterative nature of evaluation."[3] In fact, the authors may literally (with the help of computer technology) set the concentric circles spinning to reinforce that evaluation should be continuous. "Each phase uses the prior phase for validation (and) the entire evaluation process is evaluated (meta evaluation) in terms of changing needs and lessons learned."[4]

Table 7-3 compares the HPT Model and the Dessinger-Moseley Model.

Kirkpatrick Evaluation Model

The most well-known model of training evaluation is the Kirkpatrick Model.[5] Kirkpatrick originally developed the model in 1959 to clarify the concept that the potential for evaluating training programs exists at four levels (see Figure 7-5).

Although this model specifically addresses training programs, it is widely used by both Instructional Systems Design (ISD) and performance technology(PT) practitioners because it provides "not only a common language, but also a common tool that lets us compare results."[6]

Kaufman-Keller-Watkins Model

Recognizing the limits of the Kirkpatrick model, Kaufman, Keller, and Watkins (Figure 7-6) offered an expanded version designed to fit the PT environment:

> We suggest that these levels (Kirkpatrick Level 1–4) are incomplete, however, in terms of assessing performance and consequences, and as such they have encouraged many to focus narrowly on evaluating training…. Including interventions other than training into the general evaluation design will require some modification to the four levels, while incorporating existing aspects of program evaluation…. We propose that the principles and processes of training evaluation be expanded to consider all interventions associated with strategic and tactical planning, performance improvement, organizational development, customer satisfaction/total quality and societal contributions.[7]

Brinkerhoff Six-stage Model

Another evaluation model that is less well-known but also applicable to evaluating performance interventions is the Six-stage Model by Brinkerhoff.[8] Brinkerhoff looks at

---

FIGURE 7-3

GEIS AND SMITH EVALUATION MODEL

Analyze ———— *Evaluate* ———— Revise ————— Design————

Evaluate ———— Revise ———— Develop ———— *Evaluate* ————

Revise ———— Implement ———*Evaluate*——— Revise ———— *Evaluate*

evaluation as a cycle and says that his model "responds to the decisions necessary for programs (or interventions) to proceed productively and defensibly … enabling and facilitating quality efforts." In PT terms, the Six-stage Model evaluates the following:

1. Needs and goals—the value and importance of the problems or opportunities that trigger the intervention
2. Design—the practicality, soundness, and responsiveness to the needs and goals
3. Operation—the "goodness" of the installation and implementation of the performance intervention in relation to the needs, goals, and design
4. Learning—the level of the user's knowledge, skills, and attitudes when he or she first uses the intervention on the job
5. Usage and endurance—how well the intervention achieves the intended results over time
6. Payoff—the return on investment from the implementation of the intervention

FIGURE 7-4

DESSINGER-MOSELEY 360° EVALUATION MODEL

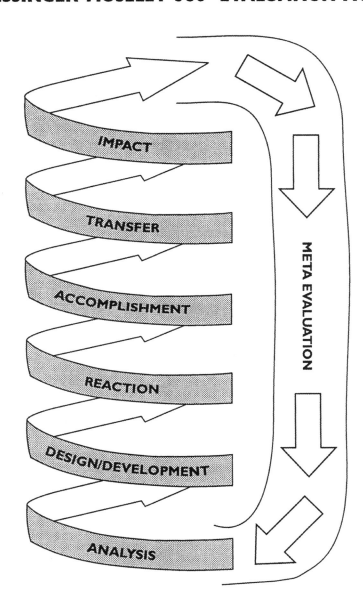

TABLE 7-3

COMPARISON OF THE HPT MODEL AND THE DESSINGER-MOSELEY 360° EVALUATION MODEL

HPT Model	Dessinger-Moseley Model
• Performance Analysis • Cause Analysis	Evaluate **analysis** process and products
• Intervention Selection • Intervention Design	Evaluate **design/development (or selection)** process and products
• Intervention Implementation • Change	Evaluate immediate user **reaction** Evaluate immediate user **accomplishment** Evaluate on-the-job **transfer** Evaluate organizational **impact**
• Formative Evaluation • Summative Evaluation • Confirmative Evaluation	Evaluate all evaluation processes and products—**Meta Evaluation**

FIGURE 7-5

KIRKPATRICK'S EVALUATION MODEL

Level 1—Immediate Reaction

Level 2—Immediate Learning

Level 3—On-the-Job Behavior

Level 4—Organizational Results

FIGURE 7-6

ADAPTATION OF THE KAUFMAN-KELLER-WATKINS MODEL

Level 1	Input and Reaction—the availability and quality of human, financial, and physical resources (input) and the perceived acceptability and efficiency of method and processes (reaction)
Level 2	Acquisition—individual and small-group mastery and competence
Level 3	Successful Application—individual and small-group utilization within the organization
Level 4	Organizational Results—organizational contributions and payoff
Level 5	Societal Consequences—societal and client responsiveness, contributions, and payoffs

FORMATIVE EVALUATION

Formative evaluation begins during the analysis stage, continues through the selection and design of interventions and, if a pilot stage is included in the intervention plan, may extend into early implementation. Formative evaluation is set apart from summative or confirmative evaluation because it is "a quality control method to improve, not prove...effectiveness."[1] Formative evaluation is conducted to improve the design of performance intervention packages. The term *performance intervention package* is defined as "any combination of products and procedures designed to improve the performance of individuals and/or organizations."[2] This section will discuss when and how to use formative evaluation to validate that the performance intervention package is:

- Designed to do what the designers/developers promise it will do.
- Grounded in the mission and values of the organization.
- Aligned with the objectives of the performance improvement effort.

Definition and Scope

Formative evaluation is largely defined by its purpose. By any other name, formative evaluation would be called *continuous improvement* or *quality control*. Originally coined to describe a "systematic process of revision and tryout"[3] to improve curriculum and instruction, formative evaluation has become a major technique for ensuring quality and consistency of performance improvement processes. Formative evaluation is diagnostic and is "used to shape or mold an ongoing process...to provide information for improvement..."[4] The word *improve* is key to understanding why formative evaluation is such an important tool in the PT practitioner's toolkit. "The immediate output of formative evaluation is an improved [performance intervention] package that provides consistent results."[5]

Purpose

Traditionally, formative evaluation takes place between the design and implementation of instruction, which would position it between the intervention selection and design and the implementation phases of the HPT Model. However, PT practitioners are beginning to take a less traditional look at when to conduct formative evaluation. Here are some of their views:

- Begin at the beginning, during the analysis stage, and continue throughout all the phases of the HPT Model.[6]

- Think about formative evaluation as a "continuous process incorporated into different stages of development of the intervention."[7]
- Integrate formative evaluation with all four levels of Kirkpatrick's Evaluation Model (see Figure 7-5). Formative evaluation is usually associated with level one (immediate reaction) and level two (immediate knowledge and skill acquisition) of Kirkpatrick's model. Integrating formative evaluation with level three (on-the-job transfer) and level four (organizational results) "is consistent with current approaches to performance technology, and provides an opportunity for the designer to become knowledgeable about the workplace, and to use that knowledge to facilitate the transfer of learning from the classroom to the performance context."[8]
- Consider formative evaluation as "an ongoing procedure for updating and upgrading the (performance improvement) package after it has been implemented in the workplace."[9] For those readers who are involved with computer information systems, the process is similar to maintaining and upgrading a computer system throughout its life cycle. (Long-term formative evaluation is discussed in the section on confirmative evaluation.)

Conducting a Formative Evaluation

There are four typical methods for conducting formative evaluation: expert review, one-to-one, small group, and field test.[10] Although these methods are traditional to the field of instructional systems design, they may also be adapted to the PT environment. Keep in mind that the methods described below are used to review the entire performance intervention package—products *and* procedures—throughout the entire PT process.

1. Expert Review

A content or performance expert provides information that aids in the selection or design of the intervention and/or reviews draft components of the intervention before implementation. The PT practitioner (or evaluator) then "reviews the review," clarifies any remaining issues, and revises the intervention.

2. One-to-One Evaluation

A potential performer or user reviews draft components of the selected or designed intervention before implementation.

The PT practitioner takes part in the review and revises the intervention as needed.

3. Small-group Evaluation

Potential performers or users review draft components of the selected or designed intervention before implementation. The PT practitioner may or may not participate directly in the review, but is responsible for establishing what the group will focus on during the review, clarifying issues that arise during the review, and making the necessary revisions.

4. Field Test Evaluation

The selected or designed intervention is tried out with target performers/users before full-scale implementation. This method is frequently followed by a debriefing session involving the PT practitioner, who then makes any necessary revisions.

Alternative Methods

Despite the usefulness and proven validity of traditional methods for conducting formative evaluation,[11] Tessmer lists two major factors that call for alternatives:

1. Special circumstances such as time or resource pressure, geographic distances, complexity of performance, or political goals, may require altering the basic methods.
2. Computer and electronic communication technologies have created new tools for gathering and evaluating information that expand basic methods for conducting formative evaluation.

Table 7-4 outlines the traditional and the alternative methods suggested by Tessmer.

The alternative methods help the PT practitioner to customize traditional formative evaluation processes to fit the context in which the package was designed and will be implemented. No matter which alternative is selected and implemented, the outcome is that the PT practitioner (in the role of evaluator/designer/developer) guides the focus and criteria for the evaluation process and revises the performance improvement package based on input from expert performers. The following discussion is based in part on Tessmer and Thiagarajan.[12]

1-A Self-evaluation (Initial Debugging)

The designer, developer, or several members of the design team evaluate the intervention before presenting it to experts or performers for evaluation. This process is frequently called an *internal review* and is conducted before presenting material to the client for the review or the review-revise-approve cycle or external review. For self-evaluation to work effectively, the designer or developer should complete the following tasks:

- Develop a set of evaluation criteria. The criteria may be the same as or different from the criteria set for the expert, performer, or client review, but it should include all the items the client or external reviewers will focus on, plus any design or development issues that the design team needs to resolve.
- Set the intervention material aside for several days to gain distance from the intervention's content and intent.

TABLE 7-4

TRADITIONAL AND ALTERNATIVE FORMATIVE EVALUATION METHODS

Traditional Method	Alternative Method
1. Expert Review	1-A Self-evaluation 1-B Panel Reviews
2. One-to-One Evaluation	2-A Two-on-One Evaluation 2-B Think-aloud Protocols 2-C Computer Interviewing
3. Small-group Evaluation	3-A Evaluation Meetings 3-B Computer Journals and Networks
4. Field-test Evaluation	4-A Computer Journals and Networks 4-B Rapid Prototyping

- Literally become the performer and try out the intervention.
- Record both positive and negative feedback.

1-B Panel Reviews

The PT practitioner directs and structures the evaluation process, preparing a set of questions to guide two or more groups of experts through their review of the performance improvement package. Ideally the experts review the package before meeting with the PT practitioner so that they can focus on areas of concern during the meeting. The PT practitioner facilitates the meeting and records the outcomes.

2-A Two-on-One Evaluation

Two performers review the performance intervention package with the PT practitioner. The performers discuss their reactions as they move through the processes and products that compose the package.

2-B Think-aloud Protocols

This method involves only one performer at a time. The performer walks through the package and verbalizes all of his or her thoughts and reactions. The PT practitioner or evaluator prompts the performer to continue thinking aloud whenever the performer becomes silent.

2-C Computer Interviewing

Computer interviewing is the visual counterpart of telephone interviewing and a very effective use of e-mail, bulletin board, and chat room technology. The PT practitioner or evaluator can send, retrieve, analyze, and respond to the e-mail, or use a software program that automatically sends questions, collects and analyzes responses to open or closed-ended questions, and even generates and distributes a customized report.

Using bulletin board technology, the PT practitioner or evaluator can post performance improvement package products, procedures, or issues that arise during design or development. Experts or performers then go into the bulletin board area, read the postings, and react to the postings by leaving messages. Bulletin boards allow for ongoing dialogue among and between the PT practitioner or evaluator, the experts, and the performers. This technology is especially helpful during rapid prototyping (see 4-B), when analysis, design, and development of the performance intervention package are conducted simultaneously.

Chat rooms allow the PT practitioner or evaluator to conduct real-time interviews with one or more experts or per-

formers and to print the discussion for further analysis. Chat room facilitation requires practice. When chat rooms contain more than two people, the facilitator must set up protocols to keep the interview focused and allow respondents to complete their responses before another respondent cuts in. The difficulty level rises exponentially with the number of people in the room.

3-A Evaluation Meetings

Evaluation meetings bring performers together to review and discuss the performance improvement package. Tessmer suggests that the PT practitioner or evaluator may attend the meeting or conduct a post-meeting debriefing session with a representative from the group.[13] Thiagarajan views this method as a "hands-on procedure (which) provides feedback on how well the package works in the absence of the designer."[14] Evaluation meetings may be repeated several times to validate revisions to the original package. For example, trainers may hold an evaluation meeting after a workshop to gather feedback from the participants to update the next session.

3-B; 4-A Computer Journals and Networks

In a situation where the performance intervention uses network software, the PT practitioner or evaluator may gather information from online journals. The expert or novice performer uses the software, keeps a journal to record reactions to the software, and makes suggestions for improvement. The PT practitioner or evaluator may then follow up by using some of the computer interviewing methods discussed above.

4-B Rapid Prototyping

Rapid prototyping is an alternative development evaluation process. During the development of the performance improvement package, the designer or developer works on one component at a time, and may simultaneously analyze, design, develop, and implement instead of working in a linear fashion. In the PT environment the sequence of activities may look as follows:

1. Analyze, design, and develop one component of the performance improvement package.
2. Develop the support products required to implement the component.
3. Field test the component immediately with experts or performers.
4. Revise as needed.
5. Repeat the process until the entire performance improvement package is completed.

The formative evaluation process during rapid prototyping is similar to a pilot. However, instead of first reviewing a plan or blueprint of the performance improvement package, the users or experts review an actual working component of the package. Reviewer input is used to revise the prototype and to develop the final version.

Advantages and Disadvantages of the Alternative Methods

Table 7-5 was adapted from Tessmer to provide an overview of the advantages and disadvantages of the alternative methods of formative evaluation. Tessmer discusses each advantage and disadvantage at length in the article.[15]

TABLE 7-5

ADVANTAGES AND DISADVANTAGES OF ALTERNATIVE METHODS OF FORMATIVE EVALUATION

Method...	Advantages...	Disadvantages...
I-A Self-evaluation	• easy to conduct • insider's viewpoint	• not rigorously conducted • sometimes don't "see the forest for the trees"
I-B Panel Reviews	• expert dialogue • negotiated agreement	• may move off task • less independence
2-A Two-on-One	• performer dialogue • performer agreement • possible time savings	• no pace/time data • no individual opinions • dialogue distracting
2-B Think-aloud Protocol	• data on mental errors • process data	• intrusive • awkward to use
2-C Computer Interviewing	• access to remote subjects • continuous evaluation	• time-consuming • training required • equipment required
3-A Evaluation Meetings	• amount of group info • quick tryout and revision	• only easy changes made
3-B; 4-A Computer Journals and Networks	• continuous evaluation • environmental variations • cost and time effective	• equipment and software • computer experience levels of users • no evaluator present
4-B Rapid Prototyping	• assess new strategies • assess new technologies	• time and cost to develop • undisciplined design

Case Study: Using Formative Evaluation Throughout the Life Cycle of a Performance Improvement Package

Situation

The Detroit Medical Center (DMC) completed a systemwide rollout in 1993 that presented the philosophy and methods of continuous improvement based on the teachings of W. Edwards Deming. Every manager and employee attended vendor-designed classes describing this new approach. One class discussed how to create a positive environment that would encourage employee participation in improvement efforts. After analyzing participant questions during this class, the corporate training and development staff recognized that there were some general misunderstandings about the roles and responsibilities of the individual manager in creating a positive environment within his or her work group.

The organizational resources expended on the introduction of a continuous improvement philosophy were tremendous by any measure. It was imperative that any follow-up effort to this implementation be well-focused and targeted. DMC had to be certain the follow-up would add to management's knowledge and be helpful in leading them in a constructive direction. Success would hinge on a clean design guided by a thorough formative evaluation.

The corporate training and development staff selected an outside vendor to help them design and implement an intervention that would help to increase awareness of the need to create a positive environment and the ability to do so. The intervention also needed to be cost efficient and ready for immediate delivery as a performance support tool for the systemwide rollout.

Intervention

Working closely together, the corporate training and development staff and the vendor constructed a highly interactive in-house workshop for managers. The goals of the workshop were to more specifically describe how a manager could contribute to a positive environment and to encourage managers to develop and follow a plan called "My Blueprint for Action."

The workshop, "Strategies for Rewarding Performance," built a philosophic bridge between two competing points of view:

1. Managers should create a positive environment using unconditional, noncontingent events such as picnics and pizza parties to foster comraderie among staff (the Deming/Alfie Kohn approach).

2. Managers should use contingent rewards and punishments to address workplace performance and nonperformance (the Skinner approach).

The workshop designers created performance objectives based on their understanding of the disconnects people had with the rollout training. An important addition was a process model for applying rewards and punishments.

The initial design was field-tested using a group of managers who had attended the earlier rollout training. The managers participated in the new Strategies workshop, followed immediately by a one-hour debriefing session. Comments were captured by the course designers and later linked to workshop content and presentation strategies.

Results

Although the structure and objectives remained intact, many important revisions were subsequently made to the workshop based on the input of this test group. The workshop was offered during the following two years to more than 150 experienced and new managers.

Participants reported that, after attending the workshop, they had greater clarity about what the organization expected of them in terms of creating a positive environment. Some participants later became involved in process improvement activities such as leading improvement teams and facilitating new-employee orientation sessions. A nucleus of "believers" was now better prepared to act within their own work group and carry the message to others in the organization.

An annual survey (*The Management Excellence and Work Environment Survey*) tracked whether or not the DMC was creating a positive environment. This survey showed that over a three-year period the DMC consistently maintained a positive relationship with its employees. Individual managers who scored "less than desirable" within their work group were offered a confidential coaching session with a member of the training and development staff.

Beginning in 1997, the DMC also held focus groups with employees whose managers were known to have particular challenges in maintaining positive, productive environments. These groups pinpointed specific issues of employee concern and provided a mechanism for getting issues addressed. At times, it was clear that other factors beyond an individual manager's performance were negatively impacting the work environment.

Lessons Learned

Formative evaluation is an important tool in the PT toolkit. The formative evaluation conducted during the preparation phase of the new workshop helped to focus DMC's efforts. However, such a large-scope organizational issue as work environment is a moving target that requires various intervention strategies. The workshop was recently dropped as a stand-alone offering; however, some of its important teachings have been incorporated into other courses.

It would also be worthwhile to attempt predicting the expected shelf life of an intervention at the outset so that the next gen-

eration of interventions could be planned. DMC successfully clarified the preexisting confusion about a manager's role in creating a positive environment. Now DMC must continue to maintain or improve the managers' performance as well as the organizational environment itself.

This case study was written by James Naughton, MA, Detroit Medical Center. Used with permission.

JOB AID 7-2: PLANNING A FORMATIVE EVALUATION OF A PERFORMANCE IMPROVEMENT PACKAGE

Directions: The columns are labeled with the first three phases of ISPI's HPT Model. (How to plan evaluation for the evaluation phase is discussed in the Meta Evaluation section.) The rows are labeled with the issues that you need to address when planning a successful formative evaluation. Start with the first phase—Analysis—and fill in each cell.

	Analysis of Performance, Gap, and Cause	Selection/Design of Interventions	Implementation and Change Management
What do we want to accomplish by evaluating this phase?			
When do we evaluate this phase?			
What resources do we need to evaluate this phase?			
What basic/ alternative methods will we use to evaluate this phase?			
What data will we collect to evaluate this phase? How? Who will analyze it?			
What type of reports do we need at the end of the evaluation? Who is our audience? What do they need to know?			
What will it cost to evaluate this phase?			

SUMMATIVE EVALUATION

Summative evaluation is the next logical step in the evaluation process and helps the organization determine whether or not to put the "soup" on its performance improvement "menu." "When the cook tastes the soup, that's formative; when the guests taste the soup, that's summative."[1] During formative evaluation, the "cooks" who prepare the performance intervention package (analysts, designers, developers) both conduct and benefit from the evaluation. On the other hand, an external evaluator frequently stirs the pot during summative evaluation and the "guests" are organizational decisionmakers and stakeholders.

Summative evaluation is the most objective way to document the strengths and weaknesses of a performance intervention package. It also "provides a public statement for use with clients, other possible consumers, funding agencies, government groups and others."[2] Yet summative evaluation is frequently omitted because it requires time, money, skilled resources, and the commitment and support of senior management.

Definition and Scope

A functional definition states that summative evaluation "involves gathering information on adequacy and using this information to make decisions about utilization."[3] Basically, summative evaluation looks at the results of a performance intervention package and gathers information that will be useful to the senior decisionmakers in the organization.

Purpose

Summative evaluation seeks to answer two major questions:
1. Did the performance intervention package solve, eliminate, or reduce the original performance problem or gap?
2. Does the performance improvement package meet the needs of the organization?[4]

During the summative evaluation phase, the PT practitioner or the evaluator gathers information on the following:
- Reactions—What is the reaction of the performers? Their peers? Their managers? The customers? The suppliers? The decision makers?
- Learning and capability—What was the level of learning and/or capability before the intervention? After the intervention?
- Accomplishments—Are the performers exhibiting a higher level of performance in their jobs?
- Results—What is the impact on the performance gap? On the bottomline?[5]

Conducting a Summative Evaluation

Summative evaluation is usually conducted during implementation and change management. In fact, Smith and Brandenburg refer to summative evaluation as "rear end analysis," as opposed to front-end analysis (performance analysis).[6]

Collecting and analyzing data is more formalized during summative evaluation than it is during formative evaluation. Summative evaluation may use some of the same tools as formative evaluation—interviews, observation, group processes, and surveys. However, unlike formative evaluation, summative evaluation relies largely on testing and measurement strategies and statistical analysis to evaluate the results of a performance intervention package and to provide an objective basis for decisionmaking. Frequently an external, expert evaluator conducts the summative evaluation.

There are eight basic steps to follow when planning a summative evaluation.[7] The steps are:
1. Identify the decisionmaker and the stakeholders and conduct interviews to specify what decision needs to be made.
2. Translate decision into research (evaluation) questions and ask the decisionmaker to review the questions.
3. Outline the design of the evaluation using three categories: strategies, standards, and participants or population.
4. Conduct a reality check; analyze constraints, resources, and opportunities to determine what is practical and possible given the existing situation.
5. Specify instruments, procedures, and sampling strategies that will collect the required data.
6. Conduct another reality check; outline the data analysis plan and make sure the data collection instruments really provide the answer to the evaluation questions and that the data are easy to tabulate.
7. Specify administration requirements for staffing, scheduling, budgeting, and reporting.
8. Document and communicate the evaluation process and the results by preparing and distributing a design document or blueprint, status or interim reports, and a final report.

The job aid at the end of this section provides a guideline for completing these eight steps. For additional job aids and guidelines read Herman, Morris, and Fitz-Gibbons.[8]

Case Study: Summative Evaluation Plan for a Performance Improvement Program

Situation

A major automotive company launched a performance improvement package for specialty vehicle dealership sales staff across the U.S. The package included a two-day road show that traveled to regional locations across the country. The road show team was composed of a product information facilitator, sales skills facilitator, two business theater facilitators (BTFs) to conduct role plays, the training designer, and a technician. The technician was there to set up, run and troubleshoot an electronic presentation system (EPS) and an audience response system (ARS). EPS made it possible to project video, slides, and MS Powerpoint presentations.

The following discussion contains an overview of the evaluation plan for the road show. The complete plan was sent to the decisionmaker and the stakeholders at division headquarters.

Evaluation Plan

The goal of the road show was to provide dealership salespeople and key personnel with the techniques and tools they needed to make the division's newly articulated vision a reality. The purpose of the evaluation plan was to help the division measure how well they met the goal.

The plan followed the four traditional levels for evaluating the results of training. [9] The following excerpt from the dealership evaluation plan lists the focus or goal of each level of evaluation (evaluation questions) and explains when (timing) and how (strategy) the team planned to evaluate participant reactions and accomplishments and the impact of the program on the dealerships and the division.

Dealership Evaluation Plan Overview

Level 1–Reaction

Evaluation Question
Did the participants like the training?

Timing and Strategy
At the end of each training day the facilitator will use the Audience Response System (ARS) to gather participant reaction to the workshop content, presentation, instructional aids, and their self-reported ability to use the new learnings or skills. The facilitator will also collect written comments from the participants. The ARS system will collect, save, and summarize the reactions.

Because the Road Show is a work in progress, the designer will use the information to revise the program as needed.

Level 2–Learning

Evaluation Question
Did the participants learn the information/acquire the skill presented in the training?

Timing and Strategy
At the beginning of Day One the facilitator will use the ARS system to pretest the participant's product knowledge.

At the end of each module, the facilitator will use performance tests with planned observation (tied to role-play scenarios) and include application of product knowledge when appropriate.

At the end of Day Two the facilitator will use the ARS system to post-test the participants' product knowledge.

Level 3–Behavior

Evaluation Question
Can the participants apply what they have learned to create business as "unusual"?

Timing and Strategy
At the end of each module, participants will complete an action plan describing how they will use the new knowledge or skill.

The evaluator will follow up in the dealerships within 30–60 days by interviewing participants, sales managers, coworkers, customers, and dealer principals.

Level 4–Impact

Evaluation Question
Did the road show have a positive impact on the dealerships and division?

Timing and Strategy
Six months after the training the evaluator will interview participants, sales managers, coworkers, customers, dealer principals, and division stakeholders.

The evaluator will also perform a before-and-after comparison of sales figures and customer service documentation.

The evaluator provided the decisionmaker and stakeholders with weekly evaluation reports while the road show was touring the U.S. The reports included the ARS results of the Level 1 and 2 evaluations and copies of the open-ended Level 1 evaluations filled out by the participants.

The evaluation team also provided the decisionmaker and stakeholders with a biweekly report of Level 3 evaluation activities. A biweekly Level 3 report was also sent to the regional managers with the names and dealerships of participants from their region who had activated their action plans and received certificates of completion.

Evaluation Report

The ARS survey measured participant reaction to the following components of the training program: facilitators, training aids, learning aids, and participant materials. The participants also indicated to what degree they felt they would be able to apply what they had learned when they returned to their dealerships.

All the questions on the ARS survey were answered on a scale of 1–6 as follows:
1 = very strongly disagree
2 = strongly disagree
3 = disagree
4 = agree
5 = strongly agree
6 = very strongly agree

The average response to the training components was 5.0. A review of the Level 1 evaluation data from 230 participants at 11 sites indicated that 98 percent or approximately 225 of the 230 participants agreed, strongly agreed, or very strongly agreed that:
- The visual components helped them learn and increased their interest level.
- The participant materials helped them to learn.
- The examples and samples helped them to learn.
- The product and sales facilitators were well-prepared, organized, easy to understand, knowledgeable, and effective at interacting with the participants.
- The BTFs were prepared, easy to understand, and effective at interacting with the participants.
- The participants will be able to apply what they have learned when they return to their dealerships.

Feedback from the approximately 100 participants who have completed their action plans and received their plaques also helps confirm that the training resources in Phase 1 were effective and that the training transferred on the job.

Exact data on the knowledge or skill accomplishments of the participants are not available at this time; however, there was a positive increase in the knowledge and skill levels.

Level 3 and Level 4 evaluation is incomplete, but the program did continue through several phases and later evolved into a corporate university format.

Lessons Learned

1. The ARS surveys and quizzes were a highlight of the program and a good incentive to participate in the evaluation components of the workshop. The participants enjoyed using their "phasars" (keypads) and rated the ARS system highly on their Level 1 evaluation. The ARS system also made it easy to gather individual and group Level 1 and 2 evaluation data and to report the results quickly, clearly, and accurately. In addition, the system made it possible to give immediate feedback to the participants by projecting histograms of the reactions and knowledge test responses made by the entire group.

2. Prizes (special road show mugs, pen holders, caps, etc.) provided incentive for learning and achieving. In addition to offering prizes to teams and individuals who excelled during the training sessions, each participant who successfully implemented a personal action plan received a Selling the Vision certificate.

3. Using professional actors (BTFs) for the role playing put the participants at ease and encouraged them to take a more active role in the performance testing activities. For example, when Dan Seller (BTF) was not listening to the customer during the listening skills module role play, the participants eagerly coached him and even offered to demonstrate active listening skills.

4. Sometimes good news is bad news. Program stakeholders discontinued the use of Level 1 evaluation because of the consistent positive feedback. In addition, the strongly positive reaction to the initial program caused stakeholders to withdraw support from the implementation of a full Level 1–4 evaluation plan and to shift the organization's resources into design, development, and implementation of new training programs that would build on the skills developed during the road show.

This case study was written by Joan Conway Dessinger, Ed.D., The Lake Group. Used with permission.

JOB AID 7-3: GUIDELINES FOR PLANNING A SUMMATIVE EVALUATION

Steps To Take	Guidelines
1. Specify the decision	Interview decisionmaker and stakeholders to determine: a. Who is the real decisionmaker? b. Who are the real stakeholders? c. What is the real decision that needs to be made? d. What data does the decisionmaker require to make the decision? e. What criteria will the decisionmaker use to make the decision? f. Are there any constraints on the evaluation (see Step 4)?
2. Translate the decision into evaluation questions	Each evaluation question should contain the following: a. What is being measured? b. Who is being measured? c. How (standard or criteria) will the data be measured? Example: Do managers (who) change (standard) their approach to self-development as a result of a new process (what)? (Data collection will provide the level of self-development before implementation of a new process.)
3. Outline the evaluation design	The outline should include the following information: a. What strategies will be used to evaluate changes in performance after the performance intervention is implemented? b. What standards will be used to determine the value of the change in performance? c. Who will participate in the evaluation?
4. Analyze constraints, resources, and opportunities	Determine the resources required to conduct the evaluation, taking into account the five major constraints: a. Time b. Staff c. Access to data sources d. Political considerations e. Budget Try to turn constraints into opportunities…Example: If the old program continues to run while the new program is being implemented, take advantage of the chance to compare the outcomes.

5. Specify instruments, procedures, and sampling	Given the evaluation questions, participants, and organizational climate…
	
	a. What data collection procedures are most effective and efficient?
	  • Analysis of existing records
	  • Interviews
	  • Surveys or questionnaires
	  • Observation
	  • Group processes
	  • Tests
	  • Other…

JOB AID 7-3: GUIDELINES FOR PLANNING A SUMMATIVE EVALUATION *continued*

Steps To Take	Guidelines
Step 5 continued...	b. Which instrument(s) will generate the required information? • Standardized or new tests • Standardized or new surveys or questionnaires • Observation checklists • Interview checklists • Group process questions • Other... c. What sampling decisions need to be made? • Selection: random, stratified random (random by group), or whole group • Sample size (the bigger the impact the smaller the sample size required to demonstrate the impact)
6. Outline data analysis	Check the logic of the data collection procedures by asking the following questions: a. What statistics will be compiled? b. How will the statistics be used? c. How will the data be summarized?
7. Specify administrative requirements	Administrative requirements include the following: a. Who will manage the evaluation? b. How will the schedule be developed? Approved? Maintained? c. How will the budget be developed? Approved? Maintained? d. How will data collection be monitored? e. How will communication (status and final report)) be handled?
8. Document and communicate the process and the results.	The following documents will help document the progress of the evaluation: a. Evaluation Plan or Design Document (blueprint for Steps 1–7) b. Status Reports (if required by stakeholders or decision maker) c. Final Report (contains overview of evaluation process, text and graphic report of results, conclusions, and recommendations for action) Distribute the reports to the decision maker, stakeholders, and participants as determined in the Evaluation Plan.

This job aid is based on the work of Smith and Brandenburg.[10]

CONFIRMATIVE EVALUATION

Confirmative evaluation is "a new paradigm for continuous improvement."[1] Twenty years ago Misanchuk introduced confirmative evaluation as a logical next step to formative and summative evaluation of instructional materials or learners.[2] Today, with the impact of the quality movement on evaluation, practitioners within the instructional and PT environments are beginning to accept the fact that "Quality control requires continuous evaluation including extending the cycle beyond summative evaluation."[3] Confirmative evaluation builds on the findings and recommendations generated during formative and summative evaluation. It enables evaluators to confirm the continuing worth of performance improvement packages and performers and helps organizations decide how to manage continuous performance improvement efforts.

Definition and Scope

The following process definition of confirmative evaluation, although written for instructional developers, easily fits the broader context of PT: "Confirmative evaluation is the process of collecting, examining, and interpreting data and information in order to determine the continuing competence of learners or the continuing effectiveness of instructional materials."[4] The definition is easy to translate into "PT-talk" by substituting the word *performers* for learners and *performance improvement package* for instructional materials.

Confirmative evaluation "challenges us to jettison linear models and integrate evaluative process throughout every phase of [PT]."[5] For further insight into what confirmative evaluation is all about, it is necessary to examine its purpose and timing.

Purpose

The major purpose of confirmative evaluation is to provide continuous quality control over the life cycle of the performance improvement package. Within the PT context, confirmative evaluation does this by placing a value on the endurance of the performance improvement package and by helping the decisionmakers establish what to do next.[6]

Confirmative evaluation identifies, explains, and confirms the value of the performance improvement intervention over time. "Enduring or long-term effects refer to those changes that can be identified after the passage of time and are directly linked to the performance improvement package."[7] Figure 7-7 below illustrates how the value of a performance intervention is equal to the *continuing* competence of the performers who participate in the intervention and the *continuing* effectiveness of the entire performance improvement package including products and processes.

Confirmative evaluation also helps decisionmakers select ways to manage the performers and the performance improvement package over time. Table 7-6 illustrates the six options that are open to the decisionmakers. The table also suggests that even if the level of performance meets performance standards or the performance package is effective, there is always the option to exceed the standards, increase the effectiveness, and delight the customer.

In addition to confirming the competency of the performers and the effectiveness of the performance improvement package, there are other reasons why PT practitioners or evaluators should conduct confirmative evaluation:

1. Confirmative evaluation may be used to link the intervention to broader accomplishments that directly affect the organization and to establish actual costs and benefits.[8]
2. Long-term formative evaluation, or confirmative evaluation, not only supports and strengthens continuous improvement efforts within an organization, but can also "feed back valuable hypotheses to researchers in

---

FIGURE 7-7

EQUATION FOR CONFIRMING THE VALUE OF A PERFORMANCE INTERVENTION

Value of the Intervention	=	Continuing competence of the performers	+	Continuing effectiveness of the performance package

pursuit of a better understanding of human behavior, performance, and accomplishment," helping to build a scientific base for PT.[9]

When Is Confirmative Evaluation Used?

There are two viewpoints on when to use confirmative evaluation. The first views confirmative evaluation as an extension of formative evaluation, and the second views confirmative evaluation as a separate and distinct form of evaluation that goes beyond formative *and* summative evaluation.

The first viewpoint stresses that confirmative evaluation should be "an ongoing process designed to 'take a pulse' before, during and after an intervention is implemented. Confirmative evaluation must be woven into the fabric of an intervention...."[10] This viewpoint is in-line with the concept of "long-term formative evaluation," which extends formative evaluation beyond implementation and summative evaluation. "Long-term formative evaluation is conducted after the newly installed intervention has been in effect for some time, and after its novelty has worn off. Ideally, this evaluation should be repeated every six months or so."[11]

This section will focus on the second and more traditional viewpoint that "the major element which distinguishes

confirmative evaluation from formative and summative evaluation is the time factor. Confirmative evaluation... takes place after implementation."[12] The heuristic, or rule of thumb, is that confirmative evaluation should take place six months to a year after implementation of the performance improvement package. The following guidelines say that confirmative evaluation should not begin *until and unless*:

1. The criteria for the formative and summative evaluation phases have been met.
2. Detailed assessment information on the participants is available.
3. Instrumentation is available to assess the areas of possible effect and other intervening factors.[13]

Another way to determine when to conduct confirmative evaluation is to use these three criteria: criticality, complexity, and frequency.[14] For example, if the performers and the organization rate the criticality, complexity, or frequency of a performance as eight or higher on a scale of 1–10, then confirmative evaluation of any intervention to improve that performance should be conducted every six months after implementation. The job aid at the end of this section will provide guidelines for determining when to conduct a confirmative evaluation based on the three criteria.

TABLE 7-6

SIX OPTIONS FOR MANAGING THE PERFORMER AND THE PERFORMANCE IMPROVEMENT PACKAGE

	If...	Then...
Continuing competence of the performer	Level of competency meets performance standards	Maintain or continue to improve performance
	Level of competency does not meet performance standards	Improve performance
	New context requires new performance standards	Change performance
Continuing effectiveness of performance improvement package	Effective	Maintain and improve package
	Somewhat effective	Revise package
	Not effective	Discard or replace package

177

Conducting a Confirmative Evaluation

Because long-term formative evaluation and confirmative evaluation are so similar in intent, the following guidelines for conducting long-term formative evaluation[15] also apply to the process of confirmative evaluation:

1. Collect data every six months.
2. Be as unobtrusive as possible; for example, incorporate data collection into ongoing activities such as performance appraisals or audits.
3. Focus on the typical effects of the package such as long-term productivity and payoff.
4. Use a form of expert review to verify that the content of the package is still valid, timely, and aligned with the latest corporate policies.

Methods for conducting confirmative evaluation may include, but certainly are not limited to, the following:

- Checklists (desired or optimal performance)
- Interviews (performer, supervisor, coworkers, customers, etc.)
- Observation (performance tests)
- Rating scales (quantifies level of actual performance)
- Assessments (printed tests of knowledge and skill; pre- and post-tests)
- Review of existing information (before-and-after data, safety reports, production reports, suggestions etc.)

These and other methods may be used separately or together. For example, in the following situation, the performance standards were known and the PT practitioner planned to train observers to use checklists and a rating scale to conduct confirmative evaluation.

One task assigned to the field service managers at automotive dealerships is to appraise leased vehicles that have been turned in at the end of a lease. The managers were not consistent in their appraisals. To minimize the variance between the appraisers, a performance improvement package was implemented. The package included classroom and hands-on training, job aids, and incentives.

In addition to formative evaluation, the evaluation plan called for both summative and confirmative evaluation. Immediately after the initial implementation of the package, and again six months later, evaluators would observe the managers as they appraised a series of vehicles with preset conditions. The evaluators would use a checklist, which included a list of the conditions, the standards, and a rating scale for each performance. The resulting data would be compared and used to determine the continuing competence of the performers and the continuing effectiveness of the package.

FIGURE 7-8

MOSELEY AND SOLOMON CONFIRMATIVE EVALUATION MODEL

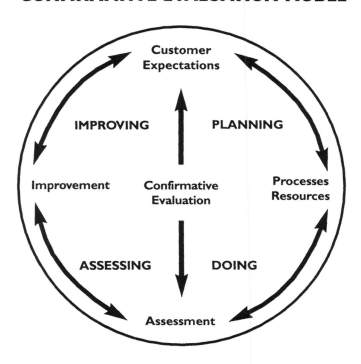

FIGURE 7-9

PRELIMINARY CHECKLIST FOR CONFIRMATIVE EVALUATION

IMPROVING
- Is the intervention effective?
- Should it be continued, improved, or terminated?

PLANNING
- What are you evaluating?
- Who are the stockholders?
- What's important to the stockholders?

ASSESSING
- What are your findings?
- What do your findings suggest?

DOING
- How will the evaluation be designated?
- How will data be collected?

Confirmative Evaluation Model

In 1997 *Performance Improvement* published a model of "confirmative evaluation-a new paradigm for continuous improvement."[16] The model divides confirmative evaluation into four phases: planning, doing, assessing, and improving. The focus of the model is on "continuous improvement, a principle driven by customer expectations."[17] The model, and its companion checklist, are shown in Figures 7-8 and 7-9.

The tasks to be conducted during each phase of the confirmative evaluation model are listed in Table 7-7.

Who Should Conduct Confirmative Evaluation?

Confirmative evaluation requires a special perspective and strong analysis skills. One option is to use a team of "unbiased evaluators"[18] to determine whether or not the performers have maintained the level of competence they achieved after the package was implemented and whether or not the package itself still meets the original objectives. The same source also suggests using an outside evaluator teamed with an expert who is familiar with the performance or the environment in which the performers function. The following case study shows how outside evaluators confirmed the effectiveness of a performance intervention package that was implemented on a grand scale.

Case Study: Confirming the Long-term Effects of a Nationwide Reading Program

Situation

In the 1990s there was a movement toward introducing reading and writing skills into the K–12 curriculum at the kindergarten and even preschool level. This is an example of how a confirmative evaluation helped to determine national educational policy.

During the 1973–74 school year, a number of school districts throughout the U.S. implemented the SWRL/Ginn Beginning Reading Program in their kindergartens. Several years later, Hanson and Siegel wrote a technical report that described how a portion of these students compared with students from the same district who had different kindergarten experiences.[19] The instrument used to compare the students was specifically designed to measure both current reading skills and other potential effects of the kindergarten reading program. The confirmative evaluation was also based on extensive summative evaluation data gathered from a large national sample of schools that implemented the program in their kindergarten classes.

Intervention

Participating school districts offered a formal beginning reading program in kindergarten instead of first grade. The goal was to

TABLE 7-7

TASKS TO PERFORM DURING CONFIRMATIVE EVALUATION PHASES

During this phase...	The evaluator will...
1. Planning	Focus and design the evaluation
2. Doing	Collect information using multiple information gathering techniques such as questionnaires, interviews, observations, focus groups, work sample analysis, performance analysis, context studies, peer-supervisor-self reports, cost-benefit analysis
3. Assessing	Gather and interpret data
4. Improving	Consider the impact, value added, and effectiveness, then recommend whether to continue, improve, or terminate the intervention

increase the reading ability of students in the K–12 system by exposing them to beginning reading concepts and skills at an earlier age than traditional school curricula allowed. Specifically, the program sought to increase reading ability, decrease the need for remediation, and foster an ongoing positive attitude toward reading.

Results

The high school students showed a clear and consistent pattern of increased reading competency as a result of receiving formal reading instruction in kindergarten. Those high school students who went through the reading program in kindergarten were superior readers to those who did not take the program. The students who took the program also had higher grades, better attendance patterns, more positive attitudes toward reading, and less need for remediation. The results of this confirmative evaluation were parallel to the results from similar long-term evaluations of early intervention programs in science curricula.

Lessons Learned

The case for using confirmative evaluation to determine policy in the field of education was affirmed by this study and can be extrapolated to other environments such as business and industry. The study provided insights on the many purposes of confirmative evaluation including:

1. Helps decisionmaker to develop policy that will produce desirable long-term effects, for example, a policy to introduce reading skills into the kindergarten curriculum based on confirmation of increased student performance.
2. Provides a rational basis for improvement during the life cycle of a program.
3. Helps resolve any gaps between the original stated goals and the actual outcomes.
4. Produces cost-benefit information, for example, the need for less remediation may decrease costs within a school district.

This case study was written by Joan Conway Dessinger, Ed.D., The Lake Group, based on personal experience and a report by Hanson and Siegl. Used with permission.

JOB AID 7-4: DETERMINING WHEN TO CONDUCT A CONFIRMATIVE EVALUATION

Here are some heuristics, or rules of thumb, for determining when to conduct confirmative evaluation based on three performance factors: criticality, complexity, and frequency. Gather responses from as many stakeholders as possible: performers, their supervisors, managers, customers, vendors, suppliers, and organizational decisionmakers. Then use this job aid to determine when to conduct a confirmative evaluation.

If this performance factor...	Is rated...	Confirm the "package" every...
How critical is the performance to the success of the organization?	• High • Medium • Low	• 6 months • 6–12 months • 12 months
How complex is the performance?	• High • Medium • Low	• 6 months • 6–12 months • annually
How often is the performance required?	• Regularly • Monthly • Annually • One time only	• 12 months • 6 months • 12 months • 6 months or do not confirm
How often is the performance intervention applied?	• Regularly • Monthly • Annually • One time only	• 12 months • 6 months • 12 months • 6 months or do not confirm

ISPI © 2000 Permission granted for unlimited duplication for noncommercial use.

META EVALUATION

Meta evaluation stands apart from the three types of evaluation discussed in the previous sections. It is a quality control process that is applied to the processes, products, and results of formative, summative, and confirmative evaluation. Meta evaluation has been around since the 1970s; however, organizational buy in to implementing meta evaluation is spotty at best. Implementation of meta evaluation is hampered by time, cost, and skill requirements. Those who do implement meta evaluation find that it enables them to:

- Improve the quality of formative, summative, and confirmative evaluation.
- Test whether or not the formative, summative, and confirmative evaluations delivered what they promised.
- Increase the probability that evaluation results will be used effectively.[1]

Definition and Scope

Basically, meta evaluation is the process of evaluating formative, summative, and confirmative evaluation by literally zooming in on the evaluation processes, products, and outcomes to take a closer look at what happened and why. There are two types of meta evaluation, and for the purposes of this section, they will be referred to as Type One and Type Two meta evaluation. The differences between the two types of meta evaluation are timing and purpose, as shown in the following Table 7-8.

Type One is very much like formative evaluation because it is concurrent and proactive. Many times an outside evaluator observes and analyzes the formative, summative, and confirmative stages of evaluation as they occur and makes recommendations for improving the evaluation process before the process is finalized. Type Two resembles summative evaluation because it places a value on the *completed* evaluation processes. Type Two is the most frequently used form of meta evaluation. It requires fewer resources (time, money, personnel, materials) and can be tied directly to the bottom line of the performance intervention. Therefore, this chapter will focus on Type Two meta evaluation.

Why Is Type Two Meta Evaluation Conducted?

The concept of Type Two meta evaluation fits in quite well with the concepts of quality control and accountability. "Evaluators will be more likely to see their studies effectively utilized when they demonstrate that their work can stand the test of careful analysis and that they themselves are open to growth through criticism."[2]

The specific purposes for conducting Type Two meta evaluation may vary, but usually involve placing a value on basic issues such as:

- Technical adequacy of the formative, summative, and confirmative evaluation processes and products.

TABLE 7-8

TIMING AND PURPOSE FOR TYPE ONE AND TYPE TWO META EVALUATION

Type of Meta Evaluation	Timing and Purpose
Type One	• Conducted **during** formative, summative, and confirmative evaluation • **Guides** the evaluator through the planning, design, and implementation of all three stages of evaluation
Type Two	• Conducted **after** the formative, summative, and confirmative evaluations are completed • Provides **feedback** on the reliability and validity of the evaluation processes, products, and results

- Usefulness of the formative, summative, and confirmative evaluation results in guiding decision making.
- Ethical significance of policies for dealing with people during formative, summative, and confirmative evaluation.
- Practical use of resources during formative, summative, and confirmative evaluation.
- Whether the formative, summative, and confirmative evaluations served the information needs of the client.
- Whether or not the formative, summative, and confirmative evaluations adequately addressed the goals and values of the performance improvement intervention and the organization.
- How well the formative, summative, and confirmative evaluations dealt with situational realities.
- Whether or not the formative, summative, and confirmative evaluations met the requirements of honesty and integrity.
- Other...as determined by the organization for which the intervention was implemented.[3]

In fact, the PT practitioner (or evaluator) could rephrase the issues stated above as questions and use the questions to focus the meta evaluation. For example, Was the formative evaluation useful for decisionmaking? Did the formative evaluation meet the informational needs of the performance intervention package designers?

How To Conduct Type Two Meta Evaluation

There are three basic methods for conducting a Type Two meta evaluation:[4]

1. Review the Documentation
Evaluators review the evaluation proposal, evaluation plan, interim reports (status reports) and/or final report. The purpose of the review is to determine whether the reviewer agrees with the data collection, data analysis, and conclusions of the original evaluator(s). Documentation review is particularly helpful when the outcomes of an evaluation are qualitative rather than quantitative. (Qualitative outcomes are based on feelings and experience and the information is often gathered through interviews or self-reporting. Quantitative outcomes are based on more objective measurement and the information is often gathered using statistical methods.)

2. Do It All Over Again
Evaluators reanalyze the quantitative data from the original evaluation to determine the "goodness" (reliability and validity) of the data and the analysis techniques. The evaluator may replicate all or part of the original evaluation or examine the effects of using different statistical procedures or asking different questions. Reanalysis is costly in terms of time and resources and is usually reserved for evaluation projects that involve major policy changes.

3. Find Others Who Did the Same Thing and Combine the Results
If an evaluation has been repeated in different settings, it is possible to gather together and integrate the results from all the evaluations. This is a statistical process that makes it feasible to draw general conclusions about the processes, products, and results of all the evaluations. The current popularity of internal or external benchmarking could be a selling point for implementing this method of meta evaluation (benchmarking compares internal performance to industry standards or practices).

For those readers who wish to explore the process of meta evaluation in more depth, Stufflebeam provides 34 standards and 68 guidelines for conducting a Type Two meta evaluation.[5] The standards and guidelines are applicable to business and industry as well as education and are useful when planning a meta evaluation.

Who Should Conduct Meta Evaluation?

The PT practitioner or evaluator conducts the meta evaluation with input and support from the performance intervention stakeholders. The stakeholders should be involved in the meta evaluation, particularly if an outside evaluator conducts the evaluation. Stakeholders can help make decisions regarding the purpose for conducting the meta evaluation and can also help select the methods to use when conducting the evaluation. The services of an external evaluator, or an internal evaluator who has not participated in planning, designing, or implementing the performance improvement package, is generally preferred to gain a fresh perspective.

Case Study: An External Evaluator Plans a Meta Evaluation of the Case Studies in Chapter Seven

For this case study, an external evaluator reviewed the case studies in the formative, summative, and confirmative evaluation sections of this chapter, provided initial reactions to the evaluation plans, and outlined plans for conducting a meta evaluation of each evaluation.

The Detroit Medical Center (DMC) Case Study (page 168): Using Formative Evaluation throughout the Life Cycle of a Performance Improvement Package

Initial Reactions to the Case Study

- This case is an example of long-term formative evaluation.
- It appears that the initial systemwide rollout was a good idea in principle, but should have included a pilot study. Including every manager and employee in the DMC is costly and time intensive. Using feedback from the participants for future planning of workshops is certainly an excellent idea.
- Additional follow-up beyond Level 1 evaluation (personal reaction to the training) is warranted when large numbers of people, money, and time are involved. The new workshop was developed based on Level 1 reports of the difficulties individuals had with the rollout training. A Level 2 pre- and post-test evaluation to compare entering knowledge and skills with exit knowledge and skills would have been more helpful to the designers of the new workshop.
- The goal of the new workshop was to describe the role and actions of a manager who contributes to a positive environment and to encourage managers to develop and follow a personal action plan for creating a positive environment within their work area. The goal is certainly an important one; however, from an evaluation perspective, it needs to be much more clearly defined and measurable. For example, the role of the personal action plan as an evaluation tool is unclear.
- The field-testing of a group of managers for this new workshop with a follow-up debriefing, was an excellent step to include in the process. However, since the goal was a positive environment for *everyone* in the workplace, greater input from both managers and employees should have been obtained.

Meta Evaluation Plan for DMC Formative Evaluation Case Study

Purpose

- Provide feedback on the design, development, and implementation of the long-term formative evaluation.
- Assess the usefulness, validity, and reliability of the results.

Foci

Original Course Materials and New Workshop Materials

- What were the specific participant reactions to the content of the original course?
- What were the specific participant reactions to the instructional strategies used in the original course?
- What content revisions were made based on participant reaction to the original course?
- What instructional strategy revisions were made based on participant reaction to the original course?

Design and Development Process for New Workshop

- What are the goals and objectives for the new workshop?
- How were the goals and objectives established?
- Was formative evaluation built in during design and development? If yes, how?

Internal Review by DMC Training Staff and Vendor

- Who participated in the review?
- How was the review conducted?
- What were the results?
- What revisions were made to the new workshop as a result of the internal review?

Field-test and Debriefing Session

- Were the participants truly representative of the target audience?
- How was the field-test conducted?
- How was the briefing session conducted?
- What were the results of the Level 1 evaluations from the field-test participants?
- What were the results of the debriefing session?
- How did the participants react to the revisions made as a result of the Level 1 evaluations from the original course?
- How did the participants react to the revisions made during the internal review?
- What revisions were made to the new workshop as a result of the field-test?

Level 1 Evaluation of the Workshops

- What were the results of the Level 1 evaluations of the new workshop over time?
- Were there any trends?
- Were revisions made to the workshop based on the Level 1 evaluations? If yes, what were they?

Action Plans

- What was the purpose of and process for the personal action plans?
- What were the results of the personal action plan?
- Were there any trends in the results?
- Were revisions made to the new workshop based on the action plan results?

Annual Survey

- To what degree of certainty can it be said that the results of the survey showed that over three years, the DMC consistently maintained a positive relationship with its employees?
- Was a pretest used for the annual survey?

Coaching Sessions

- What issues from the workshop were carried over to the coaching sessions?
- Were any trends obvious?
- What revisions were made to the new workshop as a result of the coaching sessions?

Focus Groups

- How were the focus groups conducted?
- What issues were explored?
- What new issues were raised?
- What feelings or emotions surfaced during the sessions?
- What revisions were made to the new workshop based on the focus groups?

Methods for Conducting the Meta Evaluation

- Review existing documentation and materials
- Find others who did the same thing and compare the evaluations.
- Replicate at least part of the evaluation (do it all over again).

Dealership Case Study (page 172): Summative Evaluation Plan for a Performance Improvement Program

Initial Reactions to the Case Study

- After reading the evaluation plan, it is clear that an organized and thorough approach to evaluation was conducted using Kirkpatrick's four levels of evaluation.[6] The entire evaluation was well thought out, comprehensive, and professionally completed.
- Using Kirkpatrick's four levels of evaluation provided a complete picture from the participants' immediate reaction to the training to the impact of the training on the organization's vision.
- Level 1 Evaluation (immediate reaction) was obtained through both quantitative and qualitative responses. The results from these reactions were summarized clearly and provided useful information.
- Level 2 Evaluation (immediate increase in knowledge or skill) was done by using a pre- and post-test. This was effective in assessing the acquisition of skills presented in training.
- Level 3 Evaluation (transfer back on the job) used participant action plans completed during the training to follow up on what and how the participants applied what they learned during the training. In addition, a followup in the dealerships

was conducted after 30–60 days. This was an excellent step in the evaluation process.

- Level 4 Evaluation (impact on the organization) was completed by interviewing individuals six months after the training, reviewing before and after sales, and reading customer service documentation. This information was obtained at an appropriate time interval.
- – It was still fresh to those who were being interviewed
  - There was ample time for the impact to be felt throughout the organization
  - There was ample time for objective information to be collected as to how the training impacted the dealership and the sales organization.
- Incentives were an excellent idea. Immediate feedback on surveys and quizzes was a positive aspect of the evaluation plan.
- One suggestion is that plans for a confirmative evaluation be considered. Perhaps, evaluation at six-month intervals over a three- or four-year period is needed. If another training session is conducted in the near future, it is strongly recommended that it follow a similar plan for summative evaluation such as the one conducted in this study.

Meta Evaluation Plan

Purpose

- Provide feedback on the design, development, and implementation of the summative evaluation plan.
- Assess the usefulness, validity, and reliability of the results.

Foci

Level 1 Evaluation

- What were the specific participant reactions to the program?
- Were any trends evident over time?
- Was the instrument valid and reliable?
- What revisions were made to the program based on the Level 1 evaluation results?

Level 2 Evaluation

- What were the goals and objectives for the program?
- How were the goals and objectives established?
- Do the pre- and post-test questions align with the program goals and objectives?
- Do the pre- and post-test questions align with the content of the program?
- What were the specific pre- and post-test results?
- Were any trends noted over time?

Level 3 Evaluation

- Do the action plans align with the program goals and objectives?
- What was participant reaction to the action plans?

- What were the results?
- What revisions were made to the new workshop as a result of the action plans?
- Were any trends noted over time?
- Was there a transfer of competency over time (K–12)?

Level 4 Evaluation

- What was the interview protocol? Was there a script? Were the interviewers trained?
- What was the result of the interviews?
- Were any trends noted?
- How was the before-and-after comparison of sales figures and customer satisfaction conducted?
- What were the results?
- What was the impact on the bottom line?
- Is there a final report available? Does it include recommendations for next steps?

Methods

- Review existing documentation and materials.
- Conduct a statistical analysis of Level 1–4 evaluation results.
- Interview the program designer and evaluator.
- Interview the participants.
- Interview the management.

Case Study (page 179): Confirming the Long-term Effects of a Nationwide Reading Program

Initial Reactions to the Case Study

- By its very nature, confirmative evaluation poses particular challenges that are not necessarily apparent in formative or summative evaluation. In this case, the greatest challenge was to assess the effects of a reading program implemented in kindergarten by measuring those effects 12 years later.
- The design of the study posed a problem. It does not appear that a pretest and a posttest were conducted. This may have been because a pretest to measure reading skills at the kindergarten level is particularly difficult to develop when many of the students are not yet reading. Therefore, the summative evaluation data gathered from a large national sample in which the reading program was implemented in kindergarten classes still provided a strong basis for developing the confirmative evaluation.
- The results of the evaluation need careful assessment. The design of the study did not include an experimental or quasi-experimental approach. Measuring the effects of a reading program after 12 years without either of these approaches certainly makes the findings vulnerable to biases. For example, the finding that high school students who went through the reading program had higher grades, better attendance patterns, more positive attitudes toward school, and less need for remediation is a welcomed result. However, what about the many confounding factors that

potentially affect these findings, such as IQ, motivation, perseverance, internal vs. external locus of control, family influence, and personality type.

- Ongoing evaluation after the reading program was completed and then throughout the students' K–12 years typifies a common evaluation strategy for educational studies such as this one.
- Qualitative and quantitative evaluation involving both the staff who implemented the program and the children's parents who were a part of this program may lead to some additional insights not readily apparent.
- Student achievement and the cost-benefit ratio are key factors for any district to consider when implementing a program of this type. Both types of information should be generated when evaluating the effectiveness of a program with such a broad scope.
- A well-planned evaluation design and an ongoing evaluation and tracking system are needed so that programs such as these can be assessed for their effectiveness over time.

Meta Evaluation Plan

Purpose

- Provide feedback on the design, development, and implementation of the confirmative evaluation.
- Assess the usefulness, validity, and reliability of the results.

Foci

SWRL/Ginn Beginning Reading Program

- What were the specific goals and objectives of the program?
- Was content aligned with the goals and objectives?
- Were the instructional strategies prescribed or left to the individual teacher?
- How much variation was there in the implementation of the program?
- Was the reading program subjected to a thorough product evaluation?
- Can any generalizations be made about the confirmative evaluation findings based on the reading program itself?

Design of the Evaluation Program

- What was the overall evaluation plan?
- What were the goals and objectives for the evaluation?
- How were the goals and objectives established?
- Do the pre- and post-test questions align with the evaluation goals and objectives?
- Do the pre- and post-test questions align with the content of the program?
- What were the specific pre- and post-test results?
- What was the summative evaluation plan?
- How were data on achievement and attendance generated?

Instruments Used for Follow-up Measurement of Reading Competency and Attitude

- What instrument was used to measure to test student competency at the beginning and end of kindergarten?
- What instrument was used to measure competency from grade 1 to grade 12?
- What instruments were used to measure attitude?
- How was data on attendance and achievement collected?
- Were the instruments valid and reliable?
- How frequently was competency measured?
- How frequently was attitude measured?
- How were the results of the evaluation analyzed?
- What trends were noted over time?

Summative Evaluation

- How was data gathered from schools that implemented the program in their kindergarten classes?
- Was it a random sampling?

- What were the goals and objectives of the summative evaluation?
- If instruments were used, were they valid and reliable?
- What were the results?
- What trends were noted?
- How were the data quantified and analyzed?

Methods

- Review existing documentation and materials.
- Find others who did the same thing and compare the evaluations.
- Replicate at least part of the evaluation (do it all over again).

These meta evaluations were written by Mary Jane Heaney, R.N., M.S.N., Ph.D., C.H.E.S., of Wayne State University. Used with permission.

JOB AID 7-5: WHY DO WE NEED TO CONDUCT A META EVALUATION?

One way to determine the purpose of a meta evaluation is to sit down with the stakeholders and respond together to the following questions.

Do we need to know...	Formative	Summative	Confirmative
Technical adequacy of the evaluation process and products?	❏ Yes ❏ No	❏ Yes ❏ No	❏ Yes ❏ No
Usefulness of the results in guiding decision making?	❏ Yes ❏ No	❏ Yes ❏ No	❏ Yes ❏ No
Ethical significance of policies for dealing with people?	❏ Yes ❏ No	❏ Yes ❏ No	❏ Yes ❏ No
Practical use of resources?	❏ Yes ❏ No	❏ Yes ❏ No	❏ Yes ❏ No
Whether it served the information needs of the client?	❏ Yes ❏ No	❏ Yes ❏ No	❏ Yes ❏ No
Whether it adequately addressed the goals/values of the performance improvement package?	❏ Yes ❏ No	❏ Yes ❏ No	❏ Yes ❏ No
Whether it adequately addressed the goals/values of the organization?	❏ Yes ❏ No	❏ Yes ❏ No	❏ Yes ❏ No
How well it dealt with situational realities?	❏ Yes ❏ No	❏ Yes ❏ No	❏ Yes ❏ No
Whether it met the requirements of honesty and integrity?	❏ Yes ❏ No	❏ Yes ❏ No	❏ Yes ❏ No
How well it satisfied the need for truthfulness?	❏ Yes ❏ No	❏ Yes ❏ No	❏ Yes ❏ No
Other?	❏ Yes ❏ No	❏ Yes ❏ No	❏ Yes ❏ No

CHAPTER

8

PERFORMANCE TECHNOLOGY IN THE WORKPLACE— A WORD TO THE WISE

"WHAT TYPE OF STRING DID YOU USE?"

INTRODUCTION

Performance technology is a powerful methodology because it is comprehensive and integrates many workplace sectors such as human resources, training, finance, human factors, information technology, quality control, and organizational development. It is systematic, enabling PT practitioners to adopt a consistent approach to resolving performance problems. It serves as an interface between workplace sectors that normally do not work together, except on crossfunctional teams.

Employees benefit from a coordinated performance improvement strategy. The HPT Model deals with complexity; it does not try to simplify workplace challenges. It offers a method for working through, without minimizing, the complexity. In addition, if the HPT Model is consistently applied, the interventions are reproducible.

Throughout the book, there has been a focus on one stage of the HPT Model at a time. However, in the actual workplace, it is necessary to integrate stages and often work in more than one stage simultaneously. For example, formative evaluation needs to be an ongoing process. PT practitioners constantly observe and evaluate workplace activities to ensure that the outcomes and results are what were expected and that the processes used are sound.

"Reflagging and Managing a New Hotel – Marriott International – Detroit, Michigan" is a case study that tells the story of workplace change and restructuring. It is comprehensive because it begins with performance analysis and then defines causes. The Marriott-Detroit selected and then designed several interventions to immediately address their reflagging needs. The case study discusses one intervention—communication—in greater detail and finally identifies an evaluation plan for studying and revising the entire PT application. The case study applies many of the job aids from the book to illustrate their use.

The Marriott case study represents the hospitality industry that is worldwide. Every city has a hotel, and reflagging (ownership change) is common. Marriott is a respected and familiar brand name so readers everywhere will relate to the story. In addition, most organizations face restructuring at some point to meet changing customer or external environmental demands. Marriott's positive approach provides ideas and examples for this common situation.

This chapter recognizes the complex competency and skill set necessary to be an effective PT practitioner. To integrate so many areas, PT practitioners must have a broad range of skills and competencies. For example, great flexibility and leadership are required because frequently PT practitioners serve as project leaders. PT has the model and the methodology to integrate workplace improvements.

Employees often recognize that single solutions, such as changing the culture, instituting 360° degree feedback, or creating a new safety campaign, will not fix problems that encompass many issues, such as compensation, rewards, ergonomics, or supervision.

Finally, not everyone is pleased that PT is used to solve workplace problems. Many want to punish people who cause problems or lay-off those who do not fit in. This may look like a viable solution. However, without addressing causes, the problem remains or reappears. A word to the wise for PT practitioners: Prepare for resistance and maintain a commitment to seeking solutions that are good for both the organization and the employees.

REFLAGGING AND MANAGING A NEW HOTEL: MARRIOTT INTERNATIONAL –

This comprehensive case study is designed to illustrate the implementation of the entire HPT Model. First, it highlights the complexity of performance issues and identifies numerous causes. Then, it reviews the suite of interventions that were identified and implemented. Finally, this case study also makes use of selected job aids from earlier sections of this book to demonstrate application of the HPT Model.

Scenario

Marriott International, a leader in the hospitality field, entered a partnership agreement that includes a management contract with General Motors (GM) to operate the hotel located in their new global headquarters. GM purchased the Renaissance Center in downtown Detroit, which includes the hotel and four surrounding office towers. In addition, GM bought the Millender Center across the street, which was previously operated by the Doubletree Hotel Company. Marriott now operates the Renaissance Center hotel as a Marriott full-service brand with the intent of making it a five-star hotel. The Millender Center hotel is a Courtyard brand. Marriott is one-third partner with GM in ownership and development of the hotel. Marriott, hired by the two-thirds partner to manage the hotel, reports to GM at the monthly owners meeting about profit and loss, guest statistical surveys (GSS), and associate opinion surveys (AOS).

Background

Westin Hotels, Resorts, and Suites previously operated the Renaissance Center hotel for almost 22 years. The center, sold once during this time, had been on the market again for about 8–10 years before its purchase by GM. Detroit was not a popular destination for travelers, and hotel space was too limited to attract conventions.

The Renaissance Center and the hotel had been losing money for a number of years. The owners had made minimal investments in the upkeep on the building to create the illusion of profitability on paper to attract a buyer. As a result, both equipment and technology were out of date and needed to be upgraded for the most efficient day-to-day operations.

Performance Analysis

Marriott International – Detroit conducted a performance analysis to understand the performance issues, using a process similar to the "What's Happening" Job Aid (see Job Aid 3-2).

1. Organizational Analysis Issues

What is happening when the organization interacts with the workforce, the competition, and the community?

Marriott International Brands. Marriott is a company experiencing a lot of growth. It has systematically developed a variety of brands to capture as much of the hospitality market as possible including senior living communities and services, vacation clubs, and wholesale food distribution. The Courtyard by Marriott brand was designed according to opinions from business travelers. Marriott is extremely focused on the loyalty of their customers and develops strategies to attract as much of the hospitality market as possible from the luxury, moderately priced, business, extended stay, and economy sectors. It has developed or purchased brands to address the needs of all guests and is expanding rapidly into the international market.

Community Orientation. It is important to Marriott that it is recognized as a company that cares about the community. In February 1999, Marriott called its commitment the "Spirit to Serve Our Communities," with a focus on companywide service and volunteer efforts. Through Marriott Pride and Children's Miracle Network, customers donate reward points to "Help Hospitals Help Kids" to pay for lodging when a child is receiving care. Marriott consistently receives recognition for its leadership in the area of diversity management and was awarded "Highest Rated Hotel Company" for 1999 in the NAACP's third annual report on the lodging industry. Marriott has also been recognized as one of the "100 Best Companies for Working Mothers," "Top 20 Family Friendly Companies," and "Top 25 Companies for Women."

Workforce. Approximately 700 unionized associates and 80 salaried associates work at the Detroit Marriott Renaissance Center. Many associates have been at the hotel for 10–20 years. Turnover is lower than is typical in the hospitality industry. From the time the center was

JOB AID 3-2: WHAT IS HAPPENING?

At this level of analysis...	Some of the issues are...
1. Organizational Environment Level What is happening when the organization interacts with its external stakeholders and competition? • Customers • Suppliers • Distributors • Industry regulators • Stockholders • Special interest groups • Professional associations • Competitors • Other _____	• How does the organization interact with its external stakeholders? • Which interactions are most critical to the success of the organization? • What is the effect of competition on the organization, the work environment, the work, and the worker? • What does the organization need to do to stay competitive? • How do the various stakeholders define a quality product or service?
2. Work Environment Level What is happening inside the organization to support optimal performance? • Resources (time, money, staff, tools, materials, space) • Information • Policies and procedures • Other _____	• Does the performer have adequate resources to achieve optimal performance? • Does the performer have the information required to achieve optimal performance? • Do policies for recruiting, hiring, feedback, and consequences support optimal performance?
3. Work Level What is happening on the job? • Job design • Work flow • Job responsibilities • Other _____	• Is the job designed for optimal performance? • Does the work flow foster efficient completion of tasks? • Are job responsibilities clearly established?
4. Worker Level What is happening with the workers? • Skills • Knowledge • Motivation • Expectations • Capacity or ability	• Does the performer have the requisite knowledge or skills to achieve success? • Is the performer motivated to achieve? • Do the performer's expectations match the reality of the total performance environment? • Is the performer able to achieve success?

(Based on Langdon (1995), Rothwell (1996b), Rummler and Brache (1995), and Grant and Moseley (1999).)

purchased by GM until the management company was chosen, associates waited 18 months for that decision to be made. Due to changes resulting from creating more efficient operations and the use of new technology, people have recently been assigned new duties and, as a result, are uncertain about their future. But the workforce is committed to the center and to Detroit.

2. Work Environment Issues

What is happening inside the organization while it is striving for optimal performance?

Opening. When Marriott took over management of the hotel, there was a preopening budget to purchase new uniforms, new equipment, and new technology. Town hall meetings and a family-oriented holiday party were held to introduce associates to their new company.

Renovations. Current conditions of the hotel do not attract the typical Marriott guest. Patrons are finding the hotel is not yet up to the usual Marriott standards. The situation was aggravated because the decision to choose the management company for the hotel took longer than expected. Many groups coming to the hotel expected renovations to have been completed. This was a particular problem for groups (conventions, etc.), since these events usually book 2–4 years in advance.

Budget. The partners, GM and Marriott, expect to see a profit. The transitional issues were extremely challenging and the original proformas were not being met. Initially, there was a large outlay of dollars to invest in many visible and tangible items (uniforms, computers, and kitchen renovations). What appeared to be an unlimited ability to spend during opening phase could not be continued. To associates it appears that, after the initial investment, management is settling back into some of the same challenges that were being faced under the old Westin management. However, less tangible investments continue, such as training.

Job Security. Restructuring and closures due to renovations resulted in reassignments. For example, Marriott's reservation system is centralized; therefore, within a month, management was able to downsize the reservations department. Positions were found for all associates except one who could only work a special schedule (which was not available). Management also closed one restaurant and the health club, discontinued room service's midnight shift, and downsized engineering.

Physical Appearance. Frustration with renovations was acute for guests and associates. Jack hammering often prompted complaints at the Front Desk.

Employee Development. Training is an ongoing priority. Jobs were changing as new technology was introduced. Job certification is important to Marriott—not just for hourly associates but for managers as well. Marriott requires a minimum of 40 hours of training a year for all associates (including managers).

The Detroit market is able to afford a regional training center. Marriott supports hourly associates in the advancement of their careers. A Management Candidacy Review Board meets to interview applicants and authorizes appropriate training to prepare them for a management position. Marriott introduced its "Personal Passport to Learning" program as a way for managers to map their own career path and to take initiative by choosing the applicable courses to advance themselves.

Labor Pool. There is now a lot of competition in the downtown market for labor. Since the temporary MGM Grand Casino opened, some associates have left or are working two jobs. The labor pool will have more employment options with three permanent casinos opening along with the riverfront, where development is enticing other smaller hotels. The unemployment rate is very low in Detroit.

3. Worker Issues

What is happening with the workers?

Workplace Climate. The Renaissance Center hotel has three unions, and the Courtyard across the street has one. In Marriott hotels where there is no union, peer review is used in place of the typical grievance procedure. There is a corporate-sponsored associate hotline that can be utilized to report issues or discuss problems that occur at the property level. An Associate Opinion Survey is conducted annually by a third party to identify problems pertaining to hotel climate. Each brand is rated, and the Detroit Marriott is compared to all other full-service hotels.

Workplace Benefits. Profit-sharing, tuition reimbursement, and 401k plans are automatically available at most Marriott hotels. Most of these benefits are not presently available in the Detroit hotel and will be negotiable items when the labor contracts expire.

Guest Satisfaction. Due to the condition of the facility upon takeover and the ongoing construction, the Marriott Renaissance Center's scores in Guest Satisfaction Survey (GSS) were lowest when it was compared to all other full-service Marriott brands.

Labor Pool. The Marriott hotels in the suburbs lack sufficient applicants for jobs because associates do not have transportation to properties. The downtown Detroit sites have lots of applicants because of the metropolitan bus system, but because unemployment is so low, employers are left with a less skilled labor pool from which to hire.

Worker Morale. After the excitement of a change in management and the purchases made with the opening budget, the reality of day-to-day problems returned and morale dropped to its previous level. Many associates have identified solutions to the problems, and systems are being developed that, once implemented, will facilitate their participation.

Job Security. Fear of job loss is a concern. The focus on certification with the introduction of new technology has increased this concern. Some associates have expressed interest in attaining new skills but are afraid of what will

happen if they do not meet criteria. Many associates have been at the Renaissance Center hotel for 10–20 years. They are an older work force and are afraid of being discarded if they are unable to learn the new technology.

Worker's Compensation. There is a large number of worker's compensation cases. Most of these are room attendants in housekeeping. Because the occupancy of the hotel fluctuates drastically, the schedule for room attendants can be demanding. For several weeks they may work only two to three days; then, if a convention checks in, they may work many days straight with little time off.

Management/Labor. Negotiated in the last contract, a Joint Steering Committee was created and has been meeting

JOB AID 4-2: PROBING FOR PEOPLE'S REPERTORY OF BEHAVIOR DRIVERS (OR CAUSES)

This job aid is an adaptation of Gilbert's PROBE Model. Answers to the following questions help to establish the drivers or causes of performance gaps. Some of the answers may be found in documentation for the performance gap analysis. Other answers may require additional input from actual performer(s).

Category	Questions	Yes	No
Knowledge and Training	1. Do people understand the consequences of both good and poor performance?		
	2. Do they grasp the essentials of performance? Do they get the big picture?		
	3. Do they have the technical concepts to perform well?		
	4. Do they have sufficient basic skills such as reading?		
	5. Do they have sufficient specialized skills?		
	6. Do they always have the skills after initial training?		
	7. Are good job aids available?		
Capacity	1. Do the incumbents have the basic capacity to learn the necessary perceptual discriminations with accuracy and speed?		
	2. Are they free of emotional limitations that would interfere with performance?		
	3. Do they have sufficient strength and dexterity to learn to do the job well?		
Motives	1. Do incumbents seem to have the desire to perform well when they enter the job?		
	2. Do their motives endure? Is the turnover low?		

Dean, P.J. and Ripley, D.E. (Eds.), (1997). Performance Improvement Pathfinders: Models for Organizational Learning Systems, pp. 57–58. Washington, D.C.: The International Society for Performance Improvement. Used with permission.

for the past three years. This is a management/labor committee that discusses issues that need the support of the union and invites dialogue and resolution in a proactive and constructive manner. An example: Marriott is piloting a new service initiative called "At Your Service." Since new skills are now required, management is developing a certification process to ensure the necessary levels of competency. The need to certify was first proposed in the Joint Steering Committee to discuss any concerns the union membership might have about the process and to receive feedback at the appropriate steps.

There is also an open-door policy in place that encourages all employees to meet with the general manager if they feel their concerns are not being addressed at the department level.

Labor Contracts. All contracts are usually negotiated to last for three years and to expire in different years. The largest membership is in Local 24, for hotel restaurant employees, and its contract expires this year. There are two other union contracts that offer more generous benefits than the Local 24 contract.

Cause Analysis

Marriott International identified employee-related causes of performance problems using questions illustrated in Job Aid 4-2.

Knowledge and Training

Marriott's relationship with associates is very important. The corporate philosophy, the associate handbook, and the open-door policy all focus on the practice that "if you take care of associates, they will take care of the guest." Because of the transition, associates had not built up a trust that Marriott was truly interested in helping associates succeed. Although Marriott provided training (and was planning more), a significant number of associates felt this was an attempt to weed them out. The Joint Steering Committee, composed of shop stewards and managers, meets monthly to discuss issues that might conflict with a strict interpretation of the contract. Marriott's intent, to provide associates with valuable job knowledge through certification, was discussed in great length. Pretests and posttests were introduced to the committee as a way to ensure that learning takes place. It was stated that, in reality, there may be one or two who might not be capable of performing the new tasks, but that they would be placed in other jobs suiting their qualifications. By the time this discussion was communicated to other associates, some associates believed that there were very few employees who would measure up to the new criteria and that the rest would lose their jobs.

Capacity

An all-associate meeting was planned as a special celebration, including raffles and games, to communicate the sales initiative for the next year and to thank everyone for their efforts during a difficult time. Some people felt that the purpose of the meeting was to give out layoff notices. Holding onto the old rather than embracing the new methods fostered a certain amount of negativity among the employees. Because of the history at the hotel, a "been there, done that" attitude prevailed.

Motives

In training classes and in meetings such as those held by the Joint Steering Committee, more frequent and informative communication and respectful treatment by managers were two issues that came up consistently. A needs assessment was conducted approximately three months after the change in management, and these issues were still identified as major concerns. Data from the assessment attributed this to the management before Marriott. However, it also raised the possibility that the initial hope and enthusiasm of the change in management had not been sufficiently maintained in the day-to-day challenges.

Intervention Selection and Design

To make this property a five-star hotel in General Motors Global Headquarters, Marriott realized that interventions were necessary. They conducted a needs assessment after three months of operation and identified key employee related drivers that could affect change to accomplish the transformation of the hotel. Using a process similar to Job Aid 5-1, the following viable interventions were identified: organizational communication, learning organization, job enlargement (crosstraining), and culture (trust and motivation).

1. Organizational Communication

An all-associate meeting was held to address communication. The theme was "From the Old to the New." Associates were invited to a room set up sparsely with trays of cookies and water served in paper cups. Jack hammering could be heard throughout. After 10 minutes, associates were invited to a quieter room where "Simply the Best" music played in the background as they entered the doors. They found an elegant room where tables had been set up with candles, centerpieces, wine glasses, and cloth napkins in a fancy fold. Managers poured a non-alcoholic sparkling beverage for a toast and then served a special dessert to each associate. A PowerPoint™ presentation depicted renderings of the new lobby and restaurant.

JOB AID 5-1: INTERVENTION SELECTOR

Based on the cause analysis and performance gap analysis, select interventions that would improve the situation. Place a check next to each intervention to be considered. Prioritize the possibilities and circle three interventions to begin the performance improvement effort.

Performance Support

- Instructional
- ❏ Learning Organization
- ❏ Action Learning
- ❏ Self-directed Learning
- ❏ Training
- ❏ Knowledge Capture and Management
- ❏ Education
- ❏ Interactive Technologies
    - ❏ Distance Learning
    - ❏ Telecommunications
    - ❏ Satellite Technology
- Noninstructional
- ❏ Job Aids
- ❏ Electronic Performance Support Systems
- ❏ Documentation (Job Specification) and Standards

Job Analysis/Work Design

- ❏ Job Specifications
- ❏ Job Rotation
- ❏ Job Enlargement
- ❏ Work Methods
- ❏ Quality (Control, Management, and Assurance)
- ❏ Continuous Improvement
- ❏ Value Engineering
- ❏ Interface Design
- ❏ Ergonomics
- ❏ Preventive Maintenance
- ❏ Safety Engineering

Personal Development

- ❏ Mentoring and Coaching
- ❏ Career Development
- ❏ Career Assessment
- ❏ Feedback

Human Resource Development

- ❏ Selection and Staffing
- ❏ Compensation and Benefits
- ❏ Literacy
- ❏ Retirement Planning
- ❏ Health and Wellness
- ❏ Motivation (Incentives and Rewards)
- ❏ Performance Appraisals
- ❏ Assessment Centers and Competency Testing
- ❏ Succession Planning and Career Pathing
- ❏ Leadership and Executive Development
- ❏ Management and Supervisory Development

Organizational Communication

- ❏ Networking and Collaboration
- ❏ Information Systems
- ❏ Suggestion and Grievance Systems
- ❏ Conflict Resolution

Organizational Design and Development

- ❏ Strategic Planning and Management
- ❏ Environmental Scanning
- ❏ Globalization
- ❏ Benchmarking
- ❏ Reengineering, Realignment, Restructuring
- ❏ Teambuilding Strategies
- ❏ Problem Solving and Decision Making
- ❏ Culture and Diversity
- ❏ Ethics
- ❏ Spirituality in the Workplace

Financial Systems

- ❏ Financial Forecasting
- ❏ Capital Investment and Spending
- ❏ Cash Flow Analysis
- ❏ Mergers, Acquisitions, and Joint Ventures

Other Interventions

Developed by Darlene Van Tiem, James Moseley, and Joan Dessinger.
Sources: Gayeski, Hutchinson and Stein, Stolovitch and Keeps, Hale, and Whiteside and Langdon.

Human Resources announced that the facilities were changing, but that the focus on associates was changing as well. Because communication was a major concern, the hotel was organizing an associate council on which all departments would be represented. This would be done by application, and candidates would be interviewed by a panel to choose final members. This council would identify problems, recommend resolutions, and present them to the executive committee when consensus was reached. The council would establish ground rules and participate in teambuilding training.

Corporate headquarters implemented a daily loyalty bulletin in all full-service brands. The HR department published the bulletin, rotating which of the 20 basics it highlighted. If everyone practiced these basics, management believed that the guests would remain loyal to the Marriott brand. This bulletin is also used to communicate the groups staying in the hotel, VIP guests, associate birthdays, and service anniversaries. Each department conducts daily pre-shift meetings to discuss the items listed in the bulletin. HR oversees these communication tools as well as a centrally located bulletin board to inform associates and encourage them to participate in the all-associates meetings and to apply for the associate council.

2. Learning Organization

The analysis of the needs assessment clearly indicated that associates were interested in learning. In responding to the statement "I am committed to learning," 92 percent either agreed or mostly agreed. On all training questions, more than 50 percent agreed that they needed some form of training, and more than 50 percent disagreed that "people in organizations are only motivated by rewards such as pay and bonuses." The majority of the write-in responses showed that associates wanted additional training in computers for both their job and their personal growth.

Marriott is committed to training. The Detroit Marriott Renaissance Center is looking to create a training manager position with the goal of offering ongoing classes. This would not only be for job-related training, but for learning important to individuals as well. Marriott also wanted to tap into the expertise of associates to teach such classes as diet and nutrition, financial planning, using the Internet, etc. For instance, an HR manager who was getting a master's in Adult Instruction and Performance Technology and taking a class in Creating the Learning Organization was also facilitating the associate council.

3. Job Enlargement (Crosstraining)

A manager with a background in training and social work was hired at the Courtyard across the street to facilitate the Welfare-to-Work program sponsored by Marriott. The Detroit Marriott Renaissance Center may also utilize this program at no cost as long as it can guarantee a required number of hours for on-the-job training. When hotel occupancy levels become consistent, this program will be a valuable tool to attract and retain staff.

The banquet department keeps a minimal number of regular staff, using union extras when large parties are booked into the hotel. Many associates from other departments are trained to pick up banquets after their shift is over or on their days off. Many new associates would be interested in doing this if regular ongoing training was made available.

Marriott has a certification process whereby associates are identified as trainers of new hires and then receive special training to prepare them to properly train all new hires. Ideally each department has at least one certified person; the Detroit Marriott Renaissance Center will also implement this process.

The PBX department (hotel operators) is undergoing the heaviest redesign. They are now called "At Your Service." Associates in this department will be the first to receive official certification. Typing assessments have been completed, and PBX associates are using the "Typing With Mavis" CD-ROM to improve their speed and accuracy. A criterion has been established, and typing tests will again be administered. Next the associates will undergo computer training, which will eventually become available to all associates in the learning organization. Other associates can then become certified, which would ensure that they are next in line for promotion when an opening occurs. Once this is successfully established in PBX department, the training process will be expanded to include all departments.

4. Culture (Trust and Motivation)

An associate opinion survey (AOS) will be conducted. It is anticipated that it will take time and effort to achieve satisfactory scores. This survey will help identify some key issues and the necessary steps to improve on-the-job culture.

The Detroit Marriott Renaissance Center hired a nurse manager (shared with the Courtyard across the street) to address the health and safety concerns of associates. This will save some associates from having to go to the clinic for certain complaints, and the hotel can be proactive in reducing worker's compensation issues. Associates are excited about this addition because it displays a caring attitude.

JOB AID 6-2: CHANGE MANAGEMENT EVALUATOR

Directions: Answer the following questions.

Has the change expectation been thoroughly defined?
How will this change disrupt the current organization?
Does the organization have a history of implementation problems? If so, describe.
Are the sponsors sufficiently committed to the project? If not, would education or replacing sponsors help?
Does synergy exist between sponsors, employees, and change targets? If not, what can be done to improve relationships?
What resistance is anticipated?
Is planned change consistent with organizational culture?
Are employees sufficiently ready for change effort? Would training help?
Are the right people, right communication plan, and right measurements in place?

JOB AID 7–1: TYPES OF EVALUATION: ADDRESSING THE ISSUES

Directions: The columns are labeled with the four types of evaluation; the rows are labeled to describe issues that must be addressed when planning an effective evaluation. Fill in each cell before the evaluation begins and revise as the evaluation progresses.

	Formative	Summative	Confirmative	Meta
Primary Audience				
Primary Emphasis in Data Collection				
Primary Role of PT Practitioner				
Primary Role of Evaluator				
Typical Methodology				
Frequency of Data Collection				
Primary Reporting Mechanisms				
Reporting Frequency				
Emphasis in Reporting				
Requirements for Credibility				

TABLE 8-1

EVALUATION SYSTEMS AT MARRIOTT INTERNATIONAL – DETROIT

	Type of Evaluation and Who Measured	What to Measure	How to Measure
FORMATIVE	Associates who are Council members	• Team-building training • First Council Meeting • Ongoing meetings of Council as revisions are made	Questionnaire Questionnaire Questionnaire
	Associates represented by Council members	• Department reaction	Questionnaire
	Council members	• Attendance, ideas generated, consensus	Data collected by facilitator
	Council members and Exec. Committee	• First presentation to Executive Committee	Questionnaire to Council and to Executive Committee
SUMMATIVE	Council Members	• Team building training • Council meeting after revisions have stabilized	Pre/post tests Post test
	Executive Committee	• First presentation to Executive Committee	Pre/post test to evaluate awareness of problem
	All hourly associates and management staff	• Associate Opinion Survey (AOS)	Once initial scores are established, retest at 6 months
	Managers affected by implementation	• Awareness of problem prior to implementing recommendations	Questionnaire
	Department where problem is occurring	• Collect data as pertains to each recommendation of Council	Depending on problem, cost impact, safety etc.
	All hourly associates and management staff	• Needs Assessment to compare with original	Questionnaire
	Guests of hotel	• Guest Satisfaction Scores (GSS)	Calculated quarterly by third party
	Associates and management	• Grievance Activity	Compare by month the frequency of grievances
	Associates and management	• Worker's Compensation cases	Compare by month the number of cases
CONFIRMATIVE	Guests of hotel Hourly associates	• AOS • GSS • Open up council membership annually	Administered annually Compare quarterly Compare number of applicants from year to year
	Hourly and management staff	• Needs Assessment	Yearly questionnaire

Intervention Implementation and Change

The intervention selected for focus is organizational communication, including implementation of an associate council. Because an extensive evaluation system was needed, all other interventions were developed later. Certain considerations in managing the change process (based on Job Aid 6-2) were identified:

- When the format of the council was announced, associates from all departments were invited to apply.
- HR presented the overall direction of the council to the general manager for buy-in.
- Interruption in work was anticipated and accommodated to allow associates time off to attend meetings during their scheduled shift as necessary.
- Applications were designed and criteria established for selection purposes. (Note: The original application was too extensive—associates felt the criteria were discouraging. After this feedback, they were redesigned, approved by a couple of associates, and the deadline was extended.)
- The need to overcome the belief of associates that this had been attempted before was identified and addressed.
- The need for training in teambuilding, brainstorming, and consensus was identified and the training designed.
- Choosing a facilitator committed to the success of the council was completed.
- The first meeting was committed to developing a shared vision and ground rules in how to conduct an effective meeting.

Evaluation

Currently, Marriott International – Detroit's evaluation system is in the process of design and development (see Job Aid 7-1). Marriott has outlined their intentions (see Table 8-1) for the type of evaluation, who will measure, what will be measured, and how they will measure. Fully defining an evaluation system, with consensus and approval of the director of human resources, will ensure that their goals are being met. Having reliable data will validate the success (or failure) of the council and other evaluation strategies and allow Detroit to become a benchmark in the Marriott Corporation.

Future

The future looks very bright. Having the global headquarters for one of the world's largest companies in the heart of the downtown area has contributed to the revitalization of the city. As a result of General Motor's investment, many of the offices in the Renaissance Center had to relocate to other parts of the city, which created a demand for office space. In addition, with the recent approval for three casinos to be built in the Detroit area, the city is now becoming a destination for travelers. In the next five years, Detroit is expected to undergo a complete revitalization.

Case study written by Cathy Tishhouse, Marriott International, Detroit, Michigan, October 21, 1999. Used with permission.

Conclusion—Skills and Knowledge Needed by PT Practitioners

Let your aim be the good of all.
—Bhagavad Gita (6th century B.C.)[1]

At this point, it is clear that acquiring confidence as a PT practitioner requires extensive skills and knowledge and substantial experience. Competence comes from gradually getting involved in projects that utilize the various aspects of the HPT Model. PT practitioners must be willing to learn to integrate numerous intervention techniques into a comprehensive strategy. It is then necessary to anticipate resistance to the changes brought about by implementing the interventions.

PT Competencies

Change and performance improvement happen because people work together in new ways. People commit to resolving problems. PT practitioners need empathy to influence others. They need vision and the ability to persuade people to develop new methods or to improve processes. PT practitioners need to motivate, encourage, provide feedback, and recognize successes. Due to human unpredictability, designing change activities requires faith that persistence and good sense will eventually lead to positive results. Rothwell has identified and described the major skills needed to be an effective PT practitioner.[2]

Business Savvy

(including negotiating/contracting, buy-in/advocacy, and consulting)

Education, nonprofit human services, and government organizations are adopting many businesslike practices, making business savvy a universal competency. PT practitioners need negotiating and contracting skills that depend on give-and-take discussions resulting in a common understanding of expectations. These skills require an ability to monitor agreements and the progress of vendors. Buy in and advocacy skills mean establishing support and confidence among employees and the ability to speak on behalf of others. Consulting skills involve the ability to establish new processes and procedures by working closely with many employees.

Organizational and Group Dynamics Knowledge

PT practitioners must grasp the larger perspective that takes into account the political, economic, and social systems within an organization. It is essential that PT practitioners also understand how groups function and how people are influenced by others.[3]

Systems Thinking and Problemsolving Capacity

Performance technology activities are interrelated and affect each other. PT practitioners need to identify the parts of a system—inputs, throughputs, and outputs—to understand how each one impacts the others. It is necessary for PT practitioners to realize how individuals, organizational culture, and processes influence outcomes.

Successful performance improvement efforts depend on accurately defined gaps and well-designed interventions.

Word to the Wise

It is not unusual for traditional managers to seek simple explanations for workplace problems. Unfortunately, all too often, it is believed that people are not capable or willing to work hard and reach ambitious productivity targets. Employees are then described as "not cutting the mustard." Workers appear to lack motivation, work ethic, or the ability to do their job correctly.[4]

PT assumes a more positive approach by recognizing that the changes required in the knowledge era are not fleeting. Customers expect quality, value, and service. "Whereas people were formerly concerned with issues involving price and quantity, now they are primarily concerned with value and service. The new reality is not transitory. It is a systemic and permanent change in society and the business world."[5]

Performance technology systematically describes the change process. Following the HPT Model helps organizations adapt effectively to the knowledge society.

CITATIONS

Chapter One: Fundamentals of Performance Technology: A Guide to Improving People, Process, and Performance

[1] Elsenheimer, October 1998
[2] Edvinsson and Malone, 1997; Stewart, 1997

Chapter Two: The Human Performance Technology Model

What Is the HPT Model?

[1] Slywotzky and Morrison, 1997, p. 79
[2] Deterline and Rosenberg, 1992, p. 3
[3] Deterline and Rosenberg, 1992, pp. 3–4
[4] Zuboff, 1988, p. 395
[5] Gilbert, 1978, p. 87
[6] Rummler, 1977
[7] Rummler and Brache, 1995, p. 169
[8] Mager, 1962, p. 63
[9] Harless, 1975
[10] Brethower and Smalley, 1998, p. 3

Is PT Just a Passing Bandwagon?

[1] Drucker, 1993; Carnevale, 1983
[2] AON Consulting, 1997; ASTD, 1998 and 1997a
[3] Millman, 1997
[4] Fisher and Fisher, 1998
[5] Millman, 1997
[6] AON Consulting, 1997
[7] AON Consulting, 1997, p. 7
[8] AON Consulting, 1997
[9] AON Consulting, 1997
[10] AON Consulting, 1997
[11] AON Consulting, 1997
[12] Bassi, Cheney, and Van Buren, 1997
[13] Robinson and Robinson, 1995
[14] Brethower and Smalley, 1998
[15] Bassi, Cheney, and Van Buren, 1997

[16] Dolence and Norris, 1995
[17] Bassi, Cheney, and Van Buren, 1997
[18] Bassi, Cheney, and Van Buren, 1997
[19] Danford, 1996
[20] Brethower, 1997a; Brethower, 2000, p. 474
[21] AON, 1997; ASTD, 1998 and 1997a
[22] ASTD, 1997b
[23] OCED, 1997
[24] Veum, 1996
[25] Health Alliance Plan, 1998, pp. 42–44
[26] Health Alliance Plan, 1998, pp. 8–11
[27] Fitz-enz, 1991
[28] Health Alliance Plan, 1998, p. 30

Chapter Three: Performance Analysis

Introduction to Performance Analysis

[1] Rummler and Brache, 1995, pp. 17-19
[2] Rummler and Brache, 1995, p. 17
[3] Rummler and Brache, 1995, p. 19
[4] Rosenberg, 1996b, p. 6
[5] Rossett, 1998, pp. 33-34
[6] Rossett, 1998
[7] Swanson, 1994, p. ix
[8] Rossett, 1989 and Swanson, 1994
[9] Rossett, 1989, p. 63
[10] Swanson, 1994, p. 190
[11] Swanson, 1994, p. 123
[12] Swanson, 1994, p. 151
[13] Swanson 1994, p. 151
[14] Swanson, 1994, p. 187
[15] Swanson, 1994, p. ix

Organizational Analysis

[1] Rosenberg, 1996, p. 6
[2] Grant and Moseley, 1999, p. 15
[3] Nickols, 1996
[4] Nickols, 1996
[5] Rossett, 1998, pp. 33–34
[6] Tosti and Jackson, 1997, p. 23
[7] Grant and Moseley, 1999, p. 16

[8] Brethower, 1997b, p. 21
[9] Zemke, 1987
[10] Rummler and Brache, 1995
[11] Nickols, 1996

Environmental Analysis

[1] Seels and Richey 1994, p. 89
[2] Rothwell, 1996b, p. 33
[3] Rothwell, 1996b, p. 100
[4] Rothwell, 1996b, p. 100
[5] Rothwell, 1996b, p. 102
[6] Rummler and Brache, 1995, pp. 68–69
[7] Rossett, 1999

Gap Analysis

[1] Geiss, 1986, p. 6
[2] Kaufman 1993, p. 4
[3] Rothwell, 1996b, p. 132
[4] Rothwell, 1996b, pp. 129–132
[5] Rothwell, 1996b, pp. 131–32
[6] Rothwell, 1996b
[7] Zemke, 1987
[8] Rothwell, 1996b, p. 136
[9] Bunning, 1979
[10] Mager and Pipe, 1984, p. 13
[11] Hurt, 1994, pp. 57–59
[12] Ford, 1975, pp. 35–39
[13] Zemke, 1987, pp. 141–151

Chapter Four: Cause Analysis

Introduction to Cause Analysis

[1] Gilbert, T. F., 1978, pp. 88–92
[2] Rothwell, 1996a, p. 79
[3] Rosenberg, 1996a
[4] Rosenberg, 1996a, p. 380
[5] Robinson and Robinson, 1989, p. 109
[6] Rothwell, 1996b, pp. 153–154
[7] Rossett, 1999, pp. 32–37
[8] Rossett, 1999, p. 38
[9] Robinson and Robinson, 1989
[10] Gilbert, 1978, p. 88

[11] Rothwell, 1996b, pp. 13–14
[12] Dean, 1997, pp. 45–51
[13] Rothwell, 1996b, p. 33
[14] Rossett, 1992
[15] Rothwell, 1996b
[16] Rothwell, 1996b
[17] Rothwell, 1996b, p. 170
[18] Rothwell, 1996b, pp. 170–171
[19] Rothwell, 1996b, pp. 171–173
[20] Rothwell, 1996b, p. 173

Lack of Environmental Support

[1] Gilbert, 1978
[2] Rossett,1999, p. 38
[3] Rothwell, 1996b, p. 161
[4] Rothwell, 1996b, pp. 159–160
[5] Gilbert, 1996, p. 88
[6] Dean, 1997, p. 55
[7] Rossett, 1999
[8] Rossett, 1999, p. 43
[9] Gilbert, 1982, September; 1982, October
[10] Dean, 1997, pp. 57–58

Lack of Repertory of Behavior

[1] Gilbert, 1996, p. 31
[2] Mager and Pipe, 1984, p. 31
[3] Mager and Pipe, 1984, p. 31
[4] Rosenberg, 1996a, p. 375
[5] Hutchison and Stein, 1997, p. 29
[6] Mager and Pipe, 1984, p. 17
[7] Rossett, 1999, p. 45
[8] Rummler, 1983, pp. 75–76
[9] Dean, 1997b, p. 48
[10] Rothwell, 1996b, p. 170
[11] Gilbert, 1996
[12] Dean, 1997b, p. 51
[13] Gilbert, 1996, pp. 87-88
[14] Dean, 1998b, pp. 48-49
[15] Dean, 1998b, p. 51
[16] Gilbert, 1982, pp. 21–30
[17] Gilbert, 1982, pp. 85–89

Chapter Five: Intervention Selection and Design

Introduction to Intervention Selection and Design

[1] Rothwell, 1996a, p. 79
[2] Hale Associates, 1993, p. 1
[3] Carr, 1994, p. 65
[4] Spitzer, 1992
[5] Spitzer, 1999, pp. 173–180.

Classification of Interventions

[1] Hutchison, Carleton, and Stein, 1991
[2] Hale Associates, 1993
[3] Hale Associates, 1993
[4] Carr, 1994
[5] Carr, 1994
[6] Whiteside, 1991
[7] Rosenberg, 1996a
[8] Wile, 1996
[9] Whiteside and Langdon, 1997
[10] Hutchison and Stein, 1997
[11] Gayeski, 1998
[12] Spitzer, 1992
[13] Spitzer, 1992
[14] DLS Group, 1996
[15] Performance International, 1995
[16] Langdon, Whiteside, and McKenna, 1999

Performance Support Interventions: Instructional

[1] ASTD, 1995, p. 1
[2] Gerber, 1991, pp. 23–29
[3] DeVito, 1996
[4] DeVito, 1996
[5] Marquardt, 1999, pp. 23–25
[6] Piskurich, 1996
[7] McArdle, 1989
[8] Froiland, 1994
[9] Piskurich, 1996
[10] Meister, 1998
[11] Piskurich, 1996

Performance Support Interventions: Noninstructional

[1] Rothwell, 1996b
[2] Rossett and Gautier-Downes, 1991
[3] Gery, 1989, pp. 51–71
[4] Rossett, 1996
[5] Dean, 1998, p. 11

Job Analysis/Work Design Interventions

[1] Miner, 1992
[2] Shingleton, 1992
[3] Anthony, Perrewe, and Kacmar, 1996
[4] Campion, Cheraskin, and Stevens, 1994

[5] Hellriegel, Slocum, and Woodman, 1995, p. 533
[6] Harris, 1997
[7] Rothwell, 1996
[8] Rue and Byars, 1989, p. 225
[9] Sherman, Bohlander, and Snell, 1996
[10] Ostrom, 1993
[11] Ostom, 1993, pp. 8–10
[12] Neal, 1994 and Wokutch, 1994
[13] *Partners in Quality*, 1995
[14] Hayes, 1996

Personal Development Interventions

[1] Rothwell, Sullivan, and McLean, 1995
[2] *Career Assessment Instruments*, 1998, December 16 [Online] (http:/careers.Valencia.cc.fl.us/instruments.htm)
[3] Bandura, 1991
[4] Locke and Latham, 1990
[5] Deterline, 1992

Human Resource Development Interventions

[1] McLagan, 1989, p. 53
[2] McLagan, 1989, p. 77
[3] Leibler and Parkman, 1992
[4] Sherman, Bohlander, and Snell, 1996
[5] Sherman, Bohlander, and Snell, 1996
[6] Kemmerer and Thiagarajan, 1992
[7] Nelson, 1994
[8] Nelson, 1994
[9] Wilson, 1995
[10] Gohrman, 1989
[11] Morrissey, 1983
[12] Kirkpatrick, 1986
[13] Anthony, Perrewe, and Kacmar, 1996
[14] Leibler and Parkman, 1992, p. 270
[15] *HR Measurements*, 1993
[16] Harris, 1997
[17] Walker, 1976
[18] Conover, 1996
[19] Wertz, 1996
[20] Brewington, 1996, p. 638
[21] Prokopenko and Bittel, 1981
[22] Bittel and Newstrom, 1996, p. 676
[23] Riekse and Holstege, 1996
[24] Harris and DeSimone, 1998, pp. 323–330

Organizational Design and Development Interventions

[1] Powers, 1992
[2] Saccucci, Lord, and Pagano, 1998
[3] Shepperd, 1998
[4] Saccucci, Lord, and Pagano, 1998
[5] Saccucci, Lord, and Pagano, 1998
[6] Dormant, 1992; and Thiagarajan, 1992
[7] Bud Erickson Associates, Inc., 1998
[8] Lineberry and Carleton, 1992
[9] Kotter and Heskett, 1992
[10] Gordon, 1995
[11] Westgaard, 1992
[12] Rutte, 1998
[13] Rutte and Monette, 1991

Organizational Communication Interventions

[1] Gibson and Hodgetts, 1986, p. 8
[2] Gibson and Hodgetts, 1986, p. 228
[3] *Personnel Journal*, 1988, p. 11
[4] Hellriegel, Slocum, and Woodman, 1995
[5] Hellriegel, Slocum, and Woodman, 1995

Financial Systems Interventions

[1] Render and Stair, 1997
[2] Cox, Stout, and Vetter, 1995
[3] Cleverley, 1997
[4] Rakich, Longest, and Darr, 1992

Chapter Six: Intervention Implementation and Change

Introduction to Intervention Implementation and Change

[1] Rothwell, 1996a
[2] Rothwell, 1996a

Change Management

[1] Dormant, 1997, p. 432
[2] Felkins, Chakiris, and Chakiris, 1993, p. 26
[3] Dalziel and Schoonover, 1988, pp. 108–127
[4] Grossman, 1974, pp.123–127
[5] Kirkpatrick, 1985
[6] Jellison, 1993

[7] Blanchard, Zigarmi, and Zigarmi, 1994, pp. 1–31
[8] Chang, 1992, p. 6
[9] Weisbord, 1987
[10] Deming, 1982
[11] Juran, 1992
[12] Ishikawa, 1968
[13] Greer, 1996
[14] Frame, 1987, p. 5
[15] Knutson and Bitz, 1991, p. 16
[16] Thomsett, 1990
[17] Spendolini, 1992, p. 9
[18] Cheney, 1998, p. 2
[19] Cheney, 1996, pp. 3–4
[20] Spendolini, 1991, pp. 151–172; Cheney, 1996, p. 12
[21] Kaufman, Thiagarajan, and MacGillis, 1997, p. 14

Process Consulting

[1] Bellman, 1990, p. 66
[2] Bennis and Mische, 1995, p.13
[3] Lippitt and Lippitt, 1978, pp. 9–26
[4] Lippitt and Lippitt, 1978, p. 23
[5] Robinson and Robinson, 1995; Block, 1981

Employee Development

[1] Carnegie Commission on Higher Education, 1973
[2] OCED, 1997
[3] OCED, 1998, p. 3
[4] Stata, 1989, p. 64
[5] Swotzky and Morrison, 1997
[6] Veum, 1996; Bassi, Cheney, and Van Buren, 1997; OCED, 1997
[7] Watkins and Marsick, 1993
[8] Zuboff, 1988, p. 395
[9] Galagan, 1991, p. 37
[10] Galagan, 1991, p. 38
[11] Dixon, 1992
[12] Kline and Saunders, 1993
[13] Younger, 1993, p. 1
[14] Meister, 1998
[15] Hain, 1998
[16] Eurich, 1985, p. 2
[17] Bowsher, 1989, p. 44
[18] Noe, 1998
[19] Noe, 1998
[20] McDermott, 1990b, p. 47
[21] Doyle, Mansfield, and Van Tiem, 1995
[22] McDermott, 1990a

Communication, Networking, and Alliance Building

[1] Hamilton, 1997, p. 11
[2] Hamilton, 1997, p.13
[3] Birdwhistell, 1970, p. 158
[4] Gregorc, 1985; Butler, 1984
[5] Hamilton, 1997, pp. 120–121
[6] Hamilton, 1997, p. 19
[7] Hamilton, 1997, p. 20
[8] Anderson, 1992, p. 23
[9] Hamilton, 1997, pp. 409–410
[10] Kotter, 1982, p. 67
[11] Simon and Sexton, 1994, pp. 14–17

Chapter Seven: Evaluation

Introduction to Evaluation

[1] Kaufman, Keller, and Watkins, 1997, p. 9
[2] Geis and Smith, 1992, p. 130
[3] Geis and Smith, 1992, p. 131
[4] Geis and Smith, 1992, p. 134
[5] Hanson and Siegel, 1995, p. 27
[6] Hellebrandt and Russell, 1993
[7] Madaus, Scriven, and Stufflebeam, 1987, p. 16
[8] Geis and Smith, 1992, p. 133
[9] Rosenberg, 1996b, p. 9
[10] Geis and Smith, 1992, p. 133
[11] Geis and Smith, 1992, pp. 133–134
[12] Geis and Smith, 1992, p. 134
[13] Geis and Smith, 1992, p. 138
[14] Geis and Smith, 1992, p. 139
[15] Rothwell, 1996b, p. 283
[16] Herman, Scriven, and Stufflebeam, 1987

Evaluation Models Show the Way

[1] Geis and Smith, 1992
[2] Moseley and Dessinger, 1998
[3] Moseley and Dessinger, 1998, p. 247
[4] Dessinger, 1997
[5] Kirkpatrick, 1994
[6] Carliner, 1997
[7] Kaufman, Keller, and Watkins, 1996, p. 9
[8] Brinkerhoff, 1987, p. 26

Formative Evaluation

[1] Thiagarajan, 1991, p. 22
[2] Thiagarajan, 1991, p. 22

[3] Tessmer, 1994, p. 16
[4] Geis and Smith, 1992, p. 134
[5] Thiagarajan, 1991, p. 24
[6] Moseley and Dessinger, 1998, p. 245
[7] Thiagarajan, 1991, p. 26
[8] Dick and King, 1994, p. 8
[9] Thiagarajan, 1991, p. 31
[10] Tessmer, 1994
[11] Tessmer, 1994, p. 5
[12] Tessmer, 1994; Thiagarajan, 1991
[13] Tessmer, 1994
[14] Thiagarajan, 1991, p. 30
[15] Tessmer, 1994, p. 6

Summative Evaluation

[1] Seels and Richey, 1994, p. 58
[2] Geis, 1986, p. 11
[3] Seels and Richey, 1994, p. 57
[4] Smith and Brandenburg, 1991, p. 35
[5] Rosenberg, 1996b, p. 9
[6] Smith and Brandenburg, 1991, p. 35
[7] Smith and Brandenburg, 1991
[8] Herman, Morris, and Fitz-Gibbons, 1987

[9] Kirkpatrick, 1994
[10] Smith and Brandenburg, 1991, pp. 36–42

Confirmative Evaluation

[1] Moseley and Solomon, 1997, p. 12
[2] Misanchuk, 1978, p. 15
[3] Seels and Richey, 1994, p. 59
[4] Hellebrandt and Russell, 1993, p. 22
[5] Moseley and Solomon, 1997, p. 12
[6] Brinkerhoff, 1987
[7] Hanson and Siegel, 1995, pp. 27–28
[8] Hanson and Siegel 1995
[9] Thiagarajan, 1991, p. 34
[10] Moseley and Solomon, 1997, pp. 12–13
[11] Thiagarajan, 1991, p. 31
[12] Hellebrandt and Russell, 1993, p. 24
[13] Hanson and Siegel, 1995, p. 28
[14] Hellebrandt and Russell, 1993
[15] Thiagarajan 1991, p. 31
[16] Moseley and Solomon, p. 13
[17] Moseley and Solomon, 1997, p. 13

[18] Hellebrandt and Russell, 1993, p. 27
[19] Hanson and Siegel, 1995

Meta Evaluation

[1] Posavac and Carey, 1989, p. 284
[2] Posavac and Carey, 1989, p. 282
[3] Posavac and Carey, 1989, p. 282; Madaus, Scriven, and Stufflebeam, 1987, p. 16
[4] Posavac and Carey, 1989, pp. 282–284
[5] Stufflebeam, 1978
[6] Kirkpatrick, 1994

Chapter Eight: Performance Technology in the Workplace—A Word to the Wise

[1] Frank, 1999, p. 68
[2] Rothwell, 1996a
[3] McLagan, 1989c
[4] Fournies, 1988, pp. 87-88
[5] Bennis and Mische, 1995, p. 23

GLOSSARY OF TERMS

Acquisitions – Acquisitions are when one firm acquires more than 50 percent of the voting stock of another firm and, therefore, controls that firm.

Action Learning – Action learning builds opportunities for learning around real problems brought to the workplace by employees.

Assessment Centers – Assessment centers use standardized selection criteria to identify potential managers and executives.

Benchmarking – Benchmarking is a systematic process of comparing an organization to other organizations for the purposes of identifying better work methods and determining best practices. It helps define customer requirements, establish effective goals and objectives, develop true measures of productivity, and identify education and training needs for current and future employees.

Benefits – Benefits are the noncash portion of a compensation program intended to improve the quality of work life for an organization's people.

Capital – Capital is the source of long-term financing (investments and loans) available to an organization.

Capital Investment – Capital investment refers to commitment or use of money and other assets made in anticipation of greater financial returns in the future and usually involves large sums of money.

Capital Spending – Capital spending involves risk-return trade-off analysis to secure long-term financial advantage.

Career Assessment – Career assessment uses the results of standardized interest and personal style inventories to help a person develop career goals, strategies, and a personal educational plan.

Career Development – Career development attempts to match the person's abilities and interests to the person's position and career plan with a focus on professional growth and enhancement of the work role.

Career Pathing – Career pathing is a planned sequence of job assignments, usually involving growth-oriented tasks and experiences, that people assume in preparation for future job opportunities.

Cash-flow Analysis – Cash-flow analysis provides information about inflows and outflows of cash during a specific period of time.

Cause Analysis – Cause analysis is the process of determining the root cause of past, present, and future performance gaps.

Change Management – Change management involves problem solving in a concerted effort to adapt to changing organizational needs.

Coaching – Coaching is the help that managers give to people by evaluating and guiding on-the-job performance.

Collaboration – Collaboration is cooperating by working together for an improved quality of work life.

Compensation– Compensation is pay for work and performance, plus disability income; deferred income; health, accident, and liability protection; loss-of-job income; and continuation of spouse's income when there is a loss due to a person's relocation.

Competency Testing – Competency testing examines current job knowledge and skills that will be needed for present and future performance.

Confirmative Evaluation – Confirmative evaluation provides information about the continuing competence and effectiveness of people to explain and confirm the value of the performance intervention over time.

Conflict Resolution – Conflict resolution involves alleviating a disagreement between two or more people who share differing views.

Continuous Improvement – Continuous improvement is the ongoing, organizationwide framework in which stakeholders (employees, customers, and suppliers) are committed to and involved in monitoring and evaluating all aspects of a company's activities (inputs, processes, and outputs) to continuously improve them.

Culture – Culture is a shared system of values, beliefs, and behaviors that characterize a group or organization.

Decisionmaking – Decisionmaking means making choices, ideally based on structured problem solving.

Diversity – Diversity represents differences in gender, ethnicity, economic background, age, abilities, religion, culture, and sexual orientation. Many of these differences are known as "protected categories" in U.S. equal employment legislation and executive orders.

Documentation (Job Specifications) and Standards – Documentation and standards codify information to preserve it and to make it accessible in the workplace through descriptions, policies, procedures, guidelines, reference manuals, quality assurance plans, bylaws, articles of incorporation, partnership agreements, contracts, and letters of intent.

Education – Education improves work performance in a focused direction beyond the person's current job. The emphasis is on broad knowledge, understanding, comprehension, analysis, synthesis, and evaluation, and on transferring knowledge to future objectives, as well as to immediate job-related applications.

Electronic Performance Support System (EPSS) – Electronic performance support system is a highly sophisticated job aid, offering access to large databases of information designed to coach users via a user-friendly question-and-answer format.

Employee Development – Employee development involves acquiring knowledge, skills, and attitudes through employer-sponsored learning opportunities including (1) traditional instruction, (2) newer technology-oriented formats, (3) informally by means of mentoring, coaching, or on-the-job training, and (4) by team participation.

Employee Selection – Employee selection is choosing the right person for the job.

Environmental Analysis – Environmental analysis is the process used to identify and prioritize the realities that support actual performance: organizational environment, work environment, work, and workers.

Environmental Scanning – Environmental scanning is a strategic planning technique for monitoring trends in the external environment of an organization. It involves observing, assessing, and documenting economic situations, political events, technical developments, and structural changes in similar organizations or industries.

Environmental Support Analysis – Environment support analysis seeks to define causes related to

information (data, information, and feedback), instrumentation (environmental support, resources, and tools), and motivation (consequences, incentives, and rewards).

Ergonomics – Ergonomics is the study of how physical laws of nature affect the worker and the work environment.

Ethics – Ethics defines good and bad standards of conduct. Standards are cultural and vary among countries, companies, incidents, and situations.

Executive Development – Executive development enhances senior management's ability to create vision, values, and business strategies.

Feedback – Information provided by others designed to help people adjust their behavior, continue successful performance, or establish goals.

Financial Forecasting – Financial forecasting is anticipating the future needs for money.

Financial Systems – Financial systems refer to the monetary affairs (income, reserves, expenses, and dividends) of an organization. They are usually summarized in an annual report that includes an income statement, balance sheet, cash-flow statement, and explanatory notes.

Formative Evaluation – Formative evaluation is conducted to improve the design of performance interventions. It begins during the performance and cause analyses, continues through the selection and design of interventions and, if a pilot stage is included in the intervention plan, may extend into early intervention implementation.

Gap Analysis – Gap analysis describes the difference between current results and consequences and desired results and consequences. It is the last step in the performance analysis process.

Globalization – Globalization is a means of achieving higher productivity and efficiency by identifying and focusing on an organization's efforts and resources in major world markets.

Grievance Systems – Grievance systems provide mechanisms for people or unions to dispute a decision that is believed to be in violation of a contract.

Health and Wellness – Health and wellness programs are designed to enhance employee morale and productivity and to reduce absentee rates and health care costs.

Human Resource Development Interventions – Human resource development interventions are essential to human resource management and are shaped by the organization's mission and its ability to maintain market share.

Incentives – Incentives link pay with a standard for performance, such as salary, differential pay, allowances, time off with pay, deferred income, loss-of-job coverage, or desirable working conditions, training, adequate equipment, and materials.

Information Systems – Information systems refer to the varied manual and automated communication mechanisms within an organization that store, process, disseminate, and sometimes even analyze information for those who need it.

Interactive Technologies – Interactive technologies provide a channel for interaction between learner and instructor.

Interface Design – Interface design is the linkage between machinery and processes to ensure smooth and easy, user-friendly functionality.

Interventions – Interventions are conscious, deliberate, planned activities designed to improve human performance and to solve workplace problems. They can be targeted at organizations, departments, work groups, and individuals.

Job Aids (also known as Job Performance Aids) – Job aids are used during the performance of a task to facilitate efficiency and effectiveness.

Job Analysis – Job analysis is collecting information about duties, tasks, and responsibilities for specific jobs.

Job Enlargement – Job enlargement expands the number and variety of different tasks performed by the employee so that the job is more interesting.

Job Rotation – Job rotation involves moving people from job to job within an organization for designated periods ranging from an hour or two to longer, depending upon the goal.

Job Specifications – Job specifications describe the qualifications people must have to do the job, namely, educational background, experience, knowledge, skills, abilities, etc.

Joint Ventures – Joint ventures are cooperative efforts by competitors for a specific purpose, such as to develop a new technology, enter new markets, generate new products, or meet customer demands quickly.

Knowledge Capture and Management – Knowledge capture and management is the process of acquiring, storing, and managing access to bodies of data, information, knowledge, and organizational experience that assist people in performing their jobs with focus and precision.

Leadership Development – Leadership development prepares employees to cope with changes through prioritizing, overcoming obstacles and assumptions, and initiating action.

Learning Organization – Learning organization involves the belief and practice that individuals and teams can learn continuously and cooperatively to foster an organization's competitive advantage. Hallmarks of learning organizations are sharing the organizational vision, individual excellence, team learning, creating common mental models, and use of systematic thinking to enhance the use of knowledge as a competitive strategy.

Literacy – Literacy is a person's knowledge, especially the ability to compute, read, and write, which enables the person to function in society.

Management Development – Management development prepares managers to support the organization's mission, strategy, goals, and objectives.

Mentoring – Mentoring is the offering of experience, emotional support, and guidance by an experienced person to a less experienced person.

Mergers – Mergers are when two separate companies combine operations and become one company.

Meta Evaluation – Meta evaluation is the process of evaluating formative, summative, and confirmative evaluation by literally zooming in on the evaluation processes, products, and outcomes to take a closer look at what happened and why.

Motivation – Motivation encourages behavior.

Networking – Networking means establishing patterns of interpersonal communication interactions to facilitate the dissemination and collection of information.

Organizational Analysis – Organizational analysis examines the organizational mission, vision, values, goals, and strategies.

Organizational Communication – Organizational communication refers to the transfer of information and knowledge among employees, suppliers, and customers for the purpose of accomplishing efficiency and effectiveness.

Organizational Design and Development – Organizational design and development is a process that examines the operation and management of an organization and facilitates needed changes in an effort to improve efficiency and competitiveness.

Performance Analysis – Performance analysis identifies and clarifies the problem or performance gap by focusing on three areas: desired performance state, actual performance state, and the gap between desired and actual performance. It looks at three levels—organization, process, and job/performer—and considers three variables—goals, design, and management.

Performance Appraisal – Performance appraisal is a structured process used by managers to provide feedback on an individual's performance to encourage improvement. Performance appraisals also provide information for salary decisions and promotions.

Performance Support Interventions – Performance support interventions affect the workplace, the work, and the worker through planned change efforts based on knowledge and skills transfer. They can be instructional (when the problem is a result of a lack of knowledge or skill) or non-instructional (to improve individual, group, or team performance; improve processes, products, and services; and guide business plans, deliverables, results, and success measures).

Performance Technology (PT) – Performance technology analyzes performance problems and their underlying causes and describes exemplary performance and success indicators. PT identifies or designs interventions, implements them, and evaluates the results. It is the systematic process of linking business goals and strategies with the workforce responsible for achieving the goals.

Personal Development Interventions – Personal development interventions are planned work-related activities that are the employee's personal responsibility.

Individuals assume ownership of their success or failure.

Preventive Maintenance – Preventive maintenance is a proactive approach to equipment maintenance involving such tactics as oiling and greasing gears and machinery; checking parts for flaws, cracks, chips, and replacing them; calibrating precision tools to make certain they are functioning and within established specifications; aligning vehicles and their parts to make them stable; labeling parts and fixtures; cleaning tar and grease from workstations; and a host of similar tasks.

Problemsolving – The structured process of defining the problem, gathering data about the situation and causes, considering alternatives, making choices, implementing choices, evaluating the new situation, and making adjustments based on evaluation.

Process Consulting – Process consulting results in revising processes and often involves reengineering or restructuring an entire organization.

Quality (Control, Management, and Assurance) – Quality control, management, and assurance is the system used to ensure products and services meet customer needs and exceed customer expectations. It is also known as total quality management (TQM).

Realignment – Realignment is getting the organization focused on its core competencies.

Reengineering – Reengineering is the radical redesign of processes for the purpose of extensive (not gradual) performance improvements.

Repertory of Behavior Analysis – Repertory of behavior analysis examines people-oriented factors that cause performance problems related to information (skills and knowledge), instrumentation (individual capacity), and motivation (motivation and expectation).

Restructuring – Restructuring reorganizes the units or departments, usually resulting in a new organizational chart, new responsibilities, and may involve new reporting relationships.

Retirement Planning – Retirement planning helps people prepare for financial and legal issues, housing arrangements, and health and wellness following their working years.

Rewards – Rewards are designed to change and reinforce behavior through techniques such as public recognition, gift certificates, or vacations and travel based on meeting sales quotas.

Safety Engineering – Safety engineering is continually evaluating materials and processes to eliminate or minimize hazards and conditions that cause accidents.

Self-directed Learning – Self-directed learning is training designed to master material independently and at the person's own pace.

Spirituality – Spirituality means striving for the common good for individual employees and the common good for the organization.

Spirituality in the Workplace – Spirituality in the workplace encourages organizations to recognize employee needs and to promote employee involvement.

Strategic Management – Strategic management supports the organizational vision through the day-to-day implementation of the strategic plan.

Strategic Planning – Strategic planning is the process by which an organization envisions its future and develops the necessary goals and procedures to achieve that vision.

Succession Planning – Succession planning is a systematic identification and development of employees, usually for senior management positions.

Suggestion Systems – Suggestion systems allow employees to increase workplace responsibility and accountability by offering ideas for improving products or services. Rewards are often provided for suggestions that bring positive results to the organization.

Summative Evaluation – Summative evaluation considers the usability and adequacy of the intervention and gathers information about the results that will be useful to senior decision makers in the organization.

Supervisory Development – Supervisory development enables front-line managers to establish work standards and enforce organizational policies and procedures primarily for nonmanagement employees.

Team – A team is a group of people working together as a cohesive unit to accomplish a common goal.

Teambuilding – Teambuilding is based on the philosophy that people work better and more creatively in groups than they do alone. It focuses on trust, collaboration, openness, and other interpersonal factors.

Training – Training refers to instructional experiences provided by employers for employees.

Value Engineering – Value engineering is determining the amount of value added to the organization by each job and unit or to the product by each component.

Work Design – Work design is a blueprint of job tasks structured to improve organizational efficiency and employee satisfaction.

Work Methods – Work methods are documents by which an organization defines what work needs to be done and how it will be accomplished.

REFERENCES

Anderson, K. (1992). *To Meet or Not To Meet: How to Plan and Conduct Effective Meetings.* Shawnee Mission, KS: National Press Publications (division of Rockhurst College).

Anthony, W. R., Perrewe, P. L., & Kacmar, K. M. (1996). *Strategic Human Resource Management.* Fort Worth, TX: The Dryden Press.

AON Consulting. (1997). *The 1997 Survey of Human Resource Trends.* Detroit, MI: AON Consulting, Human Resource Consulting Group.

Assessment centers help target employees for management selection. (1993). *HR Measurements* (pp. 1–2).

ASTD. (1998). *The 1998 National HRD Executive Survey: Leadership Development.* Alexandria, VA: American Society for Training and Development. [Online] http://www.astd.org/virtual_community/research/nhrd_executive_survey_98ld.html

ASTD. (1997a). *The 1997 National HRD Executive Survey: Trends in HRD.* Alexandria, VA: American Society for Training and Development. [Online] http://www.astd.org/virtual_community/research/nhrd_executive_survey_97tr.htm

ASTD. (1997b). *The 1997 National HRD Executive Survey: Measurement and Evaluation.* Alexandria, VA: American Society for Training and Development. [Online] http://www.astd.org/virtual_community/research/nhrd_executive_survey_97me.htm

Bandura, A. (1991). Social cognitive theory of self-regulation. *Organizational Behavior and Human Decision, 50,* 248–287.

Bassi, L. J., Cheney, S., & Van Buren, M. (1997). Training industry trends 1997. *Training and Development, 51* (11).

Bellman, G. M. (1990). *The Consultant's Calling: Bringing Who You Are to What You Do.* San Francisco: Jossey Bass Publishers.

Bennis, W. G. (1969). Changing organizations. In W. G. Bennis, K. D. Benne, & R. Chin (Eds.), *The Planning of Change* (2nd ed., pp. 568–579). New York: Holt, Rinehart, and Winston.

Bennis, W. G. & Mische, M. (1995). *The 21st Century: Reinventing Through Reengineering.* San Diego, CA: Pfeiffer.

Birdwhistell, R. J. (1970). *Kinesics and Context: Essays on Body Motion Communication.* Quoted in Hamilton, C., with Parker, C. (1997). *Communicating for Results: A Guide for Business and the Professions* (p. 158). Belmont, CA: International Thomson Publishing.

Bittel, L. R. & Newstrom, J. W. (1996). Supervisor development. In R. L. Craig (Ed.), *The ASTD Training & Development Handbook: A Guide to Human Resource Development* (4th ed., pp. 651–658). New York: McGraw-Hill.

Blanchard, K., Zigarmi, D., & Zigarmi, P. (1994). The organization. *Situational Leadership II Participant's Workbook.* Escondido, CA: Blanchard Training and Development.

Block, P. (1981). *Flawless Consulting: A Guide to Getting Your Expertise Used.* Austin, TX: Learning Concepts.

Bowsher, J. E. (1989). *Educating America: Lessons Learned in the Nation's Corporations.* New York: John Wiley & Sons.

Brainstorming: A problem solving activity. (1974). In J. W. Pfeiffer & J. E. Jones (Eds.), *A Handbook of Structured Experiences for Human Relations Training* (Volume 3, p. 14). LaJolla, CA: University Associates.

Brethower, D. M. (1997a). The future is bright for human performance technology. *Performance Improvement, 36* (9) 8–11.

Brethower, D. M. (1997b). Rapid analysis: Matching solutions to changing situations. *Performance Improvement, 36* (10) 16–21.

Brethower, D. (2000). The relevance of performance improvement to instructional design. In Piskurich, E.M., Beckeshi, P., and Hall, B. (Eds.), *The ASTD Handbook of Training Design and Delivery.* New York: McGraw-Hill.

Brethower, D. & Smalley, K. (1998). *Performance-Based Instruction: Linking Training to Business Results.* San Francisco: Jossey-Bass/Pfeiffer.

Brewington, E. L. (1996). Management development. In R. L. Craig (Ed.), *The ASTD Training & Development Handbook: A Guide to Human Resource Development* (4th ed., pp. 637–650). New York: McGraw-Hill.

References

Brinkerhoff, R. O. (1987). *Achieving Results from Training: How to Evaluate Human Resource Development to Strengthen Programs and Increase Impact.* San Francisco: Jossey-Bass Publishers.

Bud Erikson Associates, Inc. (1998). Problem solving and decision making. [Online] http://www.buderickson.com/psdm.html.

Bunning, R. L. (1979). The Delphi technique: A projection tool for serious inquiry. In J. W. Pfeiffer & J. E. Jones (Eds.), *The 1979 Annual Handbook for Group Facilitators* (pp. 174–181). LaJolla, CA: University Associates.

Butler, K. A. (1984). *Learning and Teaching Style: In Theory and Practice.* Maynard, MA: Gabriel Systems.

Campion, M., Cheraskin, L., & Stevens, M. (1994). Career-related antecedents and outcomes of job rotation. *Academy of Management Journal, 37* (15) 18–42.

Carliner, S. (1997, April). Adapting the Kirkpatrick model to technical communication products and services. *Performance and Instruction, 36* (4) 14–19.

Carnegie Commission on Higher Education. (1973). *Towards a Learning Society: Alternative Channels to Life, Work, and Service* (p. 43). New York: McGraw-Hill.

Carnevale, A. P. (1983). *Human Capital: A High Yield Corporate Investment.* Washington, DC: American Society for Training and Development.

Career Assessment Instruments. (1998, December 16). [Online] http://careers.Valencia.cc.fl.us/instrument.htm

Carr, C. (1994). Invasion of the performance interventions. *Training, 31* (4) 65–66.

Chang, R. Y. (1992, October). *Continuous Process Improvement: Info-line Issue 9210.* Alexandria, VA: American Society for Training and Development.

Cheney, S. (1996, January). *Benchmarking: Info-Line Issue 9801.* Alexandria, VA: American Society for Training and Development.

Cleverley, W. O. (1997). *Essentials of Health Care Finance* (4th ed.). Gaithersburg, MD: Aspen Publishers.

Conover, D. K. (1996). Leadership development. In R. L. Craig (Ed.), *The ASTD Training & Development Handbook: A Guide to Human Resource Development* (4th ed., pp. 581–600). New York: McGraw-Hill.

Cox, R. A. K., Stout, R. G., & Vetter, D. E. (1995). *Financial Administration & Control.* Cambridge, MA: Blackwell Publishers.

Dalziel, M. M. & Schoonover, S. C. (1988). *Changing Ways: A Practical Tool for Implementing Change within Organizations.* New York: AMACOM.

Danford, J. R. (1996, October 15). Interview as part of research project to study trends in Adult Instruction and Performance Technology. Warren, MI: General Motors University.

Dean, P. J. (1998b). Performance improvement interventions: Methods for organizational learning. In P. J. Dean and D. E. Ripley (Eds.), *Performance Improvement Interventions: Performance Technologies in the Workplace* (Volume 3, pp. 2–19). Washington, DC: International Society for Performance Improvement.

Dean, P. J. (1997). Engineering performance improvement with or without training. In P. J. Dean and D. E. Ripley (Eds.), *Performance Improvement Pathfinders: Models for Organizational Learning Systems* (pp. 45–64). Washington, DC: International Society for Performance Improvement.

Dean, P. J. (1998a). Performance improvement interventions: Methods for organizational learning. In P. J. Dean and D. E. Ripley (Eds.), *Performance Improvement Interventions: Instructional Design and Training,* (Volume 2, pp. 2–19). Washington, DC: International Society for Performance Improvement.

Deming, W. E. (1982). *Out of the Crises.* Cambridge, MA: Center for Advanced Engineering Study.

Dessinger, J. C. (1997, August). *A 360° Approach to Evaluating Distance Learning. Conference Presentation and Proceedings: 14th Annual Conference on Technology and Education.* Oslo, Norway.

Deterline, W. A. (1992). Feedback systems. In H. S. Stolovitch & E. J. Keeps (Eds.), *Handbook of Human Performance Technology.* San Francisco: Jossey-Bass/NSPI.

Deterline, W. A. & Rosenberg, M. J. (1992). *Workplace Productivity: Performance Technology Success Stories.* Washington, DC: International Society for Performance Improvement.

De Vito, J. D. (1996). The learning organization. In R. L. Craig (Ed.), *The ASTD Training & Development Handbook: A Guide to Human Resource Development* (4th ed., pp. 77–103). New York: McGraw-Hill.

Dick, W. & King, D. (1994). Formative evaluation in the performance context. *Performance and Instruction, 33* (9) 8.

Dixon, N. M. (1992, Spring). Organizational learning: A

ture with implications for HRD professionals. *Human Resource Development Quarterly*, 3 (1) p. 213.

DLS Group (1996). *Performance improvement interventions – Defined*. Workshop presented at the International Society for Performance Improvement Conference.

Dolence, M. G. & Norris, D. M. (1995). *Transforming Higher Education: A Vision for Learning in the 21st Century*. Ann Arbor, MI: Society for College and University Planning.

Dormant, D. (1992). Implementing human performance technology in organizations. In H. S. Stolovitch & E. J. Keeps (Eds.), *Handbook of Human Performance Technology* (pp. 167–186). San Francisco: Jossey-Bass/NSPI.

Dormant, D. (1997). Planning change: Past, present, future. In Kaufman, Thiagarajan, & MacGillis (Eds.), *The Guidebook for Performance Improvement: Working with Individuals and Organizations* (pp. 429–452). San Francisco: Pfeiffer.

Doyle, T., Mansfield, A., & Van Tiem, D. (1995). Technical and skills training suppliers. In L. Kelly (Ed.), *The Technical and Skills Training Handbook*. New York: McGraw-Hill.

Drucker, P. F. (1993). *Managing for the Future*. Oxford, UK: Butterworth Heinemann.

Edvinsson, L. & Malone, M. S. (1997). *Intellectual Capital: Realizing Your Company's True Value by Finding Its Hidden Brainpower*. New York: HarperBusiness.

Elsenheimer, J. (1998). Job aids in the technology age. *Performance Improvement*, 37 (9).

Esque, T. J. & Patterson, P. A. (Eds.). (1998). *Case Studies in Performance Improvement*. Amherst, MA: HRD Press/ISPI.

Eurich, N.P. (1985). *Corporate Classrooms: The Learning Business*. Princeton, NJ: The Carnegie Foundation for the Advancement of Teaching.

Felkins, P. K., Charkiris, B. J., & Chakiris, K.N. (1993). *Change Management: A Model for Effective Organizational Performance*. White Plains, NY: Quality Resources.

Fisher, K. & Fisher, M. D. (1998). *The Distributed Mind: Achieving High Performance Through the Collective Intelligence of Knowledge Work Teams*. New York: AMACOM.

Fitz-enz, J. (1991). *Human Value Management: The Value-Adding Human Resource Management Strategy for the 1990's*. San Francisco: Jossey-Bass Publishers.

Ford, D. I. (1975). Nominal group technique: An applied group problem solving activity. In J. W. Pfeiffer & J. E. Jones (Eds.), *The 1975 Annual Handbook for Group Facilitators* (pp. 35–39). LaJolla, CA: University Associates.

Fournies, F. F. (1988). *Why Employees Don't Do What They're Supposed to Do and What to Do About It*. New York: Liberty Hall Press.

Frame, J. D. (1987). *Managing Projects in Organizations: How to Make the Best Use of Time, Techniques, and People*. San Francisco: Jossey-Bass.

Frank, L. R. (Ed.) (1999). *Random House Webster's Quotationary*. New York: Random House.

Froiland, P. (1994, January). Action learning: Taming real problems in real time. *Training*, 31 27–34.

Gallagan, P. (1991). The learning organization made plain: An interview with Peter Senge. *Training and Development Journal*, 28 (10) 37–44.

Gatewood, R. D. & Feild, H. S. (1994). *Human Resource Selection* (3rd ed.). Fort Worth, TX: The Dryden Press.

Gayeski, D. M. (1998). Changing roles and professional challenges for human performance technology. In P. J. Dean & D. E. Ripley (Eds.), *Performance Technologies in the Workplace* (Volume 3). Washington, DC: International Society for Performance Improvement.

Geis, G. L. (1986). Human performance technology: An overview. In *Introduction to Performance Technology* (pp. 1–20). Washington, DC: National Society for Performance and Instruction.

Geis, G. L., & Smith, M. E. (1992). The function of evaluation. In H. S. Stolovitch & E. J. Keeps (Eds.), *Handbook of Human Performance Technology* (pp. 130–150). San Francisco: Jossey-Bass/NSPI.

Gerber, B. (1991). HELP! The rise of performance support systems. *Training*, 28 (12) 23–29.

Gery, G. J. (1989). Training versus performance support: Inadequate training is now insufficient. *Performance Improvement Quarterly*, 2 (3) 51–71.

Gibson, J. W. & Hodgetts, R. M. (1986). *Organizational Communication: A Managerial Perspective*. Orlando, FL: Academic Press, Inc.

Gilbert, T. F. (1978). *Human Competence: Engineering Worthy Performance*. New York: McGraw-Hill.

Gilbert, T. F. (1996). *Human Competence: Engineering Worthy Performance* (Tribute ed.). Amherst, MA: HRD Press/ISPI.

Gilbert, T. F. (1982). A question of performance, part I: The PROBE model. *Training and Development Journal*, 43 (9) 21–30.

Gilbert, T. F. (1982). A question of performance, part II: Applying the PROBE model. *Training and Development Journal*, 43 (10) p. 214.

Gohrman, A. M. (1989). *Designing Performance Appraisal Systems.* San Francisco: Jossey-Bass Publishers.

Gordon, J. (1995, May). Different from what? Diversity as a performance issue, *Training, 32* (5), 25–33.

Grant, D. A. & Moseley, J. L. (1999, July). Conducting a customer-focused performance analysis, *Performance Improvement, 38 (7) 15-21.*

Greer, M. (1996). *The Project Manager's Partner: A Step-by-Step Guide to Project Management.* Amherst, MA: HRD Press/ISPI.

Gregorc, A. F. (1985). *Inside Styles: Beyond the Basics.* Maynard, MA: Gabriel Systems.

Grossman, L. (1974). *The Change Agent.* New York: AMACOM.

Hain, T. (1998, October 15). *Presentation on GM University to the Michigan Chapter of the International Society for Performance Improvement.* Dearborn, MI.

Hale Associates. (1993). *If Training Isn't Everything, What Are the Other Interventions?* Workshop presented to the National Society for Performance and Instruction.

Hamilton, C., with Parker, C. (1997). *Communicating for Results: A Guide for Business and the Professions.* Belmont, CA: International Thomson Publishing.

Hanson, R. A. & Siegel, D. F. (1995). *The Three Phases of Evaluation: Formative, Summative, and Confirmative.* Updated draft of paper originally presented at the 1991 meeting of the American Educational Research Association, April 3–7, Chicago.

Harless, J. (1975, March). Analyzing organizational performance, *Performance Technology – Training Magazine's Best*

Thinking On: The Art and Science of Performance Technology (reprinted articles published in 1989). Minneapolis, MN: Lakewood Publishers.

Harris, D. M. & De Simone, R. L. (1998). *Human Resource Development* (2nd ed.). Fort Worth, TX: The Dryden Press.

Harris, M. (1997*). Human Resource Management: A Practical Approach.* Forth Worth, TX: The Dryden Press.

Hayes, B. J. (1996). Training in quality. In R. L. Craig (Ed.), *The ASTD Training & Development Handbook: A Guide to Human Resource Development* (4th ed., pp. 725–746). New York: McGraw-Hill.

Health Alliance Plan. (1998). *1997 Human Resources Effectiveness Report.* Detroit, MI.

Hellebrandt, J. & Russell, J. D. (1993, July). Confirmative evaluation of instructional materials and learners. *Performance and Instruction, 32* (6) 22–27.

Hellriegel, D., Slocum, J. W., Jr. & Woodman, R. W. (1995). *Organizational Behavior* (7th ed.). St. Paul, MN: West Publishing.

Herman, J. L., Morris, L. L., & Fitz-gibbons, C. T. (1987). *Evaluator's Handbook.* Newbury Park, CA: Sage Publications.

Hodge, B. J., Anthony, W. P., & Gales, L. M. (1996). *Organization Theory: A Strategic Approach* (5th ed.). Upper Saddle River, NY: Prentice Hall.

Hunt, M. (1998). *DreamMakers: Putting Vision and Values to Work.* Palo Alto, CA: Davies-Black Publishing.

Hurt, F. (1994) Better brainstorming. *Training and Development 48* (11) 57-59.

Hutchison, C. S., Carleton, J. R. & Stein, F. S. (1991). *Potential*

Strategies and Tactics for Performance Improvement [Unpublished working document]. Conifer, CO: Conifer Consulting.

Hutchison, C. S. & Stein, F. S. (1997). A whole new world of interventions: The PT practitioner as integrating generalist. *Performance Improvement,* 36 (10) 28–35.

Ishikawa, K. (1982). *Guide to Quality Control.* Toyko, Japan: Asian Productivity Organization.

Jellison, J. M. (1993). *Overcoming Resistance: A Practical Guide to Producing Change in the Workplace.* New York: Simon & Schuster.

Juran, J. M. (1992). *Juran on Quality by Design: The New Steps for Planning Quality into Goods and Services.* New York: The Free Press.

Kaufman, R., Keller, J., & Watkins, R. (1996). What works and what doesn't: Evaluation beyond Kirkpatrick. *Performance and Instruction,* 35 (2) 8–12.

Kaufman, R., Rojas, A., & Mayer, H. (1993). *Needs Assessment: A User's Guide.* Englewood Cliffs, NJ: Educational Technology Publications.

Kaufman, R., Thiagarajan, S., & MacGillis, P. (1997). *The Guidebook for Performance Improvement: Working with Individuals and Organizations.* San Francisco: Jossey-Bass Publishers.

Kemmerer, F. N. & Thiagarajan, S. (1992). Incentive systems. In H. S. Stolovitch and E. J. Keeps (Eds.), *Handbook of Human Performance Technology* (pp. 312–330). San Francisco: Jossey-Bass/NSPI.

Kerr, S. (1995). On the folly of rewarding A, while hoping for B. *Academy of Management Executives,* 9 (1) 7–16.

Kirkpatrick, D. L. (1985). *How to Manage Change Effectively:*

Approaches, Methods, and Case Examples. San Francisco: Jossey-Bass Publishers.

Kirkpatrick, D. L. (1986). Performance appraisals: Your questions answered. *Training and Development Journal, 40* 68–71.

Kirkpatrick, D. L. (1994). *Evaluating Training Programs: The Four Levels.* San Francisco: Berrett-Koehler Publishers.

Kline, P. & Saunders, B. (1993). *Ten Steps to a Learning Organization.* Arlington, VA: Great Ocean Publishers.

Kotter, J. P. (1982). *The General Managers.* New York: The Free Press.

Kotter, J. P. & Heskett, J. L. (1992*). Corporate Culture and Performance.* New York: The Free Press.

Kuntson, J. & Bitz, I. (1991). *Project Management: How to Plan and Manage Successful Projects.* New York: AMACOM.

Langdon, D. (1995). *The New Language of Work.* Amherst, MA: HRD Press.

Langdon, D. G., Whiteside, K. S., & McKenna, M. M. (Eds.) (1999). *Intervention Resource Guide: 50 Performance Improvement Tools.* San Francisco: Jossey-Bass/Pfeiffer.

Leibler, S. N. & Parkman, A. W. (1992). Personnel selection. In H. S. Stolovitch and E. J. Keeps (Eds.), *Handbook of Human Performance Technology* (pp. 259–276). San Francisco: Jossey-Bass/NSPI.

Lineberry, C. & Carleton, J. (1992). Culture change. In H. S. Stolovitch & E. J. Keeps (Eds.), *Handbook of Human Performance Technology* (pp. 233–245). San Francisco: Jossey-Bass/NSPI.

Lippitt, G. & Lippitt, R. (1978). *The Consulting Process in Action.* San Diego, CA: University Associates.

Locke, E. & Latham, G. (1990). *A Theory of Goal Setting and Task Performance.* Upper Saddle, NY: Prentice Hall.

Madaus, G. F., Scriven, M. S., & Stufflebeam, D. L. (1987). *Evaluation Models: Viewpoints on Educational and Human Services Evaluation.* Boston: Kluwer-Nijhoff Publishing.

Mager, R. F. (1975). *Preparing Instructional Objectives* (rev. 2nd ed., originally *Preparing Objectives for Programmed Instruction,* 1962). Belmont, CA: Pitman Learning.

Mager, R. F. & Pipe, P. (1984). *Analyzing Performance Problems or You Really Oughta Wanna* (2nd ed.). Belmont, CA: David S. Lake Publishers.

Marquardt, M. J. (1999). *Action Learning in Action: Transforming Problems and People for World-Class Organizational Learning.* Palo Alto, CA: Davies-Black Publishing.

Martinez, M. (1995). Equality efforts sharpen bank's edge. *HR Magazine,* (1) 38–43.

McArdle, G. E .H. (1989). What is training? *Performance and Instruction, 28* (6) 34–35.

McDermott, B. (1990a). Improving the status of training: Partnership with corporate leaders is training's key to status. *Managing the Training Function: Trends, Politics, and Planning Issues* (Book I). Minneapolis, MN: Lakewood Books.

McDermott, B. (1990b). Deciding who to train. *Managing the Training Function: The Nuts 'N Bolts of Personal, People, and Resources* (Book II). Minneapolis, MN: Lakewood Books.

McLagan, P. A. (1989a). *Models for HRD Practice: The Models* (Volume 3, p. 77). Alexandria, VA: American Society for Training and Development.

McLagan, P. A. (1989b). Models for HRD practice. *Training and Development Journal, 43 41,* 53.

Meister, J. C. (1998*). Corporate Universities: Lesson in Building a World-Class Work Force* (Rev. and updated ed.). New York: McGraw-Hill/ASTD.

Mieder, W. (1986). *The Prentice-Hall Encyclopedia of World Proverbs.* New York: MJF Books.

Millman, H. (1997, November 17). The pros and perils of mining intellectual capital. *InfoWorld, 19* (46) 128.

Miner, J. B. (1992). *Industrial-Organizational Psychology.* New York: McGraw-Hill.

Misanchuk, E. R. (1978). Descriptors of evaluation in instructional development: Beyond the formative-summative distinction. *Journal of Instructional Development, 2* (1) 15–19.

Morrissey, G. L. (1983). *Performance Appraisals for Business and Industry.* Reading, MA: Addison-Wesley.

Moseley, J. L. & Dessinger, J. C. (1998). The Dessinger-Moseley evaluation model: A comprehensive approach to training evaluation. In P. J. Dean, & D. E. Ripley (Eds.), *Performance Improvement Interventions: Instructional Design and Training* (Volume 2, pp. 233–260). Washington, DC: International Society for Performance Improvement.

Moseley, J. L., & Solomon, D. L. (1997). Confirmative evaluation: A new paradigm for continuous improvement. *Performance Improvement, 36* (5) 12–16.

Neal, W. (1994). Workplace health, safety: A continuing process. *HR News,* 18.

Nelson, B. (1994). *1001 Ways to Reward Employees.* New York: Workman Publishing.

Nickols, F. (1996). *The Mission/Vision Thing.* [Online] trdev-l@psuvm.psu.edu

References

Noe, R.A. (1998). *Employee Training and Development.* Boston, MA: Irwin/McGraw-Hill.

OECD. (1997). *Literacy Skills for the Knowledge Society.* Paris, France: Organisation for Economic Co-operation and Development.

OECD. (1998). *Human Capital Investment: An International Comparison.* Paris, France: Organisation for Economic Co-operation and Development.

Ostrom, L.T. (1993). *Creating the Ergonomically Sound Workplace.* San Francisco, CA: Jossey Bass/NSPI.

Partners in Quality (1995). *Continuous Quality Improvement Symposium.* Detroit, MI: Ford Motor Company and Wayne State University.

Performance International. (1995). *Performance Technology Definitions.* ASTD International Conference.

Performance Support 1995 Survey 2 Results. Alexandria, VA: American Society for Training and Development, p. 1.

Piskurich, G.M. (1996). Self-directed learning. In R. L. Craig (Ed.), *The ASTD Training & Development Handbook: A Guide to Human Resource Development* (4th ed., pp. 453–472). New York: McGraw-Hill.

Posavac, E. J., & Carey, R. G. (1989). *Program Evaluation: Methods and Case Studies* (3rd ed.). Englewood Cliffs, NJ: Prentice-Hall.

Powers, B. (1992). Strategic alignment. In H. S. Stolovitch & E. J. Keeps (Eds.), *Handbook of Human Performance Technology* (pp. 247–258). San Francisco: Jossey-Bass/NSPI.

Prokopenko, J. & Bittel, L. R. (1981). A modular course format for supervisory development. *Training and Development Journal, 35* 14–22.

Rakich, J. S., Longest, B. B., Jr. & Darr, K. (1982). *Managing Health Services Organizations* (3rd ed.). Baltimore, MD: Health Professions Press.

Render, B. & Stair, R. M., Jr. (1997). *Quantitative Analysis for Management* (6th ed.). Upper Saddle River, NJ: Prentice-Hall.

Riekse, R. J. & Holstege, H. (1996). *Growing Older in America.* New York: McGraw-Hill.

Robinson, D. G. & Robinson, J. C. (1995). *Performance Consulting: Moving Beyond Training.* San Francisco: Berrett-Koehler Publishers.

Robinson, D. G. & Robinson, J. C. (1989). *Training for Impact: How to Link Training to Business Needs and Measure the Results.* San Francisco: Jossey Bass.

Rosenberg, M.J. (1996a). Human performance technology. In R. L. Craig (Ed.), *The ASTD Training & Development Handbook: A Guide to Human Resource Development* (4th ed., pp. 370–393). New York: McGraw-Hill.

Rosenberg, M. J. (1996b). Human performance technology: Foundations for human performance improvement. In W. J. Rothwell, *ASTD Models for Human Performance Improvement: Roles, Competencies and Outputs* (pp. 5–10). Alexandria, VA: American Society for Training and Development.

Rossett, A. (1992) Analysis of human performance problems. In H. S. Stolotvitch & E. J. Keeps. (Eds.), *Handbook of Human Performance Technology* (pp. 97–113). San Francisco: Jossey-Bass/NSPI.

Rossett, A. (1999). *First Things Fast: A Handbook for Performance Analysis.* San Francisco, CA: Jossey-Bass/Pfeiffer.

Rossett, A. (1996). Job-aids and electronic performance support systems. In R. L. Craig (Ed.), *The ASTD Training & Development Handbook: A Guide to Human Resource Development* (4th ed., pp. 557–578). New York: McGraw-Hill.

Rossett, A. (1998). *Responding to Customers, Experts, Personnel.* [Online] http://www.jossey bass.com/rossett/respond

Rossett, A. (1989). *Training Needs Assessment.* Englewood Cliffs, NJ: Educational Technology Publications.

Rossett, A. & Gautier-Downes, J. H. (1991). *A Handbook of Job-Aids.* San Diego, CA: Pfeiffer & Company.

Rothwell, W. J. (1996a). *ASTD Models for Human Performance Improvement: Roles, Competencies, and Outputs.* Alexandria, VA: American Society for Training and Development.

Rothwell, W. J. (1996b). *Beyond Training and Development: State-of-the-Art Strategies for Enhancing Human Performance.* New York: AMACOM.

Rothwell, W. J., Sullivan, R. & McLean, G. M. (1995). *Practicing Organization Development: A Guide for Consultants.* San Francisco: Jossey Bass/Pfeiffer.

Rue, L.W. & Byars, L.L. (1989). *Management: Theory and Application* (5th ed.). Homewood, IL: Irwin.

Rummler, G. A. (1983). Training skills isn't enough. *Training, 20* (8), 75–76.

Rummler, G.A. (1977, October). Performance is the purpose. *Performance Technology–Training Magazine's Best Thinking On: The Art and Science of Performance Technology* (reprinted articles published in 1989). Minneapolis, MN: Lakewood Publishers.

Rummler, G. A. & Brache, A. P. (1995). *Improving Performance: How to Manage the White Space on the*

Organization Chart (2nd ed.). San Francisco: Jossey-Bass.

Rutte, M. (1998). *What Some Businesses Are Doing.* [Online] http://www.Martinrutte.com/whatsome.html.

Rutte, M. & Monette, M. (1991). *Bringing Spirit to Work.* [Online] http://www.Martinrutte.com/bringing.html.

Saccucci, B., Lord, B., & Pagano, P. (1998). Environmental scanning, *Greenhall Gateway Project.* [Online] http://www.uri.edu/gateway/scanning.htm.

Seels, B. B., & Richey, R. C. (1994). *Instructional Technology: The Definition and Domains of the Field.* Washington, DC: Association for Educational Communication and Technology.

Senge, P.M. (1990). *The Fifth Discipline: The Art and Practice of the Learning Organization.* New York: Currency/Doubleday.

Shepperd, F.M., Esq. (1998). *What is globalization?* [Online] http://www.quadalgroup.com/globis.htm.

Sherman, A., Bohlander, G., & Snell, S. (1996). *Managing Human Resources.* Cincinnati, OH: South-Western College Publishing.

Shingleton, K. (1992). Job audits as interviews: Define physical requirements. *HRFocus, 69* (7) 11.

Simon, F. L. & Sexton, D. E. (1992). International business: Formulating and implementing a business strategy. In J. J. Hampton (Ed.), *AMA Management Handbook* (3rd ed.). New York: AMACOM.

Slywotsky, A. J. & Morrison, D. J. (1997). *The Profit Zone: How Strategic Business Design Will Lead You to Tomorrow's Profits.* New York: Random House.

Smith, M. E., & Brandenburg, D. C. (1991). Summative evaluation. *Performance Improvement Quarterly, 4* (2) 35–58.

Spendolini, M. J. (1992). *The Benchmarking Book.* New York: AMACOM.

Spitzer, D. R. (1992). The design and development of effective interventions. In H. S. Stolovitch & E. J. Keeps (Eds.), *Handbook of Human Performance Technology* (pp. 114–129). San Francisco: Jossey-Bass/NSPI.

Spitzer, D. R. (1999). The design and development of high-impact interventions. In H. S. Stolovitch & E. J. Keeps (Eds.), *Handbook of Human Performance Technology* (pp. 136–154). San Francisco: Jossey-Bass Pfeiffer/ISPI.

Stata, R. (Spring, 1989). Organizational learning - The key to management innovation. *Sloan Management Review,* (pp. 63–74).

Stewart, T. A. (1997). *Intellectual Capital: The New Wealth of Organizations.* New York: Currency Doubleday.

Stufflebeam, D. (1978). Meta evaluation: An overview. *Evaluation and the Health Professions, 1,* 17–43.

Swanson, R. A. (1994). *Analysis for Improving Performance: Tools for Diagnosing Organizations and Documenting Workplace Expertise.* San Francisco: Berrett-Koehler Publishers.

Tessmer, M. (1994). Formative evaluation alternatives. *Performance Improvement Quarterly, 7* (1) 3–18.

The power of suggestions at Con Ed. (1988). *Personnel Journal,* p. 11.

Thiagarajan, S. (1991). Formative evaluation in performance technology. *Performance Improvement Quarterly, 4* (2) 22–34.

Thiagarajan, S. (1992). Small-group activities. In H. S. Stolovitch & E. J. Keeps (Eds.), *Handbook of Human Performance Technology* (p. 420). San Francisco: Jossey-Bass/NSPI.

Thomsett, M. C. (1990). *The Little Black Book of Project Management.* New York: AMACOM.

Tichy, N. M. & Sherman, S. (1993). *Control Your Destiny or Someone Else Will.* New York: Currency/Doubleday.

Tosti, D. & Jackson, S. D. (1997). The organizational scan. *Performance Improvement, 36* (10) 22–26.

Veum, J. R. (1995, November). Training, wages, and the human capital model. *National Longitudinal Surveys Discussion Paper,* Report: NLS 96–31. Washington, DC: U.S. Department of Labor.

Walker, J. W. (1976). Let's get serious about career paths. *Human Resource Management, 15* (3) 2–7.

Watkins, K. E, & Marsick, V. J. (1993). *Sculpting the Learning Organization: Lessons in the Art and Science of Systemic Change.* San Francisco: Jossey-Bass.

Weisbord, M. R. (1987). *Productive Workplaces: Organizing and Managing for Dignity, Meaning, and Community.* San Francisco: Jossey-Bass.

Wertz, L. H. (1996). Executive development. In R. L. Craig (Ed.), *The ASTD Training & Development Handbook: A Guide to Human Resource Development* (4th ed.), pp. 622–636. New York: McGraw-Hill.

Westgaard, O. (1992). Standards and ethics for practitioners. In H. S. Stolovitch & E. J. Keeps (Eds.), *Handbook of Human Performance Technology* (pp. 576–584). San Francisco: Jossey-Bass/NSPI.

Whiteside, K. S. (1991). *Performance Technology Interventions Checklist.* Workshop presented at the National Society for Performance and Instruction.

References

Whiteside, K. S. & Langdon, D. (1997). *Improving the Performance of Organizations.* Workshop presented at the ASTD International Conference and Exposition, Washington, DC.

Wile, D. (1996). Why doers do. *Performance and Instruction, 35* (2) 30–35.

Wilson, T. B. (1995). *Innovative Reward Systems for the Changing Workplace.* New York: McGraw-Hill.

Wokutch, R. (1994). New lessons from Japanese management. *HR Magazine,* 72–78.

Younger, S. M. (1993). *Learning organizations: The trainer's role.* ASTD Info-Line, 9306 (June 1993), 1. Alexandria, VA: American Society for Training and Development.

Zemke, R. & Kramlinger, T. (1987). *Figuring Things Out: A Trainer's Guide to Needs and Task Analysis.* Reading, MA: Addison-Wesley Publishing.

Zuboff, S. (1988). *In the Age of the Smart Machine: The Future of Work and Power.* New York: Basic Books.

INDEX

A

Acquisitions...63, 65, 100, 110–111, 113, 115, 117, 196, 207

Action learning. See Learning

Active listening...146, 173

Alliance building...3, 10, 125, 145, 147

American Productivity and Quality Center (APQC)...129

American Society for Training and Development (ASTD)...15–16, 138, 147

Analysis techniques...24–25, 182

Arbor Consulting Group...18

Assessment...47, 71, 80, 95, 103, 128, 140, 177, 185. See also Career Assessment; Needs Assessment
centers...7, 63, 65, 92–93, 196, 207
questions...85

B

Bandwagon...13, 16–17

Benchmarking...15–16, 20, 63, 65, 99–100, 127–129, 139–142, 182, 196, 207

Benefits...6, 11–12, 15–16, 19, 63, 65, 92–94, 102, 113–117, 126, 128, 143, 148, 176, 193, 195–196, 207

Bennis, Warren...67

Bid lists...140

Birdwhistell, R. L....145

Brache, Alan P....9, 47

Brainstorming...25, 27, 40, 127, 201. See also Group Processes

Brethower, Dale...xi, 8, 9

Brinkerhoff Six-stage Model...161

Buy in...29, 40, 78, 135, 181, 201–202

C

Capital...4, 63, 65, 68, 100, 113–114, 119, 138–139, 196, 207
human...4, 68, 138, 212

Career...7, 17, 55, 66, 92, 140, 149

Career, continued
assessment...63, 65, 86–89, 196, 207
development...3, 14–15, 19, 47, 63, 65–66, 79, 87–89, 92, 196, 207
opportunities...52
Guidance Model (Figure 6-3)...150–151
pathing...63, 65, 92–93, 193, 196, 207

Carr, Clay...63, 66, 67

Case studies...xi, 2, 6, 64, 69, 140, 183, 190–191
Aetna Life and Casualty Co....94
Bugaj, Incorporated...110
California-based Aerospace and Defense Corporation...80
Detroit Medical Center...168
Epilepsy Foundation of Michigan...129
Health Alliance Plan...17
J.C. Penney Company...72
Kaizen...53
Managed Care College of Henry Ford Health System...141
meta evaluation of the case studies in Chapter Seven...183
Michigan Virtual Automotive College...148
Morrison-Knudsen Corporation...102
Muller-Roberts...115
nationwide reading program...179
plastic exterior trim parts...58
Roegan Enterprises...135
statewide professional organization...28
summative evaluation plan...172
The Michael James Clinic...84
The Simonini Company...89
training legend...35
university development center...40
using formative evaluation...168
Visteon Automotive Systems...10

Cash-flow analysis...113–114, 207

Cause analysis...xi, 3, 6, 9–10, 38–39, 45–59, 62–65, 127–128, 142–143, 156–157, 163, 195–196, 207–208

Change...2, 3, 6, 9–10, 17, 19, 40, 53, 62, 64, 67, 79, 85, 87, 93, 99–102,

Change, continued
110–111, 115–116, 123–130, 145, 147, 157–158, 163, 174, 190, 194–195, 201. See also Change Management Interventions
facilitation...14
management...3, 13–14, 66, 125, 130–132, 156–157, 170–171, 198, 207

Coaching...7, 9, 19, 63, 65–66, 87, 89, 138, 140, 168, 184, 196, 207

Codes...67
nonverbal...145
paralanguage...145
verbal...145

Collaboration...7, 63, 65, 101, 107, 126, 136, 147, 196, 207, 210

Communication...7, 10, 16–17, 41–42, 66, 70, 80, 84, 93, 94, 107–112, 125, 130, 132–133, 136, 139, 145–147, 165, 175, 190,195, 197–198, 201, 208–209. See also Organizational Communication
skills...81

Compensation...10, 19, 63, 65, 92, 196, 207. See also Worker's Compensation

Competency...9, 15, 41, 68,–69, 83, 92–95, 138, 149–150, 176–177, 180, 185–186, 190, 195, 202, 210
modeling...14
testing...7, 63, 65, 196, 207

Computer interviewing...165–167

Confidentiality...40, 129, 141

Confirmative evaluation. See Evaluation.

Conflict...52, 80, 110
management...66
resolution...7, 63, 65, 107, 109–110, 196, 207

Conifer Consulting Group...66

Consequences...3, 6, 9, 33, 37–39, 48–49, 51–52, 56, 59, 66, 161, 163, 192, 194, 208

Consultants...11, 18, 110, 125, 133–134, 139, 140–141

Continuous improvement...53, 63, 65, 79, 82–84, 126, 133, 141–142,

161, 164, 168, 176, 179, 196, 207

Continuous Quality Improvement (CQI)...141–142

Corporate
culture...27, 139
libraries...140
policies...178
restructuring...15
strategies...27
training...168
universities...139, 173

Cost-benefit analysis...10, 11, 140, 179

Creativity...14, 102, 106

Crosby, Philip B....84

Crosstraining...195, 197

Culture. See Organizational Culture

Customizing...140

D

Data analysis tools...25

Data collection tools...24, 80

Dealership evaluation plan...172

Decision making...xi, 17, 63, 65, 71, 84, 92, 94, 99, 100–101, 110, 139, 147, 151, 158, 171, 182, 187, 196, 207

Delphi group...40

Deming, W. Edwards...84, 168

Dessinger-Moseley 360° Evaluation Model...161–163

Deterline, William...xi, 6

Detroit...17–18, 110, 133, 141, 190–191, 193, 197, 201

Distance learning. See Interactive Technologies; Learning.

Diversity...101, 105, 109, 146, 191, 207

Dixon, Nancy...139

DLS Group...67

Documentation...24, 28, 48, 53–54, 56–57, 59, 63, 65–66, 68, 71–72, 74, 78, 172, 182, 184–186, 194, 196, 207. See also Job Specifications

Drucker, Peter...67

E

Eastern Michigan University...18, 151

Education...7, 20, 33, 42, 48, 63, 65, 67–68, 70, 73, 77, 87, 94–95, 99–101, 110, 127, 129–130, 132, 138–139, 141–142, 148–149, 151, 180, 182, 196, 198, 201, 207, 208
Training and Development (ET&D)...10–11

Effectiveness report...17–18

Electronic Performance Support Systems (EPPS)...63, 65, 68, 71, 78, 196, 208

Employee
development...3, 8, 125, 138, 139–141, 143–144, 193, 208
selection...57, 71, 88, 92, 208

Enterprise resource planning (ERP)...108

Environmental
analysis...3, 23, 33–35, 57, 208
drivers...23
engineering...66
factors...2, 52
general...6, 35, 42, 58, 167, 190
interventions...66
remediation...102
scanning...63, 65, 99–100, 196, 208
support...8, 33, 51, 54–56, 208
lack of...7

Equal employment opportunity (EEO)...15

Ergonomics...3, 33, 63, 65–66, 79, 82, 190, 196, 208

Ethics...63, 65, 72, 99, 101, 107, 196, 208

Evaluation...xi, 6, 8–11, 67, 70, 74, 83, 88, 102, 127–128, 134,–136, 142, 144, 155–187, 201, 208, 210
confirmative...3, 156–160, 163–164, 176–180, 207, 209
formative...3, 64, 142, 157, 159–160, 163–170, 190, 208
meta...3, 157–160, 181–187, 209
type one...181
type two...181
model(s)...161–163
one-to-one ...164–165
self-...69
small-group...165
summative...3, 156–157, 159–160, 171–175, 210
two-on-one...165–167

Evaluation, continued
type, purpose, timing...157
types of...199, 200

Executive development...63, 65, 92–94, 96, 196, 208

Expectations...3, 6, 14, 22–23, 26–28, 33–34, 36–37, 42, 48, 51, 56–58, 66–67, 93, 126–127, 129, 131, 133, 136–137, 141, 146, 179, 192, 202, 210

Expert review...164–165, 178

Extant data analysis...24. See also Performance Analysis

F

Feedback...3, 6–7, 9–11, 13–14, 19, 28, 33, 37, 42, 47–48, 51–52, 54, 56, 63, 65–66, 70, 87–90, 93, 102, 107, 109, 126–127, 134–135, 138–140, 146–147, 149, 158, 166, 173, 181, 183–185, 190, 192, 195–196, 201, 208, 209

Field-test evaluation...165

Financial forecasting...63, 65, 113, 196, 208

Financial systems...7, 63, 65, 67, 113, 196, 208
interventions. See Interventions.

Flow chart...xi, 50

Focus groups...25, 27, 40, 50, 168, 179, 184. See also Brainstorming; Group Processes

Formative evaluation. See Evaluation

Frame of reference...145

Front-end analysis (FEA)...8, 9, 158, 171

G

Gantt chart...127–128

Gap analysis...10, 23, 27, 34, 36, 38–42, 53–54, 56–57, 59, 65, 127, 143, 194, 196, 208. See also Rothwell's Six Cell Gap Analysis

Geis and Smith Evaluation Model (Figure 7-3)...161

Gilbert's Behavior Engineering Model (Table 2-2)...8–9, 46–47, 51, 56

Gilbert's PROBE Model...54, 59, 194

Gilbert, Thomas...57

Globalization...63, 65, 99, 100, 196, 208

GM University...139

Grant and Moseley Customer-Focused Performance Analysis Model (Figure 3-2)...27

Gregorc's Learning Styles (Table 6-1)...145. See also Styles

Grievance systems...63, 65, 107, 109–110, 196, 208. See also Suggestion Systems

Group processes...24–25, 27, 34, 40, 171, 174. See also Brainstorming; Focus groups

H

Handbook of Human Performance Technology, 2nd Edition...xi

Harless, Joe...8–9, 47, 67

Health and wellness...63, 65, 92, 94, 196, 208, 210

Hierarchy model...66

Histograms...49, 84, 127, 173

Human Performance Technology (HPT) Model...2, 3, 6, 9–11, 22–23, 26, 33, 38, 46, 49, 62, 64, 67–68, 79, 87, 92, 99, 107, 113, 124–125, 156–159, 161, 163–164, 170, 190–191, 201–202

Human Resource(s) (HR)...7, 13, 15, 17–19, 58, 64, 70, 92–93, 95, 139, 190, 197, 201
    development (HRD)...63, 65–67, 69, 79, 92, 208
    management...66, 79, 211
    planning...93

I

Implementation...xi, 3, 6, 8–10, 39, 64, 67, 95, 99, 101, 107, 123–126, 132, 134, 136, 138, 145, 148, 156–157, 159, 162–165, 168, 170–171, 173–174, 177–178, 181, 183–184, 191, 198, 200–201, 208, 210

Incentives...3, 6, 8–9, 47–49, 51–52, 56–58, 63, 65–66, 89, 92, 126, 178, 184, 196, 208

Incentives, continued
    career development opportunities...52
    monetary...52, 92
    nonmonetary...52, 55, 92

Individual capacity...3, 48, 51, 56–57, 59, 210

Information
    systems...17, 19, 63, 65, 72, 107–109, 164, 196, 208
    technology...15, 190

Innovation...14, 38, 139

Instructional System Design (ISD) Model (ADDIE)...161

Instrumentation...8, 47, 51, 56, 177, 208, 210

Integrated work project (IWP)...142

Interactive technologies...63, 65, 67–68, 70, 73, 196, 208. See also Learning, distance; Satellite Technology; Telecommunications

Interface design...63, 65, 79, 82, 84, 196, 208

Internal customers...10–11, 16, 127

International Society for Performance Improvement (ISPI)...x, 6, 147, 156

International Standards Organization (ISO)...89

Internet...16, 35, 70, 149, 197

Interpersonal
    communications...145–146, 209
    factors...101, 210
    relationships...139, 140, 145
    skills...14, 140

Intervention Resource Guide: 50 Performance Improvement Tools...xi

Interventions...2, 4, 6, 8, 10, 13, 15, 47, 62–122, 127, 134–135, 142, 146, 157, 161–162, 169, 190–191, 195–196, 201–202, 208
    change management...3, 13
    classification of...66–67
    financial systems...3, 113–122
    human resource development...3, 92–96, 208
    job analysis...79–86
    list of (Table 5-1)...63
    organizational communication...3, 107–112

Interventions, continued
    organizational design and development...3, 99–106, 209
    performance support ...67–78, 209
    personal development...3, 87–91, 209
    selection and design of...xi, 3, 157, 164, 170, 208
    selector (Job Aid 5-1)...65, 196
    work design...3, 79, 82

Intranet...16, 70, 108, 149, 151

J

Japanese safety approaches (Table 5-8)...83

Job
    aids...xi, 4, 6, 9–11, 20, 57, 59, 63–66, 68, 71, 78, 82, 102, 125, 138, 140–141, 171, 178, 190–191, 194, 196, 209
    analysis...209. See also Interventions, job analysis
    applicant weaknesses...14
    descriptions...71, 79–80, 94, 207
    design...2, 10, 15, 23, 33–34, 37, 82, 83, 192
    enlargement...63, 65, 79, 195–197, 209
    performance aids...71, 74, 78
    rotation...63, 65, 79, 125, 140, 196, 209
    specifications...63, 65, 71, 78, 79, 83, 196, 207, 209

Joint ventures...63, 65, 100, 113, 115, 117, 196, 209

Juran's Quality Trilogy...84

Juran, Joseph M....84

K

Kaufman's Definition of Need (Figure 3-4)...39

Kaufman-Keller-Watkins Model (Figure 7-6)...161, 163

Kirkpatrick's Evaluation Model (Figure 7-5)...161, 163

Kline, Peter...139

Knowledge. See also Task analysis, knowledge.

Knowledge, continued
capture and management...63, 65, 67–68, 70, 73, 77, 196, 209
era...13, 138, 202
management...7

L

Labor relations...19, 64, 109

Leadership...13–14, 16, 20, 63, 65, 87, 92–95, 100–102, 126, 133, 135, 138–139, 141, 190–191, 196, 209
development...93, 96

Learning...6, 17, 41, 58, 68–70, 74, 87–88, 125, 135–136, 138, 140–43, 145, 149, 162–164, 171–173, 193, 195, 197, 207–208. See also Interactive Technologies
action...63, 65, 67–69, 73, 76, 139, 143, 196, 207

Learning, continued
distance...16, 63, 65, 67–68, 70, 73, 78, 139, 148, 196
events...16, 139–140
organizations...16, 63, 65, 67–68, 76, 101, 138–139, 196–197, 209
self-directed...63, 65, 67–69, 73, 76, 196, 210
technologies...16, 70, 149, 151

Literacy...63, 65, 92, 94, 138, 196, 209

Local area networks (LANs)...108

M

Mager, Robert...8–9, 47, 67

Management...2, 9–10, 13–17, 23–24, 30, 34, 47, 49–51, 53, 59, 63, 65–67, 69, 70, 72, 77, 79, 82, 84, 92–96, 99–101, 105, 110–111, 113–116, 125–127, 129–130, 134–135, 138–139, 141, 143, 147, 168, 171, 185, 191, 193–197, 200, 208– 210. See also Performance Management; Total Quality Management (TQM)
development...209
process...23, 127
project...127–128
strategic...210

Meetings...2, 11, 28, 40, 70, 116, 128, 141, 146–147, 165–167, 193, 195, 197, 200–201, 211

Mentoring...7, 16, 19, 63, 65, 69, 87, 89, 91, 125, 138, 140–141, 208–209

Mergers...63, 65, 110–111, 113, 115–117, 196, 209

Meta evaluation. See Evaluation

Moseley and Solomon Confirmative Evaluation Model (Figure 7-8)...178

Motivation...3, 6, 8, 10, 33–34, 37, 47–48, 51, 56–58, 63, 65, 92–93, 134, 138, 185, 192, 195–197, 202, 208–210

Multirater process...14

Myers-Briggs Type Indicator...88

N

National Committee for Quality Assurance...17

Needs analysis...24, 25, 102. See also Needs Assessment

Needs assessment...24, 38, 136, 158, 195, 197, 200

Networking...3, 10, 63, 65, 70, 79, 84, 107, 112, 125, 140, 145, 147, 152–153, 196, 209

Networks...70, 107, 108, 112, 145, 147, 165–167

Nominal group technique...40

O

Objectives...8–10, 13, 23, 26,–28, 30, 53, 69, 70, 82, 94–95, 100, 113, 115–116, 125, 135–136, 138, 141, 143, 147, 159, 164, 168, 179, 183–186, 207, 208, 209

Odiorne, George...67, 140

On-line journals...166

Organisation for Economic Co-operation and Development (OCED)...17, 138

Organizational
analysis...3, 23, 26–28, 30–32, 57, 191, 209
buy in...101, 181. See also Buy In
change...14, 63, 99, 133, 142
chart...9, 210
communication...3, 16–17, 63, 65, 67, 79–80, 107, 110–112, 195–196, 201, 209.
interventions. See Interventions

Organizational, continued
culture...15, 80, 101, 107, 110–111, 132, 141, 198, 202, 207.
design...20, 64, 65–67, 99, 100, 196, 209
design and development interventions. See Interventions
development...67, 161, 190, 209
effectiveness...92, 107, 210
environment...6, 7, 25, 33–34, 37, 49, 57, 79, 130, 169, 174, 192, 208
general...42, 64, 70, 91, 134, 144, 147
goals...10, 82, 93, 134
impact...7, 157–158, 163
implementation. See Implementation
initiatives...138, 143
learning...68, 73, 138
needs...10–11, 142, 207
performance...19, 23–24, 29, 62, 66, 92, 100, 102, 124
policies...51, 210
resources...168
results...163–164
scan...62, 66
strengths, weaknesses, opportunities, and threats (SWOTs)...135
structure...27, 78, 125, 138
systems...66, 202
vision...139, 209, 210

Outsourcing...13, 15, 100

Ownership...87, 99, 101–102, 110, 125–126, 210

P

Panel reviews...165–167

Pareto charts...49, 85

People orientation...9

People-thing...24

Performance...x, 2
-based incentives...52
monetary...52, 92
bonuses...52
profit sharing...52
stock options...52
suggestion systems...52
nonmonetary...52
-based instruction...8–9
analysis...xi, 3, 6, 22–27, 33, 38, 40, 46–47, 53, 56, 72, 156–157, 163,

Performance, continued
171, 179, 190–191, 208–209
appraisal…14, 71, 93, 209
consultants…11, 15, 35
drivers…23, 47–48
goals…66
improvement…6, 8–12, 15–16, 24, 38–40, 42, 53, 65–67, 69, 124, 126, 158, 161, 164–168, 170–172, 176–179, 182–184, 187, 190, 196, 201–202
indicators…16, 127
interventions…10
management…14, 79
outcomes…9–10, 15–16, 24, 135
state…23–24, 27, 30, 38–39, 209
support…3, 9, 33, 51, 63, 65, 67–68, 72–73, 76, 140, 196
   interventions. See Interventions
   systems…74, 213. See also Electronic Performance Support Systems
tools…4, 168
technology (PT)…x, 2, 6, 8–10, 12–13, 15–17, 33, 67, 72, 95, 161, 164, 190, 197, 202, 209
competencies…201
   practitioners…6–11, 13, 15–16, 38, 47, 64, 80, 124–127, 133, 135, 140–141, 145–147, 156, 158, 161, 164, 176, 190, 201, 202

Performance Improvement Tool Kit…11

Performance Technology Interventions Checklist…66

Personal development interventions. See Interventions

Presentations…102–103, 128, 146–147, 172

Preventive maintenance (PM)…63, 65, 82, 196, 210

Priority Matrix (Job Aid 3-3)…40, 43

PROBE Model…53–54, 59, 194

Problem solving…x, 2, 8, 14, 63, 65, 94, 99, 101, 104, 125, 127, 139–140, 151, 196, 207, 210

Process consulting…3, 8, 125, 133, 137, 210

Productivity…2, 6, 13–14, 16, 38, 52, 72, 79–80, 93–94, 100, 127–129, 133–134, 138, 178, 202, 207–208,

Project management. See Management

Project meetings. See Meetings

Proposals…102, 141. See also Request for Proposals (RFPs)

Q

Quality…9–11, 14, 23, 27, 34–37, 51–52, 63, 65, 71, 79–82, 84, 89, 92, 94, 101–102, 107, 116, 125, 127, 139, 143–144, 146, 162–164, 176, 181, 192, 196, 202, 207, 208, 210.

See also Total Quality Management (TQM; Continuous [Quality] Improvement (CQI)
   assurance…84, 141, 144
   control…24, 84, 181, 190
   improvement…x, 66, 84, 85, 142

R

Rapid prototyping…166, 167

Rating scales…40, 93, 178

Realignment…63, 65, 99–100, 196, 210

Reengineering…x, 2, 20, 63, 65, 83, 99–101, 125, 133, 140, 196, 210. See also Corporate Restructuring

Repertory of behavior…3, 56, 57, 210

Request for Proposals (RFP)…141

Requesting departments…140–141

Resistance…8, 13, 125–126, 130, 132–134, 136, 145–146, 190, 198, 201

Resource(s)…x, 3, 6, 14–15, 27, 29, 33, 37, 48, 51–53, 55–58, 66–67, 69, 83, 100–101, 113, 115, 125, 129, 134–135, 139–142, 147, 152, 156, 159, 163, 168, 170–171, 173–174, 181–182, 187, 192, 208. See also Human Resources (HR)
   allocation…33, 36

Restructuring…16, 63, 65, 99–101, 125, 190, 193, 196, 210. See also Corporate Restructuring

Retirement planning…63, 65, 92, 94, 97, 98, 196, 210

Return-on-Investment (ROI)…3, 10–11, 14, 114, 125, 157–158, 162

Rewards…3, 6, 8, 48–49, 51–52, 56, 63, 65, 68, 89, 92–93, 95, 127, 138, 168, 190, 197, 208, 210

Role…10, 17, 50, 69, 85, 87, 88, 93, 101–102, 113–114, 126, 133, 135, 156, 159–160, 165, 169, 172–173, 183, 199, 207

Rosenberg, Marc J.…xi, 6, 47, 66, 72, 95, 103, 158

Rothwell's Environments of Human Performance (Figure 3-3)…33

Rothwell's Six Cell Gap Analysis (Figure 3-5)…39

Rummler, Geary…9, 47, 67

Run charts…49, 84

S

Safety engineering…63, 65, 79, 82–84, 196, 210

Saratoga Institute…17

Satellite technology…63, 65, 67, 68, 70, 73, 196. See also Interactive Technologies

Saunders, Bernard…139

Schedule…35, 82, 127, 175, 193–194

Self-directed learning. See Learning

Senge, Peter…138

Situational analysis…12, 128

Skills…3, 6, 13–16, 33–34, 37–38, 40–42, 47–49, 51, 56–57, 59, 66, 68, 71, 77–81, 87, 92–94, 96, 101–103, 125–126, 128, 133, 135–136, 138–140, 149–150, 153, 157–158, 162, 172, 179–180, 183–185, 190, 192, 194–195, 201–202, 207–209
   and knowledge…3, 48, 50, 56, 57, 201
   development worksheet (Job Aid 6-6)…153
   requirements…15

Spirituality in the workplace…63, 65, 99, 102, 196, 210

Spitzer, D. R.…64, 67

Sponsor…10, 12, 64, 133, 137

Staffing…13–14, 20, 63, 65–66, 141, 171, 196

Standards…8, 16, 23, 27, 30, 48, 53–54, 56, 63, 65–66, 68, 70–72, 74,

Standards, continued
78–79, 83–84, 89, 100–101, 118, 129, 133, 136, 143–144, 149, 171, 174, 176–178, 182, 193, 196, 207–208, 210

Strategic planning...10, 14, 26, 28–29, 63, 65, 67, 99–100, 135, 196, 208, 210

Styles...146–147. See also Gregorc's Learning Styles (Table 6-1)
abstract random...145–146
abstract sequential...145–146
concrete random...145–146
concrete sequential...145–146

Succession planning...63, 65, 92, 93–95, 138, 196, 210

Suggestion systems...7, 52, 110, 210. See also Grievance Systems

Summative evaluation. See Evaluation

Supervisory development...63, 65, 92, 94, 96, 196, 210

Survey...13–14, 16–17, 19, 28, 30–32, 53, 88, 104, 106, 173, 184
Associate Opinion Survey (AOS)...193, 197, 200
The 1997 Survey of Human Resources Trends Report...13
The Management Excellence and Work Environment Survey...168

Systematic and reproducible...x, xi

Systems task analysis. See Task Analysis

Systems thinking...138, 202

T

Tailoring...140

Task analysis...56, 80. See also Performance Analysis
checklist (Job Aid 5-5)...81
knowledge...24–25
procedural...24–25
systems...24–25

Team(s)...9, 13, 34, 40, 53, 73, 80, 85, 87, 102, 104–106, 125, 127–128, 133, 135–142, 144, 151, 165, 172–173, 179, 208–210
-based management...101
-building...20, 66–67, 84, 99–102, 116, 127, 197, 200–201
-oriented...9–10

Team(s), continued
approach...64
attitudes (Job Aid 5-13)...104
leadership...101
learning...68, 138, 209
playing...13
skills...14

Teamwork...x, 108, 133, 142

Telecommunications...63, 65, 67, 68, 70, 73, 78, 196. See also Interactive Technologies

The Fifth Discipline...138

The Society for Human Resource Management (SHRM)...13, 63, 65, 99–100, 102, 196, 210

Think-aloud protocols...165–166

Tools...x, 3, 6, 9–11, 24, 27, 33–34, 37, 40, 47–49, 51–52, 54, 56, 66, 70–71, 80, 82–83, 110, 113, 141, 165, 171–172, 192, 208, 210. See also Performance Support Tools
cause analysis...49–50
communication...197
data analysis...25
data collection...24
empowerment...101
evaluation...144
mathematical...85
On-line Analytical Processing (OLAP)...108
qualitative and quantitative analysis...25
quality...84, 127

Tosti, Donald...67

Total Quality Management (TQM)...xi, 84, 101, 110, 210

Trainers...9, 15, 72, 140, 166, 197

Training...6, 9–11, 13–17, 20, 35–36, 47–49, 52, 57, 59, 63–72, 75, 77, 79, 80, 83, 85, 88–89, 92–95, 99–100, 102, 108–110, 115–116, 125, 127, 139, 142–143, 147–149, 151, 153, 161, 167–168, 172–173, 183–184, 190, 193–194, 196–198, 200–201, 207–208, 210
on-the-job...9, 125, 138, 140, 197, 208

Trends...13–17, 39–40, 99, 125, 150, 183–186, 208

U

U.S. Department of Labor...15, 17, 138

V

Value engineering...63, 65, 79, 82–83, 151, 196, 210

Vendors...140–141, 202

Virtual...13, 151
organizations...16
performance analysis job aid...25
reality...70–71
university...148

W

Whiteside, Kathleen...66–67

Work
-related feedback...54
-related function...88
-related learning...76
activities...51, 147, 209
analysis...33
area...35, 53, 85, 183
assignments...94
attitudes...14
behavior...2, 24
changes...82
design...3, 20, 63, 65, 67, 79, 82, 196, 210
interventions. See Interventions
duties...82
effort...107
environment...3, 10, 12, 33–34, 36–37, 49, 51–52, 56–58, 79, 82–83, 116, 141, 143, 168–169, 192–193, 208
ethic(s)...72, 202
experience...89
flow...3, 34, 37, 52, 66, 79, 83, 192
group(s)...63, 106, 133, 148, 168, 208
level...37, 192
life...82, 92, 107, 207
method(s)...63, 65, 66, 79, 82–83, 196, 207, 210
performance...89, 208
practices...142
problems...133
process(es)...66, 128, 133

Work, continued

    projects…142

    record…89

    role…87, 207

    setting…88

    space…34

    standards…133, 210

    task…52

    tools…66

    unit(s)…80, 84, 89

Worker's compensation…194, 197, 200

Workforce…2, 3, 13, 17, 34, 101, 116, 125, 135, 140, 148, 191, 193, 209

    capabilities…125

    diversity…15

    performance…7, 38

Workplace…2, 4, 6, 13, 15, 47, 56–57, 67–68, 70–71, 78, 82–84,

Workplace, continued

87, 89–90, 102, 117, 139, 140–141, 146, 164, 183, 189–201, 207, 209–210

    activities…190

    behavior…2, 4

    benefits…193

    challenges…190

    change…190

    climate…193

    communication…94

    culture…2

    diagnosis and documentation…24

    dynamics…110

    expertise…24

    improvements…13, 190

    inspections…83

    nonperformance…168

    performance…x, 6, 16, 66, 79, 168

Workplace, continued

    play…83

    problems…190, 202, 208

    safety…84

    sectors…190

    spirituality. See Spirituality in the Workplace

    wellness programs…94

Workstation…52, 83

Worthy performance…8

Y

Younger, Sandra…139

Z

Zoloft, Beth…89

APPENDIX ONE
STANDARDS OF PERFORMANCE TECHNOLOGY AND CPT DESIGNATION PROGRAM

So You Want to Be a CPT...

Credentialing is an important step in any professional career. Before taking this step, it is important to reflect on the appropriateness and value of the credentialing process, as well as the Standards of Performance Technology, and the Code of Ethics. For example, performance technology (PT) practitioners who are considering the value of becoming a Certified Performance Technologist (CPT) may want to consider three major issues:

1. What's in it for me? Why should I dedicate time, energy, and money to become certified?
2. Why should performance improvement practitioners all follow the same set of structured standards? Many successful practitioners have their unique way of doing performance improvement. Following structured standards will stifle creativity.
3. Preparing the documentation that is required to qualify for the designation as a CPT is difficult and time-consuming. Is it worth the effort?

This book provides an overview of the Standards of Performance Technology and the CPT designation program—definitions, history, and process—to help PT professionals and others in related fields make an informed decision about the value of becoming a CPT. The book also discusses the importance of integrating the Code of Ethics into both the certification process and the practice of performance technology.

What is a profession?

When practitioners join together to support a code of ethics and standards of practice, they can establish a *profession*. Based on the Society for Human Resource Management (SHRM) and the U.S. Department of Labor, there are five characteristics of a profession (Hale, 2002):

- An organization that speaks with a unified voice for members and fosters development of the field.
- A code of ethics that identifies standards of behavior, such as fairness, justice, truthfulness, and social responsibility.
- The existence of applied research related to the field.
- A defined body of knowledge, such as the CPT standards.
- Credentialing based on professional standards.

Is performance technology a profession?

A field such as performance technology is based on three factors: theory, intellectual technique, and practical application (AECT, 1977; Seels & Richey, 1994). Theory provides a framework and set of principles based on research, which systematically explains phenomena. Intellectual technique describes methods for solving problems using analysis, restructuring, and creating solutions. Practical application describes the unique methods practitioners use to approach work, such as performance improvement. The Association for Educational Communications and Technology (AECT, 1977) defines a profession as having all of the three characteristics of a field, plus training and certification; standards and ethics; self-acknowledgment as a unique, concerned profession; strong association and communication among members enabling the association to vigorously enforce practices, standards, and ethics; leadership, and relationships to other professions operating in the field (p. 22-24). Silber, one of the authors of the 1977 AECT "Characteristics of a Profession" (title page and p. 19), noted that the CPT certification program enabled performance technology to become a true profession by addressing all three characteristics. "ISPI has taken a giant step forward with its Certified Performance Technologist Program. In one fell swoop, it has addressed all three of the criteria. It has said, 'Yes we are a unique profession ...'" (Silber, 2002).

What is CPT?

CPT is a credential designed for practitioners in HPT, performance improvement, training, psychology, organizational development, human resource development, and other related fields of workplace learning. Performance technologists focus on results, take a systems viewpoint, add value to the organization, and establish partnerships. They use systematic approaches to assess needs; analyze causes; and design, develop, implement, and evaluate projects or their workplace activities.

What triggered the need for CPT?

For many years, clients and practitioners in the field of workplace learning and performance improvement requested a credential to distinguish those practitioners who are accomplished in producing desired results in a systematic way. Prior to CPT, there was little guidance for clients to differentiate between the knowledgeable, skillful practitioner and one who claimed to be an expert in performance improvement but lacked the experience and knowledge to actually improve performance. Skilled practitioners proposing appropriate methods were losing work to those who claimed to be capable but proposed inappropriate approaches. PT practitioners felt the need for a credential to signify their capability. Hale (2003, p. 31) states that prior to CPT it was:

> "difficult for clients to distinguish those who have, can, and will from those who'd like to, or perhaps did it once and think they can do it again. Clients want and deserve a way to distinguish those of us for whom improving human performance is a career of choice from the wannabes, transients, and dabblers. What certification promises and delivers is the recognition and confirmation that a person is a proficient practitioner, has committed to a code of ethics, and engages in efforts to improve his or her own performance."

How were CPT competencies derived?

In order to create a credential, it is necessary to establish the competencies or standards needed for successful practice. In the case of PT, there was considerable previous work to use as a foundation. Under the leadership of Judith Hale, president of the International Board of Standards for Training, Performance, and Instruction (IBSTPI), *Instructional Design Competencies: The Standards* was published in 1986 (Foshay, Silber, and Westgaard, 1986). Pat McLagan (1989) defined the competencies needed for Human Resource Development (HRD) through an American Society for Training and Development (ASTD) study. These HRD and ISD competencies have been widely respected for many years, and serve as models for practitioners and researchers. William Rothwell's research led to defining competencies for human performance improvement (HPI), which were also published by ASTD (1996). In addition, William Rothwell created a self-assessment tool to help practitioners determine strengths and areas to develop. Rothwell broke down the jobs in human performance improvement into analyst, change manager, intervention specialist, and evaluator. Rothwell, McLagan, and IBSTPI efforts and competency research studies (such as Guerra, 2003) provided the basis for defining the standards and validating the competencies needed for performance technology.

How did ISPI design and develop a certification process?

The International Society for Performance Improvement (ISPI) took the lead on designing and developing the CPT certification. During 2000, Dale Brethower, President of IPSI, and the ISPI board voted to endorse and support the creation of a certification process. In 2001, ISPI President John Swinney and the ISPI board established a CPT task force with President-elect Judith Hale as chair. Judith Hale convened the CPT task force, known as the "Kitchen Cabinet," from business, government, academia, and independent practitioners (see Table API-1).

The CPT Standards were validated by Indiana University graduate students under the direction of Professor James Pershing, then editor of ISPI's *Performance Improvement* journal. The graduate students conducted literature reviews to confirm that the Standards appear in practice. In addition, ISPI asked companies and independent practitioners to confirm the usefulness of the Standards and the workability of the certification process.

Why are ISPI and ASTD affiliated?

ISPI and ASTD affiliated to sponsor this CPT credential. When ISPI developed and launched the CPT Standards, they were widely acclaimed as representing best practices, or what ought to be best practices, in the field of performance improvement. ASTD decided to support the ISPI standards rather than create a competing performance improvement certification. ISPI and ASTD believe that it is critical to have a single professional voice regarding performance technology qualifications and practice. Both professional associations are highly regarded for their leadership in performance improvement. ISPI has approximately 10,000 members representing a broad spectrum of the field. ISPI promotes theory and models, giving academics and practitioners alike a chance to become visible and influential in the field. With regard to CPT, ISPI was the "incubator" in defining, field-testing, and launching the credential. ASTD also represents a broad spectrum of the profession with a membership of approximately 70,000. ASTD offers a large international presence, extensive benchmarking studies and data, and influence in public policy. ASTD is often quoted in national and international media, which broadens exposure for the CPT, the Standards of Performance Technology, and the Code of Ethics.

What kind of professional has already added the CPT credential?

Many internal and external performance consultants or vendors and academics who provide PT services have become CPTs. Internal consultants work within their organizations to implement PT in a collaborative systemic, systematic manner, focused on results. Vendors or external performance consultants use PT to provide another pair of skillful "eyes," bringing experience with different clients, different cultures, and different successes. The CPT website, www.certifiedpt.org, has the most current list of professionals who hold the CPT credential.

How does the certification process work?

A performance improvement professional who wishes to add the CPT designation to his or her list of credentials must describe the work he or she has done in the past to demonstrate how he or she has met each of the Standards of Performance Technology. A supervisor or client who has knowledge of the work and its results must attest to this description.

There are 10 Standards for Performance Technology and a Code of Ethics that serve as the basis for certification. The Standards are as follows:
1. Focus on results and help clients focus on results.
2. Look at situations systemically taking into considera-tion the larger context including competing pressures, resource constraints, and anticipated change.
3. Add value in how you do the work and through the work itself.
4. Utilize partnerships or collaborate with clients and other experts as required.
5. Systematic assessment of the need or opportunity.
6. Systematic analysis of the work and workplace to identify the cause or factors that limit performance.
7. Systematic design of the solution or specification of the requirements of the solution.
8. Systematic development of all or some of the solution and its elements.
9. Systematic implementation of the solution.
10. Systematic evaluation of the process and the results.

The Code of Ethics is intended to promote ethical practice in the profession. In order to be certified or re-certified, an applicant must sign a statement of agreement with the principles on which the Code is based. The Code of Ethics is based on six principles that guide the performance improvement process:
1. Adding value
2. Using validated practices

TABLE API-1

KITCHEN CABINET CPT TASK FORCE

Business/Government	Academia	Practitioners
Aid Association for Lutherans, Lorrie Formella	Boston University, Reza Sisakhti	Ann Battenfield
Argonne Laboratory, Karen Kroczek	Indiana University, James A. Pershing	France Gagnon
Canon USA, Daniel Messick	Western Michigan University, Dale Brethower	Judith Hale
Johnson Controls, Donald Kirkey	Northern Illinois University, Ken Silber and Bob Sheets	Lynn Kearny
Lucent, Skip Douglas	Florida State University, Roger Kaufman	Mark Lauer
Maritz Corporation, Rodger Stotz		Cindy Schaefges
Omnicell, Deb Barrett		Kelly Smith
Plato, Rob Foshay		Guy W. Wallace
Rockwell Automation, Jim Momsen		Stacy Yusim
Source One, Gail Hahn		
Technip, Ray Robertson		
U. S. Steel–Gary Works, Dean Larson		
U.S. Department of Treasury, Elaine Rand		
Walgreens, Annemarie Laures and Karen Preston		

3. Collaborating with others
4. Continuously improving ones proficiency
5. Demonstrating integrity
6. Upholding confidentiality

Applicants must use three to seven past projects to describe how they have met the first four Standards three times and the remaining six Standards twice. In addition, applicants must also sign the Code of Ethics. For the most current information and application forms, visit www.certifiedpt.org.

What Are the Issues?

Now it's time to respond to the issues posed at the beginning of this section.

What's in it for me? Why should I dedicate time, energy, and money to become certified?

Prior to CPT certification, anyone could claim that he or she was a training, performance consulting, human resource development, or performance improvement professional. There was no definition of what constituted the performance improvement profession. CPT certification brought definition to the profession and a means to measure accomplishment of Standards and ethics. It is based on the previous work of many practitioners and researchers who have defined and refined the elements that make up CPT competencies and standards. According to Judith Hale:

> "Being certified demonstrates that you engage in a different level of conversation with clients prior to offering the solution. Being certified means you have proven you focus on results, consider the larger context including conflicting pressures, work as part of a team, follow a systematic process, and in the end add value. Your methods are not arbitrary; your aim is toward something that matters. Whether the bulk of your work is designing training, building job-aids, or redesigning work processes you begin with assessment and diagnosis integrated with evaluation." (Hale, 2003, p. 31)

Now, people who actually know how to and practice performance technology can identify their skills and accomplishments and be recognized by clients as true professionals.

Why should performance improvement practitioners all follow the same set of structured standards? Many successful practitioners have their unique way of doing performance improvement. Following structured standards will stifle creativity.

The first four Standards are principles that guide every intervention as the PT practitioner focuses on results, sys-

tematically looks at performance improvement opportunities, adds value, and partners with others. The remaining six Standards guide the performance technologist in a systematic approach to improving performance. CPT Standards represent the concept of "ideal" and best practice. However, no situation is "ideal." In fact, in most situations, it would be inappropriate to use every item under each CPT Standard. Each unique situation requires decisions by the PT practitioner as to which items under each Standard are appropriate and needed.

Preparing the documentation that is required to qualify for the designation as a CPT is difficult and time consuming. Is it worth the effort?

It is quite a lot of work to prepare the CPT documentation for submission. However, because of the difficulty, the CPT credential has real meaning and significance. If obtaining the CPT were easy, it would not separate well-prepared and successful practitioners from those who merely claim to be performance improvement professionals. For CPTs to be respected, the certification process needs to be rigorous and be based on a proven record of accomplishment in the use of PT.

Standards of Performance Technology

There are 10 Standards of Performance Technology: Standards 1-4 reflect the four basic principles that underlie all successful performance improvement efforts; Standards 5-10 represent a systematic process for implementing the four principles. The following section briefly describes each of the Standards and suggests some potential examples and outputs.

PT practitioners who have earned the CPT designation provided the following comments. These comments and more are on www.certifiedpt.org.

"…the certification is an indication for me to show others that people in our profession aspire to high standards…"

Debbie Simpson, CPT, Texas
Instruments, DFAB Training Manager

"When clients ask about the CPT designation, I have an opportunity to explain my systemic approach to solving their performance problems. I find this distinction sets me apart from other organizational consultants.

Jeanne Strayer, CPT,
Performance Solutions Group

"The first time I showed the CPT designation to a client, he said, 'What the heck (edited version) is that?' After I explained what it meant, he was intrigued, saying, 'It's about time you got some standards and rigor into your profession.' Then I told him that there always were standards and rigor, but now you will know if the HPTer in front of you practices the standards with rigor. Now he was very intrigued."

Miki Lane, CPT, Senior Partner, MVM Communications

"CPT signifies that the HPT field is maturing, and recognizing its accomplishments in establishing an important body of knowledge and principles for practice. My CPT signifies a commitment to mastering and contributing to that body of knowledge. The CPT assures my clients that my practices represent the state of the art, based on sound principles and ethics."

Rob Foshay, PhD, CPT, Vice President – Instructional Design and Quality Control, PLATO Learning, Inc.

"Watch the charlatans and one-week-workshop-wonders quiver as the real CPTs arrive."

Kenneth H. Silber, PhD, CPT, Associate Professor, Educational Technology, Research and Assessment, Northern Illinois University.

"Certification as a Performance Technologist says you know how to make it happen. You can get the results."

John Amarant, CPT, Principal, Vanguard Consulting

The Standards are as follows:

Performance Standard 1: Focus on Outcomes

Focusing on outcomes and results helps your clients focus and validate the vision, mission, and business goals of the organization and client. You determine what it is you are trying to solve by focusing on accomplishments and what will be measured or accepted as evidence that the business need was met. Examples may include helping clients reach consensus on what outcomes add value or conducting thorough performance analyses (operational, environmental, gap).

Performance Standard 2: Take a Systems View

Look at situations systemically taking into consideration the larger context including competing pressures, resources constraints, and anticipated change. Taking a systems view is essential because organizations are complex, dynamic systems that affect organizational and group performance. A systems approach considers the larger environment that affects processes and other work. You consider alignment issues and determine areas of leverage affecting work, worker, and workplace. Examples may include considering the larger environment when you analyze, design, develop, implement, and evaluate a plan; or modeling systems thinking to address business needs.

Performance Standard 3: Add Value

Adding value is inextricably related to how you do the work and the work itself. Value is the constant at the heart of all important ideas concerning strategy and management. When you approach your work systematically with passion and thoroughness, you add value. You paint a landscape that will help your clients fully understand the implications of their choices, set appropriate measures, identify barriers and tradeoffs, and take control. Examples may include focusing on issues that matter to clients, or presenting facts and evidence related to problems, opportunities, and changes.

Performance Standard 4: Work in Partnership with Clients and Other Specialists

Utilize partnerships or collaborate with clients and other experts as required. The essence of partnership is collaboration involving all stakeholders, as well as experts and specialists in the fact-finding, planning, and decision processes. Working collaboratively means leveraging the expertise and influence of others while trusting and respecting each other's knowledge and expertise. Solid listening and communicating skills are paramount. Examples may include establishing relationships with clients by including all stakeholders and other specialists in identifying business needs and making decisions; or working toward common goals and using energy to find solutions to potential problems, opportunities, and challenges.

Performance Standard 5: Be Systematic—Needs or Opportunity Analysis

Be systematic in all aspects of the process including the assessment of the need or opportunity. Needs or opportunity analysis examines the current situation at any level to identify the external and internal pressures affecting it with the ultimate goal of aligning the client's activities and priorities. In a systematic way, you determine the type of functional analysis required and develop a plan or process for conducting it in collaboration with your client. Based on output, a business case is built for action or non-action. Examples may include determining the scope of the analysis including objectives, personnel, data requirements, sources, uses, tools, and time frames; or determining hypotheses regarding why the current situation at any level (society, organizational, process or work group) exists. The output is a statement describing the current state, the projected future state, and the rationale or business case for action or non-action.

Performance Standard 6: Be Systematic—Cause Analysis

Cause analysis is about working in collaboration with your client to determine *why* a gap exists between desired and actual performance or performance expectations. Examples of causes for poor performance are lack of the knowledge or skill required to perform successfully or insufficient feedback from managers and supervisors. The output of cause analysis is a statement of why performance is not happening or will not happen without some intervention.

Performance Standard 7: Be Systematic—Design

Design is about identifying the key attributes of a solution to the performance problem. You, as the performance improvement specialist, will identify and describe one or more performance improvement interventions in detail. Examples of designing performance improvement interventions may include designing a blueprint for an education and/or training program to improve the knowledge or skill level of performers; or redesigning a job, process, or system.

The output is a communication that describes the features, attributes, and elements of your recommended performance problem solution and the resources required to actualize it:

- What intervention(s) do you recommend? Why?
- What will be required to develop and implement the intervention(s)?
- Which is preferred? Why?

Performance Standard 8: Be Systematic—Development

Development is about creating or acquiring some or all of the elements of the solution. You may choose to do it personally or as part of a team, or you might outsource the effort. Examples of elements that may need to be developed include training materials for instructors and participants tools; or techniques to support a new or re-engineered process; the physical components for a redesigned workspace; or changes in policy or procedures for HRD practices such as hiring, retention, compensation, or benefits. The output is a complete performance intervention (product, process, system, or technology with all its elements and components) that is ready for implementation.

Performance Standard 9: Be Systematic—Implementation

Implementation is about deploying the solution and managing the change required to sustain the solution. In general, you help clients adopt new behaviors or use new or different tools. Examples of development activities may include helping the client track change, identify and respond to problems, communicate the results, and make recommendations for continuous improvement; or train people who will deliver the training; or assist the target audience in adopting the new behaviors, executing the new process, or using the new tools. The desired output is an implementation strategy that supports changes in or adoption of behaviors that are believed to produce the anticipated results or benefits.

Performance Standard 10: Be Systematic—Evaluation

Evaluation is about measuring the efficiency and effectiveness of what you did, how you did it, and the degree to which the solution produced the desired results so you can compare the cost incurred to the benefits gained. This Standard involves identifying and acting on opportunities throughout the systematic process to identify measures and capture data that will help identify the results of the program in terms of merit and value to the worker, work, work environment, and organization environment. Examples of actions you may take during evaluation include evaluating the results of a program or project by gathering data and comparing what you find to some standard, goal, or client expectation; or modeling the importance of evaluation by evaluating your own methods and processes. The output is an evaluation report that documents the evaluation process and findings and makes recommendations for future improvement.

Code of Ethics

The Code of Ethics for the Performance Improvement Standards is intended to promote ethical practices for guiding performance improvement. The Code supports six principles:

Principle 1: Add value

You add value by conducting yourself, and managing your projects and their results, in ways that add value for your clients, their customers, and the global environment. Approaching work with passion, thoroughness, and in collaborative effort also adds value. Examples may include basing recommendations and actions on an objective needs assessment conducted in partnership with the client; or serving clients with integrity, competence, objectivity, and respect in applying human performance techniques.

TABLE API-2

How to Use *Fundamentals of Performance Technology* and *Performance Improvement Interventions* to Explore the Performance Improvement Standards

Performance Standard 1: Focus on outcomes
Chapters 3-5, 7 in *Fundamentals*, Chapters 2-9 and the Intervention Selection Tool (Appendix) in *Interventions*, all include information on how to:
- Assist in fact-finding and designing analysis
- Facilitate the focusing on accomplishments
- Measure outcomes and results and provide evidence

Performance Standard 2: Take a systems view
Chapters 1-5 in *Fundamentals* and Chapters 2-9 and the Intervention Selection Tool (Appendix) in *Interventions* all include information on how to:
- Focus on larger environment that influences organizational and group performance
- Consider alignment issues between or among goals and objectives, performance measures, job/work designs, resources, expectations
- Present a broader and more realistic approach to analyzing the workplace environment

Performance Standard 3: Add value
Chapters 3-8 in *Fundamentals* and Chapters 2-9 and the Intervention Selection Tool (Appendix) in *Interventions* all include information on how to:
- Present a systematic approach to handling issues that affect business needs
- Identify interventions that are cost-effective, organization appropriate, and result from thorough analysis
- Approach clients and work with insight, honesty, and respect

Performance Standard 4: Work in partnership with clients and other specialists
Chapters 3-7 in *Fundamentals* and Chapters 2-9 and the Intervention Selection Tool (Appendix) in *Interventions* all include information on how to:
- Establish relationships that focus on accomplishments, priorities, and solutions
- Leverage expertise and influence of others based on honesty and trust
- Generate energy about best choices that are fundamentally beneficial

Performance Standard 5: Needs or opportunity analysis
- Chapter 3 in *Fundamentals* supports a thorough needs or opportunity analysis including functional analysis at any level and suggests a plan or process for determining and conducting the analysis
- Chapter 8 in *Fundamentals* (case study) offers a rationale for why analysis occurs at the beginning of a project
- Chapters 2-9 in *Interventions* provide information and case studies on how to plan and conduct analysis related to specific interventions

Performance Standard 6: Cause Analysis
- Chapter 4 in *Fundamentals* presents an overview of cause analysis definition and scope, how to conduct cause analysis, and Gilbert's discussion of potential causes of poor performance. Also includes a job aid, and a case study

- Chapter 9 in *Interventions* includes cause analysis in a case study on implementing interventions in the workplace.
- The Intervention Selection Tool in *Interventions* (Appendix) describes cause analysis as part of the preliminary phase of intervention selection and includes a job aid

Performance Standard 7: Design
- Chapter 5 in *Fundamentals* describes the performance intervention classifications found in the HPT model
- Chapters 1-8 in *Interventions* give detailed information on specific performance interventions within each HPT model classification and suggest guidelines for designing specific interventions
- The Intervention Selection Tool in *Interventions* (Appendix) includes a job aid for selecting the most appropriate intervention(s) and helps designers focus on the purpose of the intervention (why the intervention was selected)

Performance Standard 8: Development
Chapter 5 in *Fundamentals* and chapters 1-8 in *Interventions* all:
- Focus on the performance interventions as classified in the HPT model
- Suggest possible elements of specific interventions that may require development; for example, Chapter 5 in *Interventions* also includes a financial statement template that may be used for training purposes.

Performance Standard 9: Implementation
- Chapter 6 in *Fundamentals* presents an overview of intervention implementation and change, including implementation methods, change management, continuous improvement, problem solving, and project management. The chapter also includes a change management job aid and a case study.
- Chapters 1-8 in *Interventions* embed implementation and change strategies within each chapter.

Performance Standard 10: Evaluation
- Chapter 7 in *Fundamentals* describes formative, summative, confirmative, and meta evaluation and includes job aids and a case study.
- Chapters 1-8 in *Interventions* embed information related to evaluation within each chapter; for example, knowing the intended purpose of an intervention is vital to evaluating program effectiveness.
- Chapter 2 in *Interventions* includes a discussion on how to evaluate knowledge management (KM) and learning organization interventions.
- Chapter 5 in *Interventions* includes job aids for evaluating performance appraisal processes and management development programs and discusses how to evaluate health and wellness programs

This matrix contains the most extensive references for each book. For additional references, see the glossaries and indexes of both books.

Principle 2: Use Validated Practices

You use validated practices that are discipline-specific and that address the Standards. When validated practices are absent, you use practices that are consistent with an existing body of theory, research, and practice. Examples include committing to the implementation of socially and fiscally responsible practices; or delivering activities, methods, and procedures that reflect positive values, worth, and significance.

Principle 3: Collaborate

You collaborate with others in fact-finding, planning, and decision processes while functioning as a trust-worthy strategic partner. Examples may include integrating the organization's needs, constraints, and concerns when devising solutions to problems, opportunities, and challenges; or cooperating fully with clients' requests to partner, even when the requests represent personal competition.

Principle 4: Focus on Continuous Improvement

You focus on continuously improving your personal proficiency and remaining current in the performance technology field. Some examples include reading professional materials, participating in professional organizations, attending professional development events, and sharing and networking with other specialists. You investigate new methods, concepts, tools, strategies, and technologies that may be beneficial to both you and your clients; or you periodically evaluate your personal knowledge, skills, and attitudes related to performance technology, performance improvement, and performance consulting.

Principle 5: Maintain Integrity

You demonstrate integrity through personal honesty and truthful negotiations with stakeholders and others. Examples may include accepting only those performance improvement projects for which you are qualified by experience and competence or informing clients when you believe they are heading in the wrong direction.

Principle 6: Uphold Confidentiality

You uphold confidentiality by protecting the client and guarding against conflict of interest. Examples may include respecting the intellectual property of clients, other consulting firms, and sole practitioners by not using proprietary information, strategies, tools, or methodologies without permission; or by refusing to disclose information without appropriate authorization.

TABLE API-3

How to Use *Fundamentals of Performance Technology* and *Performance Improvement Interventions* to Explore the Code of Ethics

Code of Ethics: 1-6

Chapters 5 and 8 in *Fundamentals* and Chapters 7 and 9 in *Interventions:*

- Suggest a model to guide the performance improvement process

- Provide myriad of examples for adding value, validating practices, and collaborative efforts

- Encourage personal and professional integrity through client negotiations

References

Association for Educational Communications and Technology. (1977). *The Definition of Educational Technology.* Washington, DC: Association for Educational Communications and Technology.

Foshay, W., Silber, K., & Westgaard, O. (editors). (1986). *Instructional Design Competencies: The Standards.* Iowa City, Iowa: International Society for Training, Performance, and Instruction.

Guerra, I.J. (2003). Key competencies required of performance improvement professionals. *Performance Improvement Quarterly, 16 (1).*

Hale, J. (2003). Certification: How it can add value. *Performance Improvement, 42* (2), pp. 30-31.

McLagan, P.A. (1989). *The Models: Models for HRD Practice.* Alexandria, VA: American Society for Training & Development.

Rothwell, W.J. (1996). *ASTD Models for Human Performance Improvement: Roles, Competencies, and Outputs.* Alexandria, VA: American Society for Training & Development.

Seels, B.B. & Richey, R.C. (1994). *Instructional Technology: The Definition and Domains of the Field.* Washington, DC: Association for Educational Communications and Technology.

Silber, K.H. (2002, November 1). From the president, *Chicago ISPI Newsletter.*

APPENDIX TWO

MOVING FROM THEORY TO PRACTICE: STANDARDS OF PERFORMANCE TECHNOLOGY

The Certified Performance Technologist (CPT) process promotes the systematic and systemic identification and removal of barriers to individual and organizational performance by providing performance improvement practitioners with 10 Standards of Performance Technology and a Code of Ethics. CPT practitioners exercise creativity and flexibility when it comes to applying the Standards. Each workplace situation requires a different approach, using different tools and techniques. Each situation results in different outcomes based on different needs. However, in the end, performance technology (PT) practitioners improve the workplace for individuals, organizations, and society by staying focused on the Standards.

CPT performance and criteria indicators for operationalizing the Standards are summarized in the following matrix. The complete, detailed performance and criteria indicators can be found at www.certifiedpt.org.

PERFORMANCE STANDARD 1 – FOCUS ON OUTCOMES

Performances	Criteria
You— Determine the outcome or expected result of the assignment. You may— • Help clients specify what they expect to change, or what benefit they expect to gain as a result of the effort or assignment. • Help clients come to agreement on what they expect to accomplish. • Guide or facilitate clients in focusing on accomplishments in deference to activities or events. • Determine what will be measured or accepted as evidence that the business need was met. • Explain the importance of focusing on accomplishments.	**So that you and the client can—** • Better evaluate if the effort was successful and produced outcomes of worth. • Determine in the beginning what information will be collected and how it will be collected to measure accomplishment of the desired outcome. • Communicate what the expected outcome is to team members and other stakeholders. • Establish goals and performance measures with staff and key clients. • Design your fact-finding (analysis) efforts and recommend solutions that are more likely to accomplish the desired outcome. • Celebrate and recognize those efforts that accomplished desired outcomes. **So that—** • The results of your work and how you went about producing those results supported the client, the organization, or society's goals.

PERFORMANCE STANDARD 2 – TAKE A SYSTEMS VIEW

Performances	Criteria
You—	**So that you and the client can—**

You—

1. Identify the current work, workplace, or market environment in terms of how it affects organizational and group performance.
2. Identify the environment and culture of the work and workplace and how it affects organizational and group performance.
3. Identify if there is a lack of alignment between or among the following:
   - Goals and objectives
   - Performance measures
   - Rewards and incentives
   - Job, work, or process designs
   - Available systems, tools, and equipment
   - Expectations and capacity
4. Identify barriers and leverage points, both in the workplace and surrounding your project, in terms of how these factors could affect processes; organizational and group performance; and the development, implementation, and outcome of your proposed solutions. You may identify—
   - Key political players and stakeholders
   - Issues affecting the larger environment
   - Pressures on key players, the business, the audience, managers, etc.
   - Expectations around the project
   - Workplace constraints and surrounding the project
   - Consequences of various solutions or in not pursuing a solution
5. Drive conversations around the barriers and leverage points that have been identified. Discussions could include the following issues:
   - Constraints or pressures related to:
     - Deadlines
     - Budget
     - Politics
     - Time
     - Regulatory issues
     - Product launch
     - Safety
   - Leverage points, including:
     - Political players
     - Stakeholder support
     - Related initiatives within the workplace that support the goals of the proposed solution
6. Explain the benefits of taking a systems approach in a conversation, design document, or project plan. You may—
   - Point out the knowledge gained by looking at the larger picture surrounding a project or performance issue.
   - Show how identified leverage points could be used to positively affect the project.
   - Discuss how identified barriers need to be considered in order to increase the probability of a project's success.

So that you and the client can—

- Determine if and how the work, workplace, or industry environment supports or impedes the desired organizational and group performance.
- Determine if and how the current culture supports or impedes the professed performance.
- Identify if and where there is a lack of alignment between or among key factors affecting the success of the solution.
- Determine if and how the barriers and leverage points support or impede the proposed solutions and the desired organizational and group performance.
- Analyze how the proposed solutions will affect the greater environment of the organization as a whole.
- Determine whether and how the results of your work and how you plan on producing those results might jeopardize the client, the organization, or society's well-being.
- Help ensure that the methods of deploying and the results of the project will have a positive impact on the client, the larger environment, and society.
- Increase awareness throughout the workplace of the benefits of a systems approach.

PERFORMANCE STANDARD 3 – ADD VALUE

Performances	Criteria
You—	**So that you and the client can—**
1. Identify two or more possible solutions or courses of action.	• Establish at the start what will be used as evidence of success, accomplishment, or worth and communicate that to all vested parties (stakeholders).
2. Identify the worth of the requested solution or those under consideration, by comparing factors such as:	• Determine that a mechanism exists to establish whether the gain was realized and to track early indicators of success so corrections are made.
• Cost to design, develop, implement, and maintain each	
• Likelihood of adoption or use by the target audience	• Determine if the assumptive base and the argument for or against a course of action is documented and communicated.
• Probability of each solution achieving the desired goals	• State what tradeoffs were made and what value was gained, and conclude that the value outweighed the cost.
• Implication or possible impact on the target audience, other employees, consumers, the community, etc.	• State that what you do adds value and how you go about your work adds value.
• Ability of the organization to support each solution (reward the appropriate behaviors and results; provide the appropriate communication and information systems; tools and equipment; maintain sponsorship; etc.)	**So that—**
• Risks associated with the success or failure of each solution in terms of threats to safety, health, financial return, customer satisfaction, etc.	• The product of the assignment or the goal of the task is sound and beneficial to the organization.
3. Recommend solutions that add value, are feasible, and are more likely to accomplish the goals or aims of the project with minimal risk.	
4. Describe the potential value added and how that value will be measured, such as:	
• Increased safety, utility, or customer or community satisfaction	
• Increased revenues	
• Avoided costs	
• Decreased errors, lost time to accidents, time to market, cycle time, processing time, wait time, etc.	
• Increased on-time delivery	
• Increased customer and employee retention	
5. Point out the risks, tradeoffs, and assumptions on which decisions or choices are based	
6. Document using a contract, memo of understanding, or description in project description—the expected value added, the costs (materials, resources, time, etc.), and a schedule of deliverables	
7. Explain the importance of doing work that adds value and the importance of demonstrating the value gained	
8. Contribute insights and call out implications throughout the work	
9. Display honesty; push back, challenge assumptions.	
10. Represent yourself honestly, not as having expertise beyond your capabilities	

PERFORMANCE STANDARD 4 – WORK IN PARTNERSHIP WITH CLIENTS AND OTHER SPECIALISTS

Performances	Criteria
You— 1. Collaborate with stakeholders, experts, and specialists, making use of their knowledge, capabilities, and influence. You may— • Identify stakeholders. • Determine if other content expertise is required. • Solicit other content expertise as needed. • Incorporate stakeholders, experts, and specialists as part of the team, involving them as required. • Establish collaborative relationships. • Leverage the expertise and influence of others for the benefit of the client. 2. Take the initiative to define your expectations, working relationships, roles, responsibilities, etc. You may— • Point out the benefits of collaboration and partnering. • Increasingly expect to work in collaboration or in a partnership with each other. • Anticipate resistance and respond accordingly. • Anticipate issues and barriers. • Bring misunderstandings to the surface to reconcile them. • Give credit and acknowledge the support, endorsement, and contributions of your partners.	**So that you and the client can—** • Trust and respect each other's roles, knowledge, and expertise. • Leverage expertise and influence of others to the client's benefit. • Ensure the voices of all vested parties are sought and integrated into the design of the instructional program. • Share responsibility for all decisions concerning goals, next steps to take in the process, and implementation. • Make the best choices about accomplishments, priorities, and solutions because you understand your client's needs, challenges, and culture. • Support the product of the assignment or the goal of the task. **So that—** • All stakeholders are involved in the decision making around every phase of the process, and specialists are involved in their areas of expertise.

PERFORMANCE STANDARD 5 – BE SYSTEMATIC— NEEDS OR OPPORTUNITY ANALYSIS

Performances	Criteria

You—
 	
1. Determine the type of analysis required.
2. Develop a plan or process for conducting the analysis, including any of the following:
  • Hypotheses
  • Data-collection methods
  • Audiences to be polled
  • Sampling method
  • Statistical treatment
  • Sequence of activities
  • Timeline
  • Resources required
3. Develop any tools or documents, such as interviews, surveys, or observation forms required to capture the data.
4. Conduct the analysis.
5. Analyze the data.
6. Interpret the results. You may—
  • Determine the magnitude of the gap in terms of criticality, frequency, cost or exposure, or lost benefit.
7. Build a business case for action or non-action.
8. Make recommendations based on the results.
	So that you and the client can—
	
	• Use analysis methods appropriate to the situation.
	• Determine the question (hypothesis) you want to answer.
	• Carry out the analysis at the appropriate level: individual, group, process, organizational, or societal.
	• Develop recommendations on whether to act on the findings and how.
	• Use data-gathering methods appropriate to the situation.
	• Use sampling methods that follow recommended practices:
	  – If a representative sample was used, it lists the criteria for being selected.
	  – If a random sample was used, it (1) was of sufficient size to generalize from the results and support the statistical analysis used, (2) lists the criteria for being part of the population, and (3) describes how the sample was chosen.
	  – If a stratified sample was used, the strata are listed, the size of the strata is shown, and the size of the sample by strata is shown.
	• Use a survey format that complies with recommended practice, if a survey is used:
	  – Consistent use of scales
	  – Sufficient number of questions for statistical analysis
	  – Clear directions on how to complete the survey
	  – Piloted to confirm the questions and directions work as intended
	  – Standard method of analysis
	  – Documented method of analysis
	• Use an interview format that complies with recommended practice, if interviews or observation are used:
	  – Documented format
	  – Piloted questions
	  – Documented analysis method
	  – Accepted analysis method
	• Correctly use documents or work products as a source of data:
	  – Documented sampling method
	  – Accepted sampling method
	  – Documented evaluation or comparison criteria for documentation or work products
	• Identify the physical and technological opportunities and constraints in the work environment.
	• Identify the actual work processes used to accomplish work.
	• Identify the actual and expected outputs of the work.
	• Identify the consequences and who the receivers of those consequences are.
	• Identify what feedback systems are or are not in use and how effective they are.
	• Identify the inputs that the workgroup has available. (Inputs include information, directions, requirements, expectations, etc.)
	• Identify gaps between what is required and what actually occurs.
	• Discriminate causes due to lack of information, knowledge, or skill from those due to inadequacies in the work environment, poor job design, inadequate feedback systems, lack of consequences, or poorly designed processes.
	• Determine the feasibility or probability of eliminating the gap.
	
	So that—
	
	• The plan is feasible, given organizational time and resource constraints.
	• The results are useful and valid.
	• The process for conducting the analysis is cost- and time-efficient.
	• Findings serve as guides for future work and provide information for later evaluation.
	• The process for conducting the analysis is administered consistently and includes the voices of all stakeholders.
	• The analysis method is applied to the level of completeness and accuracy required by the problem and its risks, and no more.

PERFORMANCE STANDARD 6 – BE SYSTEMATIC—CAUSE ANALYSIS

Performances	Criteria

You—
 	
1. Use the gap to help determine the worth of determining the cause and establish criteria for measuring the effectiveness of a chosen solution.
2. Develop a hypothesis for why the gap exists.
3. Develop a plan or approach to test your hypothesis and identify the cause of the gap.
4. Implement the plan and identify the cause of the gap, such as:
   • Lack of skills or knowledge
   • Insufficient environmental support
   • Inappropriate rewards or incentives or measures
   • Poorly designed jobs or processes
5. Report your findings.
	So that you and the client can—
	
	• Differentiate performance problems that are caused by lack of knowledge and skill from those that are due to environmental, job, or process design; inadequate feedback or performance support systems; insufficient or inappropriate tools and equipment; conflicting objectives; or inappropriate performance measures.
	• Determine how much certainty is required to support a solution.
	• Determine which hypotheses (the cause of turnover, high cost of recruitment, poor morale, customer dissatisfaction, etc.) are supported by the data.
	• Note those instances where a solution is predetermined, such as training done in order to comply with regulations or for new hires who are known to lack the required skills and knowledge.
	
	So that—
	
	• Future design and development will address the real need(s) cost effectively.

PERFORMANCE STANDARD 7 – BE SYSTEMATIC—DESIGN

Performances	Criteria

You—
 	
1. Decide on one or more solution set(s), such as:
   • Process redesign
   • Training
   • Change/benefit
2. Define the desired performance.
3. Identify the objectives of the solution and all elements of the solution.
4. Develop a plan that includes strategy and tactics for accomplishing the objectives and addressing all elements of the solution.
5. Agree on roles and responsibilities for stakeholders, high performers, and subject matter experts to be involved in the development and implementation of the solution.
6. Identify key attributes of the proposed solution—such as learning strategy and tactics, transfer systems, feedback, etc.—for:
   • Data and communication systems
   • Job or process elements
   • Management practices (feedback, rewards, scheduling, promoting, performance measures, etc.)
7. Identify how the solution will be produced or actualized.
8. Identify the resources required.
9. Identify methods for delivering or deploying the solution.
10. Identify how the solution will be maintained or reinforced.
11. Identify methods for evaluating the effectiveness of the solution.
12. Explain the rationale for the proposed methods, such as:
   • Evaluation
   • Strategy and tactics
	So that—
	
	• The objectives, conditions, performances, performance elements, and criteria for judging learning, transfer, or adoption are sufficiently detailed.
	• The assumptions, the aims or intent of the solution, the strategy for development and deployment, and the criteria for judging adoption and success are sufficiently detailed and sound.
	• The required terms, concepts, rules, heuristics, principles, and procedures key to performance are present.
	• The sequence of the content and tactics is sufficiently detailed.
	• The materials used to actualize the solution are designed following instructional methods designed to enhance the likelihood of attaining the intended outcomes.
	• The strategy and tactics for accomplishing the objectives (transferring knowledge, building skills, supporting performance, redesigning work processes and feedback systems, and aligning rewards and consequences) are sufficiently detailed.
	• The method for evaluating the accomplishment of the objective and the effectiveness of the solution is feasible and sufficiently detailed.
	
	So that—
	
	• The methods for deploying the solution are described.
	• The methods for maintaining or reinforcing the solution over time are described. The client understands the investment in time and resources necessary to develop and implement the solution and can provide the resources to actualize the design.
	• The target audience can participate in testing the solution.
	• The information serves as a guide for future work and provides information for later evaluation.

PERFORMANCE STANDARD 8 – BE SYSTEMATIC—DEVELOPMENT

Performances	Criteria

You—
 	
1. Ensure that the chosen solution is developed according to design specifications. You may—
   • Assist in the development of electronic support systems, such as help screens or help desks.
   • Participate in the development of a job, task, or process redesign.
   • Participate in the development of a feedback system, reward and recognition system, communication system, or information system.
   • Participate in the development of a change strategy.
   • Develop materials or methods to improve team processes, job procedures, work practices, or individual or group decision making.
2. Conduct formative, pilot, and user evaluations of all elements of the chosen solution or product to determine if it performs as expected and accomplishes the desired goal(s). You may—
   • Engage high performers or experts in reviewing all materials or in creating a new process or system.
   • Design and conduct a formative evaluation of all elements of the solution.
   • Design and conduct pilot and user tests to determine readability, functionality, usability, etc.
   • Compare formative, pilot, and user test results against design standards.
   • Determine if the physical elements of the solution support the objective(s), are usable to the target audience, can be administered in the way intended, and can be maintained over time.
   • Ensure that learnings are fed back into development.
	So that you and the client can—
	
	• Determine if the physical elements of the solution support the objective(s), are usable to the target audience, can be administered in the way intended, and can be maintained over time.
	• Get timely, relevant data for the pilot or user tests.
	• Provide mechanisms for feedback.
	
	So that—
	
	• The solution is effective or performs as expected and accomplishes the desired goal.

PERFORMANCE STANDARD 9 – BE SYSTEMATIC—IMPLEMENTATION

Performances	Criteria

You—
 	
1. Design a change strategy that includes the following:
   • How the effort (the message) will be communicated and to whom
   • What implementation materials and messages will be required and how they will be produced
   • A schedule of the rollout, including milestones, timelines, etc.
   • How the new behaviors and other evidence of adoption will be recognized and rewarded
   • What to do in case of resistance
   • Who will provide support and reinforcement during deployment
   • Roles and responsibilities of management, the target audience, and other vested parties
2. Develop tools and procedures to help those involved in the implementation. For example:
   • Train-the-trainer sessions
   • Job aids
   • FAQs
3. Participate in the implementation or deployment of the solution.
4. During implementation, solicit feedback related to the utility and relevance of the solution and use the information obtained in the following ways:
   • As a guide for future work and evaluation
   • To look at what worked and feed it back into the solution
   • By sharing it among key players to improve the solution and ongoing rollout
	So that you and the client can—
	
	• Send a uniform message about the why, what, and how of the solution.
	• Determine what tools and procedures the team responsible for implementation or deployment requires to effectively support implementation.
	• Determine how best to track the speed of the deployment and any resistance.
	• Determine how to identify and best handle resistance.
	
	So that—
	
	• The information serves as a guide for future work and provides information for ongoing evaluation.
	• The solution is delivered to the target audience.
	• Change is sustained over time.

PERFORMANCE STANDARD 10 – BE SYSTEMATIC—EVALUATION

Performances	Criteria
You—	**So that you and the client can—**
1. State outcomes of the evaluation effort in measurable terms.	• Determine whether the solution fulfilled the goal or satisfied the need.
2. Design a measurement strategy or plan based on the program's or project's goals and outcomes. The plan includes the following:	• Determine whether data are valid and useful.
• The program or project's key success indicators or goals in measurable terms	• Determine if the measurement methods and metrics are valid and useful.
• How data will be collected and results validated	• Make timely decisions about the need to change, alter, or intervene to better ensure the effectiveness of the solution.
• The standard or goal against which results will be compared	
• How data from others will be incorporated or leveraged	**So that—**
• If and how evaluation expertise may be required	• Reports are useful and relevant to the reader(s).
3. Develop the tools, instruments, and guidelines for collecting and interpreting data and selecting samples.	• Your methods and processes for analysis; selection and comparison of alternative solutions; and the design, development, deployment, and maintenance of solutions are improved.
4. Measure the results of the solution or help the client evaluate the impact of the solution.	
5. Identify what can be done in the future to improve the way in which needs and opportunities are identified and solutions selected, valued, developed, and deployed.	• The efficacy of the solution is ensured.
6. Report your findings and recommendations.	
7. Explain the value of evaluating (ethics).	

Using the Standards and their associated criteria as a performance support tool, the CPT practitioner can take a proactive approach to continuous performance improvement and apply the Standards to a variety of performance improvement opportunities and challenges.

Authors' Biographies

Darlene M. Van Tiem

Dr. Darlene Van Tiem is an associate professor in the School of Education, University of Michigan – Dearborn. From 1992 to 1996, Darlene was the training director in the Human Resources (HR) Department at Ameritech advertising services (yellow pages business unit). She was responsible for HR training (not sales or software) for four states (Michigan, Ohio, Indiana, and Wisconsin). From 1986 to 1992, Darlene was with General Physics Corporation. She was curriculum manager for General Motors Technical Curriculum and program manager for materials management curriculum, which included training GM suppliers. She also was project manager for Ford Motor Company's failure mode effects analysis curriculum development. From 1978 to 1986, Darlene was on the faculty of Marygrove College as director of the Learning Skills Center.

Darlene is a member of the International Society for Performance Improvement (ISPI) and is active in the Michigan chapter. In the American Society for Training & Development (ASTD), she is a past-president of the Greater Detroit chapter and a former national director of the Technical and Professional Skills Practice Area. She received the ASTD National Technical Trainer of the Year Award for 1992 and the National Excellence in Leadership Award for her work with the automotive industry. Currently, Darlene is the field editor for human performance improvement for ASTD's electronic newsletter, *ASTD Links*. Her academic credentials are as follows: BA, Albion College; MSA, Central Michigan University; MEd, Marygrove College; MA, Michigan State University; and PhD, Wayne State University.

James L. Moseley

Dr. James L. Moseley is an associate professor of Community Medicine in the School of Medicine, Wayne State University, Detroit. He returned to his faculty position after 22 years of administrative experience in medical education. Jim is a specialist in educational gerontology and teaches Gerontological Health Care, Designing Instruction for Older Learners, Health Care Management and Community/Public Health. He also enjoys full faculty graduate status in Wayne State's College of Education. Jim teaches Human Performance Technology, Performance Consulting, and Program Evaluation there, and he directs and serves on dissertation committees. Jim has received teaching and service awards from the university and from professional organizations. Before his university affiliation, he was a successful high school English teacher, guidance director, and principal of two different high schools. He served as president of the International Society of WORK-SHOP WAY® Educators and as president of the Michigan Society of Gerontology.

Jim is a member of the local and international chapters of ISPI, and he has published in that organization's journals and monographs. He is also a member of ASTD. He has conducted workshops at the conferences of both organizations and has consulted in a variety of settings. His academic credentials are as follows: AB, MA, University of Detroit; MSA, Central Michigan University; MSLS, MEd, EdS, and EdD, Wayne State University. In addition to his degrees, he holds numerous certifications and licenses.

In 2004, Jim co-authored *Confirmative Evaluation: Practical Strategies for Valuing Continuous Improvement* (Pfeiffer) with Joan Dessinger.

Joan Conway Dessinger

Dr. Joan Conway Dessinger is a senior consultant with The Lake Group, Inc., a performance improvement company that she founded in 1989. She specializes in performance analysis, program and product evaluation, and distance learning design. Her clients include national and international organizations such as Ford, GM, Procter and Gamble, Control Data Corporation, PioneerHi-Bred, and National Steel. Prior to becoming a performance consultant, Joan designed, implemented, and evaluated reading and writing workshop programs for adult learners at the adult basic education, high school completion, and college levels. She continues her interest in adult education by designing and teaching a graduate course needs analysis for the Instructional Technology Department at Wayne State University. She also designed and teaches a course on health care education program administration for the University of Detroit-Mercy and Madonna University.

Joan is active in ASTD and ISPI. Since 1980, she has made presentations and facilitated workshops for more than 50 state, national, and international conferences, including those sponsored by the Michigan Council on Learning for Adults, the Michigan Association for Adult and Continuing Education, the American Association of Adult and Continuing Education, ASTD, ISPI, and the International Coalition on Technology in Education.

In addition to *Confirmative Evaluation: Practical Strategies for Valuing Continuous Improvement* (Pfeiffer, 2004), Joan and Jim have co-authored several articles on the adult learner and evaluation. In 1998, they co-authored a chapter on the Dessinger-Moseley Evaluation Model for ISPI's *Performance Improvement Series*. Joan also co-authored a chapter on evaluating satellite training in *Distance Training* (1998), published by Jossey-Bass, and on the Ford Motor Company Distance Training program for dealerships (*Sustaining Distance Learning*, Jossey-Bass, 2001).

Made in the USA
Lexington, KY
02 February 2012